Researches in Sinai

First Edition . . . *May* 1906
Reprinted . . . . . . *October* 1906

THE HEIGHTS OF SERABIT, NORTH OF THE TEMPLE.

RESEARCHES IN SINAI

BY W. M. FLINDERS PETRIE
D.C.L., LL.D., LITT.D., PH.D.,
F.R.S., F.B.A., HON. F.S.A. SCOT.

MEMBER OF THE IMPERIAL GERMAN ARCHAEOLOGICAL INSTITUTE
MEMBER OF THE SOCIETY OF NORTHERN ANTIQUARIES, ETC.
EDWARDS PROFESSOR OF EGYPTOLOGY, UNIVERSITY COLLEGE, LONDON

WITH CHAPTERS BY
C. T. CURRELLY, M.A.
OFFICER OF THE IMPERIAL ORDER OF THE MEDJIDIE

WITH 186 ILLUSTRATIONS AND 4 MAPS

LONDON
JOHN MURRAY, ALBEMARLE STREET, W.
1906

PRINTED BY
HAZELL, WATSON AND VINEY, LD.,
LONDON AND AYLESBURY.

DS 110,5
P4

125679

PREFACE

WHEN first I went to Egypt, twenty-six years ago, I read and noted the accounts of Sinai, in the hope that I might be able to visit the monuments there; and this hope was not extinguished by all the intervening years of other work. The recent reports of monuments of the early dynasties gave additional reason for a search which might supplement the discoveries at Abydos. And the reduction of the resources for my work with the Exploration Fund made it imperative to take a site where copying was more required than excavation. Hence it came about that last winter we lived for four months in the wilderness instead of in the green plains of Egypt.

First of all, acknowledgment should be made to those previous labours which aided our work. The *Ordnance Survey of the Peninsula of Sinai*, in 1868-9, by Wilson and Palmer, is the geographical basis for all later explorers; and I have specially to thank the committee of the Palestine Exploration Fund for generously giving me copies of the map for our use. And the *Memoir on the Physical Geology and Geography*, by Dr. Hull, issued by the Palestine Fund, is a standard work which I have read with advantage. The labours of Captain Raymond Weill, during the last three years, in collating all the copies and paper squeezes of the Egyptian inscriptions from Sinai, resulted in his publication, *Recueil des Inscriptions Égyptiennes du Sinai*, 1894. This work was of great use as indicating what inscriptions should be sought, and providing a text which we had to exceed in accuracy and completeness in our work from the original stones. Captain Weill also joined our party at first, and checked over a large part of our copies during the time he was with us.

The cost of the main expedition described here was borne by the Egypt Exploration Fund, and the expenses of three workers; while the expenses of two other workers of our party were from private means. That Fund will also publish the atlas of inscriptions and plans, which will be discussed and translated by Mr. Alan Gardiner. The present volume is a separate publication apart from the Fund, and is not, therefore, given to the subscribers. The expedition described in Mr. Currelly's chapters was undertaken for the Egyptian Research Account, in the next volume of which it will be published in detail.

I much regret that the increased burdens of the Exploration Fund at Deir el Bahri have resulted in that society ceasing to provide for my researches. It has, therefore, been needful for me to trust for the future to the growth of another basis of work, in the Egyptian Research Account and British School of Archaeology in Egypt. I have to thank most sincerely the large number of authorities in history, archaeology, and science who have consented to form the general committee of the

PREFACE

new school. On this basis it will now be possible for me to continue my researches without interruption, thanks mainly to the exertions of my wife.

The general results of the season's work here described fulfil most of our expectations; many new inscriptions were found at Serabít, and the whole relation of the remains is now clear. But, as is often the case, the unexpected results even exceed in value those for which we had hoped; and the arrangements of a Semitic ritual earlier than any yet known in Syria or Arabia, and the discovery of a writing peculiar to the region some centuries earlier than the Exodus, are results of the first importance.

Our camp of workers amounted to thirty-four persons, the largest number that have resided for work in this region since the old Egyptian mining expeditions. The needs of providing every mouthful of food at five days' journey from our base, and bringing every drop of water many miles' distance, have given an insight into the conditions there, which is of great importance for comprehending the life of earlier residents, Egyptian and Israelite.

In another manner, also, a knowledge of the country at present is essential to understanding the past. Perhaps no writer on the historical relation of Palestine to Egypt has ever realised the conditions on the spot. Some have argued that because Sinai belonged to the Egyptians, therefore no Israelites would have gone there; others have argued that Egypt (*Musri*) ceased at the Red Sea, and therefore nothing east of that could bear that name. Both of these arguments are falsified by the present facts, in which the ancient conditions are evidently continued. At present the dominion of Egypt extends to the Gulf of 'Aqabah; all Sinai is under Egypt, and is part of Egypt politically. The frontier of Egypt runs from 'Aqabah to El Arish; and there was great excitement among our Bedawy friends when a rumour came that some Turkish soldiers had violated this frontier. To touch Sinai was to attack the independence of Egypt. Thus it was with *Musri* in the Old Testament. Yet, on the other hand, there is not an Egyptian to be found in Sinai, except a small guard on the pilgrim road at 'Aqabah, and the entirely modern quarantine station at Tor, which is a recent creation to disinfect pilgrims before entering at Suez. In the same manner, we see that anciently the Egyptians sent expeditions to mine during the winter; but there is no trace of any permanent garrisons, and the Israelites would find the land quite empty before them.

The study of the climate, and the indications of its ancient uniformity with the present state, are also of historical value. I may add, to the evidence mentioned in this book, that the carrying of heavy loads of copper ore long distances, to smelt it at places where fuel can be now obtained (as at the plain of El Márkha, and Wady Gharándel), shows that there were anciently no nearer supplies of fuel, and therefore, that the vegetation and rainfall were the same as at present.

These inquiries lie at the basis of an historical treatment of the Exodus questions. I fear that neither of the

PREFACE

extreme parties will be pleased with the conclusions which I have drawn from a criticism of the accounts. But these conclusions are based on a practical acquaintance with the conditions which has seldom underlain other views. One possible misunderstanding should be here guarded against. It must not be imagined that the Semitic ritual of the temple at Serabít had any direct connection with the Exodus some centuries later. I do not suppose the Israelites ever saw either the temple or the mines.

In the arrangement of this book some repetitions of facts and arguments in different forms has been tolerated, as it was not desirable for a reader to need to refer to various chapters in order to find the material on a single subject. The system of numbering all the blocks of illustration, instead of numbering plates, has been used in order to simplify references. In the spelling of names I have tried to be consistent. The use of *g* for *qaf* in the maps is misleading, as it is usual for *gim*; in this case, *q*, which is the genetic representative of that letter, is here used. The termination of Magháreh is adopted to mark that its final is not *alif*, but *hê*; and for *ye* the letter *y* is used so far as possible. The accents show the pronunciation of the names, and will, I hope, do away with the curious mistake of Serâbit instead of Serabít, which name has scarcely a clear vowel in it except the final.

As personal details are sometimes wanted for reference, it may be said that we left Suez on December 3rd; were at Magháreh, December 10th to January 11th; at

Serabít, January 11th to March 18th; and returned to Suez by March 23rd. Of our party, Mr. Button and myself were present throughout, December 3rd to March 23rd; Mr. Currelly, December 18th to February 7th; Miss Eckenstein, January 21st to March 23rd; Mr. Frost, December 3rd to February 7th; Mrs. Petrie, January 21st to March 23rd; Mr. Porch, December 3rd to 19th; and Captain Weill, December 3rd to January 28th. The work of copying and surveying went on continuously day by day; and I was never an hour off work, as we had to secure our results and copy 250 inscriptions before the hot season. The last four chapters by Mr. Currelly refer to several places which I had no time to visit; and these separate expeditions occupied him from February to May.

I have to thank those who smoothed our way. My friend the late Sir Charles Wilson, whose recent loss we mourn, gave much kindly advice and information about the practical life. A new friend, Mr. Bush, of Suez, assisted all the arrangements of our base there in the kindest manner. Messrs. Guétin & Charvaut, from their works at Tor, helped Mr. Currelly, and most politely cashed cheques and allowed us to draw on their stores when delays occurred with our own. Captain Lyons, R.E., the director of the survey of Egypt, permitted me to order copies of the unpublished government map; but, unfortunately, it scarcely included Serabít el Khádem. For the purpose of copying and taking impressions I had obtained a quarter of a mile of *Times* printing-paper, but the roll was stolen by

PREFACE

some of the mining riff-raff at Magháreh, who are under no control; and we owed our next stock of paper to the kindness of Dr. Nimr, the editor of the *Mokattem* in Cairo, who presented us with a large stock on hearing of our difficulty.

A note of the current prices in the peninsula at present may be useful to future travellers. Camel hire is the great item of expense. Abu Qudéyl's terms are 20 piastres, or 4s., a day for camel and man. Contract terms for pilgrims were 16 piastres, as I heard. We succeeded in bargains at having work done at about 12 piastres a day. And the bottom price in contracts with Sheykh Mudakhel at Tor is 10 piastres. All of these are without any back fare, if only going one way and not returning for the sender. For attendance and security we paid Sheykh Abu Ghanéym £4 a month. He offered to do this duty for 10 piastres a day at first, but rose when it came to an official contract at Suez; and as he or his brother lived over at Serabít, far from all their concerns, I tolerated the extra. For an excellent and sturdy guard I gave Sheykh Mudakhel 4 piastres a day. All these charges are more or less blackmail; yet as the time and attention of responsible people is given in return, it is really no more unfitting than police-rates at home. The prices of grain at Suez and Tor are about half as much again as in England; and hence it is cheaper to have out all flour from England. Moreover, it is thus secured in boxes, which prevent camel-men feeding on it by the way; and much better quality can be obtained, the brown-meal flour being greatly preferred to the white flour of Suez, both by Egyptians and by ourselves. All stores are of better quality and cheaper direct from England than bought in Cairo. Only lentils and petroleum should be provided from Egypt.

To any one who has a moderate stock of spoken Arabic, and who knows which sheykhs to agree with beforehand, there is no difficulty about travelling in Sinai; and the points of precaution mentioned in this account will show how to accommodate European ideas to the actualities of life under such conditions. I would sooner go with my Sinai friends than travel in most countries of Europe.

W. M. FLINDERS PETRIE.

UNIVERSITY COLLEGE, LONDON, W.C.

ERRATA

Map 1, Detail, *for* Nagh *read* Naqb.
Add "Maghareh" *at* "Mines."

LIST OF KINGS NAMED IN THIS VOLUME

Ist Dynasty.
SEMERKHET . . 5291—5273 B.C.

IIIrd Dynasty.
SA·NEKHT . . . . 4945—4917
ZESER . . . . . 4917—4888
SNEFERU . . . . 4787—4757

IVth Dynasty.
KHUFU . . . . . 4702—4639

Vth Dynasty.
SAHURA . . . . . 4426—4413
MEN·KAU·HOR . 4292—4283
ASSA . . . . . . 4283—4239
UNAS . . . . . 4239—4206

VIth Dynasty.
PEPY I . . . . 4167—4114
MERENRA . . . 4114—4107
PEPY II . . . 4107—4012

XIth Dynasty.
MENTUHOTEP III   3500?

XIIth Dynasty.
AMENEMHAT I . 3459—3429
SENUSERT I . . 3439—3395
AMENEMHAT II 3397—3362
SENUSERT II . 3365—3341

XIIth Dynasty—continued.
SENUSERT III . 3341—3303 B.C.
AMENEMHAT III 3303—3259
AMENEMHAT IV 3259—3250

XVIIIth Dynasty.
AMENHOTEP I . 1562—1541
TAHUTMES I . . 1541—1516
TAHUTMES II . 1516—1503
HATSHEPSUT . . 1503—1481
TAHUTMES III . 1481—1449
AMENHOTEP II . 1449—1423
TAHUTMES IV . 1423—1414
AMENHOTEP III 1414—1383

XIXth Dynasty.
RAMESSU I . . 1328—1326
SETY I . . . 1326—1300
RAMESSU II . . 1300—1234
MERENPTAH . . 1234—1214
SETY II . . . 1214—1209
TA·USERT . . . 1208—1203
SET·NEKHT . . 1203—1202

XXth Dynasty.
RAMESSU III . . 1202—1171
RAMESSU IV . . 1171—1165
RAMESSU V . . 1165—1161
RAMESSU VI . . 1161—1156

CONTENTS

PREFACE, LIST OF KINGS NAMED IN THIS VOLUME, CONTENTS, LIST OF ILLUSTRATIONS

CHAPTER I.—ON THE SINAI ROAD

Conditions of the journey, 1—Preliminaries at Suez, 4—The start, 5—Camel-men, 6—Ayūn Mūsa, 8—Roman station, 9—Wady Werdán, 10—Wady Gharándel, 12—Hisán Abu Zena, 13—Wady Uséyt, 14—Gravels, 15—Wady Taÿibeh, 16—Abu Zenýmeh, 17—Furnace at Seih Bába, 18—Naqb el Budérah, 19—Magháreh, 20

CHAPTER II.—THE BEDAWY AND THE DESERT

Making a contract, 21—Tribal system of service, 22—Road to Serabít, 23—Descent from Serabít, 24—Camp in the Wady Nasb, 26—Copper smelting, 27—The camel-child, 28—Return to Suez, 29—Advantages of Bedawy life, 30—Position of women, 32

CHAPTER III.—WADY MAGHÁREH AND ITS SCULPTURES

Mountains at Magháreh, 34—The strata, 35—The views, 37—Miners' huts and wall, 38—Sculpture of Ist dynasty, 41—Portrait of Sa·nekht, 43—Later sculptures, 44

CHAPTER IV.—THE MINERS OF WADY MAGHÁREH

The modern destroyers, 46—The earliest mining, 48—Later methods, 49—Use of flints, 50—Miners' huts, 51—Major Macdonald, 53

CHAPTER V.—SERABÍT EL KHÁDEM AND THE BETHELS

The map, 55—History of the valleys, 57—Geology, 58—The views, 59—The mines, 60—The original road, 62—The upright stones, 63—The groups of stones, 64—Stones with enclosures, 65—Enclosures without upright stones, 66—Sleeping in sacred places, 67—The Bethel custom, 68—Adoption of local worship, 70

CONTENTS

CHAPTER VI.—THE TEMPLE OF SERABÍT

The approach to the Temple, 72—Enclosure walls, 74—Entrance, 75—Cubicle chambers, 75—Pylon, 79—Outer steles, 82—Shrine of Kings, 84—Side door, 85—Hat·hor *hanafiyeh*, 86—Lesser *hanafiyeh*, 87—Approach of Sopdu, 83—Hall of Sopdu, 89—Sanctuary, 89—Porch, 91—Portico, 93—Cave of Hat·hor, 94

CHAPTER VII.—THE HISTORY AND PURPOSE OF THE TEMPLE

Begun under Sneferu, 96—The XIIth dynasty builders, 97—The bed of ashes, 99—Semitic burnt sacrifices, 100—Offerings of the XVIIIth dynasty, 102—Building by Hatshepsut, 102—Change in direction of axis, 103—*Hanafiyehs*, 105—System of ablutions, 106—Later additions to temple, 108

CHAPTER VIII.—THE MINING EXPEDITIONS

The organization, 109—The directors, 110—The controllers, 112—The Old Kingdom system, 114—The chief workmen, 115—The labourers, 117—The foreigners, 118—The system at work, 119

CHAPTER IX.—THE LESSER AND FOREIGN MONUMENTS

Hawk of Sneferu, 122—The four kings, 123—The XIIth dynasty figures, 124—The Hat·hor figures, 125—The head of Thyi, 126—Stele of Sutekh, 127—The Ramesside sculptures, 128—The inscriptions in a new alphabet, 129

CHAPTER X.—THE ALTARS AND THE OFFERINGS

The altars, 133—Early head of Hat·hor, 135—Conical stones, 135—Alabaster vases, 137—Glazed objects, 138—Vases, 139—Menats, 141—Bracelets, 143—Wands, 144—Ring-stands, 145—Sistra, 146—Tablets of Hat·hor, 147—Tablets of cats, 148—Totals of offerings in each reign, 149—Smaller objects, 150—Polychrome vases, 151—Beads, 152

CHAPTER XI.—THE MINES OF SERABÍT EL KHÁDEM

Main group, 154—Inscribed mines, 156—Largest cavern, 159—Stone tools, 159—Flints used, 160—Copper tools, 161

CHAPTER XII.—THE REVISION OF CHRONOLOGY

The Sothis period, 165—Dates fixed by it, 166—Interval of the XIIIth to XVIIth dynasties, 167—Season of mining, 168—Dates given by Sinai steles, 169—Value of Manetho, 171—His agreement with the earlier date, 173—Dates in Old Kingdom, 174—List of dynasties, 175—The intervals of the *Sed* festival, 176—The *henti*, 177—List of *Sed* festivals, 178—List of chief *Sed* festivals, 180—Nature of the *Sed* festival, 181—Parallel deaths of kings, 181—Details of *Sed* festival, 183—Origin of the festival, 185

CONTENTS

CHAPTER XIII.—THE WORSHIP AT SERABÍT EL KHÁDEM

Burnt sacrifices, 186—Incense altars, 189—Conical stones, 189—Ablutions, 190—Dreaming, 190—Hat·hor and Ishtar, 191

CHAPTER XIV.—THE CONDITIONS OF THE EXODUS

Literary criticism, 194—Variability of Phraseology, 196—Early use of Writing, 199—Misuse of the word Miracle, 201—Direction of Exodus, 203—Road to Sinai, 205—No change in rainfall, 206—Small population, 207—Corruption of Israelite census, 209—Original form of census, 211—Tests, 212—Later numbers in the desert, 214—Levites a later organization, 215—Numbers in Palestine, 217—The Egyptian point of view, 221—Summary, 223

CHAPTER XV.—TOR TO MAGHÁREH. By C. T. Currelly

At Tor, 224—Bedawy travel, 225—Flints on the G'aa desert, 227

CHAPTER XVI.—GEBEL MUSA AND THE NAWAMIS. By C. T. Currelly

The road to Gebel Musa, 229—Manna, 230—Traditions of the Bedawyn, 232—Life of the Bedawyn, 233—The monastery, 237—Gebel Musa, 238—Settlement, in Wady Ahmar, 239—Strayed workmen, 241—Circles and furnace in Wady el Gow, 242—Nawamis in Wady Nasb, 243—Stone circles, 244

CHAPTER XVII.—MOUNT SINAI AND GEBEL SERBÁL. By C. T. Currelly

Start from Tor, 246—The centre for defence, 247—Rephidim, 249—Water by coast, 249—Sinai not at Gebel Musa, 251—Mount Serbál the Mount of the Law, 252—The Feirán, 255—Removing the sculptures of Magháreh, 256

CHAPTER XVIII.—TOR TO 'AQABAH. By C. T. Currelly

Bedawy tombs, 260—Ain Hudherah, 262—Pearl divers, 264—'Aqabah, 265—Turned back by Turkish troops, 266—The pilgrim road, 267—Population of Sinai, 268

INDEX

LIST OF ILLUSTRATIONS

		PAGE
1. The Heights of Serabít, North of the Temple	*Frontispiece*	
2. In Wady Gharándel, looking North	*Facing*	12
3. In Wady Gharándel (Elim)	,,	12
4. Palms in Wady Gharándel	,,	13
5. Broom-Rape in Wady Gharándel	,,	13
6. The Heap of Abu Zena	,,	14
7. Two Stone-heaps by the Wayside	,,	14
8. Road North-West of Wady Uséyt	,,	15
9. Faulted Marl Strata in Wady Uséyt	,,	15
10. Palm-trees in Wady Uséyt	,,	18
11. Cliffs in Wady Tayíbeh	,,	18
12. Head of the Seih Bába	,,	18
13. North from Budérah Pass	,,	20
14. Sandstone Ridge, Wady Shellál	,,	20
15. Camels climbing the Naqb Budérah Pass	,,	20
16, 17, 18. Views in the Wady Dhába, North of Temple	,,	24
19. Hill at Mouth of the Wady Nasb	,,	26
20. East Side of Wady Nasb. +, Tablet of Amenemhat IV	,,	26
21. Wady Lahyan, from + in View 20	,,	26
22. Garden in the Wady Nasb	,,	28
23. Arab Grave in the Wady Nasb	,,	28
24. Arab Grave in Enclosure, with Doorway	,,	28
25, 26, 27. Camels on the Road	,,	29
28, 29. Camels in the Desert	,,	30
30. White Broom, Retameh	,,	30

MAGHÁREH

31. Et Tartír ed Dhami, Basalt Hill in Front. Top of Lower View	*Backing*	34
32. Et Tartír ed Dhami, from Maghâreh	,,	34
33. Top of View 34	,,	35
34. Mountains North-East of Maghâreh	,,	35

LIST OF ILLUSTRATIONS

			PAGE
35.	MOUNTAINS NORTH-EAST OF MAGHÁREH, AND WADY IQNEH	Facing	36
36.	CAMEL'S SKULL ON "FORT" HILL, WADY IQNEH BELOW	,,	36
37.	THE EASTERN MOUNTAINS, FROM MAGHÁREH	,,	37
38.	THE SOUTHERN MOUNTAINS AND SERBÁL, FROM MAGHÁREH	,,	37
39.	NUMBERED POSITIONS OF INSCRIPTIONS	,,	38
40.	INSCRIBED BLOCK IN VALLEY APPROACHING MAGHÁREH	,,	38
41.	HUTS OF XII DYNASTY. WALL. MINE OF XII DYNASTY	,,	39
42.	VALLEY. HUTS OF IV DYNASTY ON HILL IN FOREGROUND	,,	39
43.	TABLETS OF SAHURA AND SNEFERU	,,	40
44.	CHISEL-CUTTINGS ON ANCIENT MINE	,,	40
45.	SCENE OF SEMERKHET AND GENERAL. I DYNASTY	,,	41
46.	GENERAL OF SEMERKHET	,,	41
47.	SCENE OF SEMERKHET SMITING THE BEDAWY CHIEF. I DYNASTY	,,	42
48.	HEAD OF SA'NEKHT. III DYNASTY	,,	43
49.	SA'NEKHT. III DYNASTY	Backing	44
50.	TABLET OF SNEFERU. III DYNASTY	,,	44
51.	GROUP OF FIGURES OF SNEFERU. III DYNASTY	,,	45
52.	TABLET OF SAHURA. V DYNASTY	Facing	45
53.	TABLET OF RA'N'USER. V DYNASTY	,,	45
54.	TABLET OF MEN'KAU'HOR. V DYNASTY	,,	46
55.	TABLET OF AMENEMHAT III. XII DYNASTY	,,	46
56.	STONE POUNDERS FOR CRUSHING SANDSTONE	Backing	48
57.	STONE PICKS STONE VASE GRINDER	,,	48
58.	STONE MAULS AND HAMMERS FOR CRUSHING SANDSTONE	,,	49
59.	SERABÍT. BLACK STONE TRIPOD, ONE LEG REMAINING	,,	49
60.	FLINT TOOLS USED FOR WORK IN SANDSTONE, AND OTHERWISE	Facing	50
61.	POTTERY, XII DYNASTY, BURIED UNDER HUT	,,	52
62.	POTTERY AND CORN-GRINDERS. XII DYNASTY	,,	52
63.	MAJOR MACDONALD'S HOUSE AT MAGHÁREH	,,	54
64.	TYPES OF GRAVES IN ARAB CEMETERY	,,	54
65.	THE CAMP KITCHEN	,,	54

SERABÍT

66.	WADY DHÁBA, LOOKING NORTH FROM ANCIENT ROAD TO TEMPLE	Facing	56
67.	HEAD OF VALLEY 2, SOUTH OF TEMPLE	,,	56
68.	MINE BANKS AT F. STELE OF SETY IN DISTANCE	,,	58
69.	GORGE OF VALLEY 3, FROM F. RAS SUWÍQ IN DISTANCE	,,	58
70.	GEBEL UMM RIGLAYN AND BRANCH OF WADY BÁTAH	,,	59
71.	CAMP AT TOP OF WADY UMM AGRÁF	,,	59
72.	QUARRYING IN MINE AT L. XVIII DYNASTY	,,	60
73.	INTERIOR OF MINE AT M	,,	60
74.	ROCK SHRINE ON ANCIENT ROAD TO TEMPLE	,,	64
75.	UPRIGHT MEMORIAL STONES AND HEAPS	,,	64
76.	GROUP OF UPRIGHT STONES	,,	65
77.	ENCLOSURE AND STELE OF SENUSERT I	,,	65

LIST OF ILLUSTRATIONS   xxi

		PAGE
78. Enclosure and Stele of Sebek·her·heb, looking West. XII Dynasty	Backing	66
79. Enclosure and Stele of Sebek·her·heb, looking North	,,	66
80. Altar and Stele of Sebek·her·heb; Amenemhat III	,,	67
81. Shelters of Stones on Hill before Temple	Facing	68
82. Shelter of Stones on Hill before Temple	,,	68
83. Shelters of Stones on Hill before Temple	,,	70
84. The Best-built Stone Shelter before Temple. Ras Suwiq in Distance	,,	70
85. Approach to Temple from West. Stele of Sety I	,,	72
86. North-East side of Temple	,,	72
87. The Temple, from Western Quarry	,,	73
88. The Temple, looking up Axis	,,	73
89. The Temple, looking West, from Top of the Knoll over the Sacred Cave	Backing	74
90. Enclosure Walls of Temple, from same point as 89	,,	74
91. Enclosure Walls of Temple, looking up to Knoll over the Sacred Cave	,,	75
92. Enclosure Wall around the Knoll. Haematite Hill behind	,,	75
93. Model of Temple, from the North	Facing	75
94. Model of Temple, from the North-West	,,	75
95. Hat'hor Pillars of Amenhotep III. XVIII Dynasty	,,	80
96. West Front of Pylon, carved by Tahutmes III and Sety II	,,	80
97. Hatshepsut's Shrine of Kings, on North of Temple	,,	84
98. Figures of Sopdu and Amenemhat III, Shrine of Kings	,,	84
99. North Doorway of Temple, Hat'hor Hanafiyeh behind	,,	85
100. Hat'hor Hanafiyeh, from East Side	,,	85
101. Hat'hor Hanafiyeh, from South-West	,,	86
102. Hat'hor Hanafiyeh, from North	,,	86
103, 104. Heads of Pillars in the Hat'hor Hanafiyeh, of Tahutmes III	,,	87
105. Lesser Hanafiyeh, looking East	,,	88
106. Lesser Hanafiyeh, looking North	,,	88
107. Outside of Sanctuary Wall, Ramessu IV and Amen	,,	90
108. Inside of Sanctuary Wall, Altar and Hat'hor	,,	90
109. North-East Corner of Portico before Sacred Cave	,,	94
110. Hat'hor and Khnumu, East Side of Hanafiyeh	,,	94
111. Hat'hor Hanafiyeh, of Tahutmes III	,,	106
112. Pillars of Ramessu VI	,,	108
113. Stele of Amenemhat III	,,	108
114. Stele of Hor·ur·ra, in XII Dynasty Approach	,,	110
115. Stele of Si·sopdu, Amenemhat IV	,,	.112
116. Set Stele of Uza·hor·em·sa, Amenemhat IV	,,	112
117. Stele of Sinefert	,,	114
118. Stele of 100 Names, Upper Half. Year 4, Amenemhat III	,,	114
119. Stele of Sebek·her·heb. Year 40, Amenemhat III	,,	116

LIST OF ILLUSTRATIONS

120.	BASES OF STELES, FACING THE SACRED CAVE	*Facing* 116
121.	OBELISK OF THREE SEMITES, IEHANEM, B'AASHA, AND KENI	„ 118
122.	GRANITE STELE OF PTAH'SEANKH AND BEBU	„ 118
123.	STELE OF YEAR 27, TAHUTMES III	„ 119
124.	STELE OF YEAR 11, QUEEN RANEFRU	„ 119
125.	STELES OF XII DYNASTY, PARTLY RE-WORKED BY RAMESSU III	„ 120
126.	GREY MARBLE HAWK OF SNEFERU, III DYNASTY	„ 122
127.	BABOON IN SANDSTONE	„ 122
128.	GROUP OF SENUSERT I, AMENEMHAT I, MENTUHOTEP III, AND SNEFERU	„ 124
129.	BASE OF FIGURE OF SNEFERU MADE BY SENUSERT I, AND ANOTHER EARLY BASE	„ 124
130.	HAT'HOR, DEDICATED BY SHIPMASTER SNEFERU, AND FIGURE OF UNKNOWN KING	„ 125
131.	UNKNOWN QUEEN, OF LOCAL WORK	„ 125
132.	HAT'HOR, LIMESTONE, XII DYNASTY	„ 125
133.	HEAD OF STATUETTE OF QUEEN THYI. DARK GREEN STEATITE. XVIII DYNASTY	„ 126
134.	MENTU'NEKHT OFFERING TO SUTEKH	„ 127
135.	STELE OF RAMESSU I, NAMING THE ATEN. XIX DYNASTY	„ 127
136.	BACK OF STATUE OF RAMESSU II	„ 128
137.	FIGURE OF BANTANTHA	„ 128
138.	SANDSTONE FIGURE, FOREIGN WORK AND INSCRIPTION	„ 130
139.	FOREIGN INSCRIPTION ON ABOVE. XVIII DYNASTY	„ 130
140.	QUEEN NEFERTARI AS HAT'HOR. XIX DYNASTY	„ 132
141.	SPHINX OF FOREIGN WORK AND INSCRIPTION. XVIII DYNASTY	„ 132
142.	ALTARS, AND EARLY HAT'HOR CAPITAL	*Backing* 134
143.	CONICAL STONES, ALTARS, AND TANK	„ 135
144.	FLINT KNIFE, XII DYNASTY. ALABASTER VASES INSCRIBED, XVIII-XIX DYNASTIES	*Facing* 136
145.	PIECES OF LOTUS CUP, AMENHOTEP III. PIECES OF ALABASTER STATUETTES	„ 138
146.	PIECES OF GLAZED VASES	„ 140
147.	PIECES OF GLAZED BOWLS	„ 141
148.	GLAZED MENATS	„ 142
149.	GLAZED BRACELETS	„ 143
150.	GLAZED WANDS AND RING-STANDS	„ 144
151.	GLAZED RING-STANDS AND SISTRA	„ 146
152.	GLAZED PLAQUES OF HAT'HOR	„ 147
153.	GLAZED HEADS OF HAT'HOR AND ANIMAL FIGURES	„ 148
154.	GLAZED PLAQUES OF SERVAL CATS	„ 149
155.	GLAZED FIGURES AND PIECES OF BOWLS	„ 150
156.	PIECES OF GLAZED VASES WITH ANIMALS AND PLANTS	„ 151
157.	PIECES OF TWO JARS WITH RELIEFS, RAMESSU III	„ 152
158.	PIECES OF TALL JARS WITH COLOURED GLAZES, RAMESSU III	„ 153
159.	GLAZED BEADS OF XVIII-XIX DYNASTIES	„ 154
160.	COPPER CHISELS FROM TEMPLE. XIX DYNASTY	„ 162

LIST OF ILLUSTRATIONS   xxiii

		PAGE
161. Crucible for melting Copper, from Temple	.	Facing 162
162. Wrought Flints from Gravels	.	,, 163
163. Wrought Flints from Tih Plateau	.	,, 163
164. The Monastery of St. Catharine, from Gebel Musa	.	,, 238
165. The Monastery Garden	.	,, 238
166. The Charnel House	.	,, 238
167. Views from near the Top of Gebel Musa	.	,, 239
168. View looking towards the Top	.	,, 239
169. Chapel of Elijah	.	,, 239
170, 171. Worked Flints from the Wady Ahmar	.	,, 240
172. Section of a Furnace	.	,, 242
173. Plan of a Tomb Circle	.	,, 242
174. Section of a Nawami	.	,, 242
175. Method of Binding the Chisel-shaped Arrow-Points	.	,, 242
176, 177, 178. Three Views of the Nawamis near the Wady Solaf	.	,, 243
179. Shell Bracelets and Beads, Flint Arrow-Heads, and Copper Tools from the Nawamis	.	,, 244
180, 181, 182, 183. Views in the Wady Feirán	.	,, 254
184. Ain Hudherah (Hazeroth)	.	,, 262
185. The Great Bowl of Rocks around Ain Hudherah	.	,, 262
186. Leaving Ain Hudherah for the Wady Ghazaleh	.	,, 262

MAPS

1. The Sinai Peninsula	.	Facing 34
2. Wady Magháreh, with Positions of Steles and Levels in Feet	,,	38
3. Valleys of Serabít el Khádem	.	,, 55
4. Plan of Temple of Serabít	.	At End of Book

CHAPTER I

ON THE SINAI ROAD

THE conditions of travelling and of working in Sinai are very different from those of life in a fertile country such as Egypt, and are still further from the ways of any European land. In Egypt most long distances can be traversed on the railway, and to go a few miles from a station means only an hour or two of donkey ride; whereas in Sinai the tedious camel is the only vehicle, and you may well spend six days on a distance which would be crossed in two or three hours in a train. In Egypt there is always water of some quality near at hand, and it only needs boiling before use; in Sinai the water sources are a day's journey apart, and you may be glad to be within such a distance that a camel can go to the water and back in the day. The beginning is the worst of all, for on the road down is the serious bar of three days without water. In Egypt the rich fertility of the land provides an abundance everywhere; excellent birds, fish, good native bread, eggs, milk, and vegetables are almost always to be had. But in Sinai grim nature gives you the stone and the serpent instead of the bread and the fish, and the utmost that can be obtained from the desert valleys is an occasional tough sheep or goat.

And if the conditions are thus different, so also are the people. In Egypt the fellah is one of the pleasantest of good fellows, where yet uncursed by the tourist: always obliging and friendly, and being generally intelligent within the scope of his ideas, he is capable of being trained to a high degree of care and skill; moreover, his industry is amazing, and can always be had by good treatment and pay. But the poor Bedawy of the desert is a very different man: he has been on short commons for untold generations, and has parted with every ounce of his anatomy, and every thought from his mind, that was not essential in his hard struggle. The simplest reckoning puzzles him; he is incapable of foresight or of working for a given end, and he is physically unfit for any continuous labour except that of slowly wandering on foot all day with his camel. A few more persevering men are found, who drift to the turquoise mines and spend a few hours a day, with many rests between, in rude blasting and breaking up the rock. One or two important chiefs show more capacity; by far the strongest of these is Sheykh Mudakhel, who has developed a good character and power of business in his dealings at Tor. So different are these people from the Egyptians, that our men from Upper Egypt consorted with us far more than with the Bedawyn; and, indeed, they had benefited by some years of training, so that they were much nearer to us mentally than they were to the men around. The natives were incessantly quarrelling over trying to get the better of one another, while a squabble was unknown among our Egyptians.

Without the Egyptians we could have done nothing in excavation, for it was only on their steady work and skill that we could rely. We wrote to our old friends at Quft, in Upper Egypt, selecting about thirty of the strongest among them; and Mr. Currelly headed them across more than three hundred miles of the deserts and the Red Sea, up to our camp in Sinai, as he will describe in due course.

Having a camp of thirty-four persons is a serious responsibility in the midst of such a wilderness. The

ARRANGEMENT OF THE EXPEDITION

ordinary traveller goes through with perhaps one or two men beside the Bedawyn, and those men are generally his providers, who look after him, instead of his having to think about looking after their needs. Very few, if any, travellers have been through here without having everything arranged for them by a dragoman; and certainly no such party as thirty men staying for some months has ever been here since the old mining expeditions of the Egyptians, which came to an end three thousand years ago. To read most narratives of visitors to Sinai is only to hear of the inevitable fat Mūsa or Suleyman, who was so devoted, yet so domineering; who cheated over the tents, and doled out such versions of the way as he thought would interest the helpless employers who paid him. The negotiations in a grand hotel in Cairo, the days of delay while the retinue was being collected at Suez, the bargains and contracts with official sheykhs, all these form the threshold of most narratives. Here I shall state the steps of a very different way of proceeding, without any of those complications which are useless if you have a small knowledge of Arabic, and give some outline of the management which is required when dealing with a large camp in such a life.

Our stores were a vital question, and we carefully planned them, and had them sent from England to Suez. Such details as may be useful, regarding rations for natives and the food needful for good health, have been stated in the preface. The essential facts are that it is cheaper and better to have everything—even flour—out from England; and that by properly assorting the boxes, and planning their storage until required, everything can be at hand without encumbering the movements of the party to a serious extent.

The dominant factor in every arrangement is the camel—how much it can carry, how long it will take on the road, and how its loads can be arranged. And the camel-driver is the next factor, as his tariff will determine what is worth while in transport, and how to plan affairs, and his possibilities of peculation will settle how much you will receive of what he brings. Very few camel-men can resist taking toll from food in sacks—sometimes a large proportion, worth nearly as much as their wages; so it is needful to secure all stores in nailed-up boxes, which they have not the tools or the wits to tamper with.

On December 2nd our party assembled at Suez, and preliminary business was settled. At Cairo I had picked up two of my old workmen, one of whom, Erfay, walked with us all the way to Sinai, while the other went down with the store boat. The first lesson to learn was that camels can only be secured through a head man of some sort; the individual camel-man will not (as in Egypt) make agreements with strangers, but only works for superiors of his own kin. Had we but known that Abu Ghanéym, the sheykh of Wady Magháreh, was in Suez at the time, we should have done far better to settle affairs with him at once. But all that I could reach from official sources was the chief grain merchant, contractor, and middleman of Suez, Abu Qudéyl. At first I had intended taking stores down by camel from Suez; but Abu Qudéyl's terms of £2 a camel made this impossible. He then proposed a boat for the stores, but as he demanded £15 for it down to Burdéys, the nearest landing-place on the Red Sea, I left the Consulate with only an agreement for four camels to take our camping stores and stuff.

The next lesson to learn in Suez was that the shipping agents, Messrs. Beyts & Co., were the indispensable basis for affairs. To any one in Sinai it may be said that Beyts is Suez and Suez is Beyts. From the first hour that I went to inquire about our stores, to the end of all our work, the constant kindness and courtesy of Mr. H. B. Bush, who was the partner in Suez at the

THE START FROM SUEZ

time, was an unfailing help to us. Every week our camel-men went to the office to deposit our antiquities and to get fresh stores; the post office sent all our letters there, and the Consulate deputed making contracts to the same friendly care. So soon as I named Abu Qudéyl's demand of £15 for a boat, Mr. Bush set his staff on the matter; and though the astute old middleman had cornered every likely boat, so as to force our hands, another new man was found to do the trip for £4. This we raised to £5 on condition of the boat waiting any time required, till all our boxes were removed by camel. We could not have succeeded nearly as well without Mr. Bush's help, but not every traveller could hope to find in all these ways so much assistance so readily granted; our work, however, appealed to his old university interests in history, and so our kind friend did everything to make our path easy.

On December 3rd we left Suez (properly Soweys or Sueys) by boat to Esh Shatt, on the other side of the Canal. This is some three miles' run, doubling the promontory of Port Ibrahim at the mouth of the Canal, and turning up the Canal a short way. Here is an elaborate quarantine station, with every facility for isolation and disinfection, and a good water supply from the Nile, which should be taken in here for the three days' journey to Gharándel. We had the offer of quarters in the station, as it was unoccupied; but I thought it more prudent to practise pitching our tents, and make sure that everything was complete. We had some Egyptian army tents and some English army tents, all bought from disused stores; the former were far more comfortable, as the sides were higher, and a thin muslin lining made them warmer.

The agent of Abu Qudéyl here brought up the four camels that were allotted to us, and they were anything but satisfactory. I had been assured that four kantars (400 lb.) was the recognised load for a camel here; but none of these were fit for more than three kantars, and one of them was always breaking down under much less, and had to be left after a day, and another camel substituted from another party. There was an hour and more wasted in squabbling about the loads, and I learned that it is best to make up equal loads oneself, and then let the men have the choice of them, for this course at Wady Magháreh saved all disputes.

The camel-men were varied. The best of them was Sálah Abu Risq, who evidently belonged to some old aboriginal race before the Semites. He was short and very dark brown, with a Socratic face and a cheerful, friendly manner. He could not resist joining in a plot to screw us later on, and making up a fabulous item in accounts; but he was always reasonable and quiet, except when he blazed up if he were being imposed on by the others. His wrath, however, was good-tempered, though fierce, and had none of the wearisome snarl in it of some other men. He was afterwards my wife's camel-man when she came down to join us, and was liked for his good-humoured, childish ways.

The most distinguished of our men was M'teyr, a pure Semite with long face and nose, of a light yellowish complexion and with a greyish beard. He was cousin of a sheykh, and made claim to considerable authority. For heartless unpleasantness there was not his equal; he could fawn, he could palaver, but once let him feel that he had a real hold on you and his bullying was insufferable. More than once the honest indignation of little Sálah burst out upon him, and reproached his shameless grasping. The other two men were non-entities.

But on the way we were joined by the wily Khallýl Itkheyl. He was a most picturesque rascal, with fine regular features, light brown skin, and a short black beard. He could smile marvellously and show the whitest of teeth, could dance to perfection, and look all the time capable of cutting any man's throat, if it were quite safe to do so. For sheer push, insinuation, and wile he had not his equal.

During part of the first day we had with us old Abu Ghanéym, the sheykh of the Wady Maghâreh and Serabít el Khádem. Had I known of his position beforehand I should have made a contract with him at once, which would have saved annoyances later. He is an old man for a Bedawy, for he was a small boy in the time of Major Macdonald, about 1862, and so must be about fifty now. He is hardly more than skin and bone, dark brown from exposure, and of a middle height. He has a good, courteous manner, and is more sincere and honest than any of the others we had to deal with, though he naturally follows his ethics and not ours in a bargain. He is intelligent in things that pertain to his life; and has a real care and interest in carrying out his engagements and maintaining his relations with others. We saw a good deal of him later on, when he camped by us in charge of our affairs at Serabít; and even when his loquacity was too much, one could not but feel a real friendship for the old man. His brother, Ra'abíyeh, was much of the same character, rather younger, with a better head, and more command about him; altogether, he is much the best man with whom to do business for anything at Maghâreh.

On December 4th at last we were on the way by 10.30, going down the old road that every one has trodden from prehistoric days—turquoise hunters eight thousand years ago, Egyptian conquerors of the 1st dynasty, miners of all ages, the tribes of Israel, and the hosts of pilgrims to Mount Sinai in later ages.

The track (see Map 1 at end) lies along the nearly level plain of raised sea-bed which stretches from the present shore, back over more than ten miles, to the foot of the great limestone plateau of the Tîh. The surface is thickly strewn with flints, washed down from the limestones behind. But a way had been cleared through these flints, much as roads have been cleared on the Egyptian desert from Memphis to the Oasis, or at Tell el Amarna. The flints were swept up to either side into two ridges, and in various parts I measured the clear road as 320 and 310 in. wide, which is 15 cubits of Egyptian measure; the roads to the Oasis and the Fayum were 50 cubits wide (PETRIE, *Season in Egypt*, pp. 34-5). This road could not be traced on descending to the clear marly plain before Ayūn Mūsa; and beyond that no trace of such a road could be seen, even where the track was strictly confined by passing over gaps in the ridges of the plain. It seems, therefore, that this road only led from Arsinoë to Ayūn Mūsa, and no farther.

We walked on to Ayūn Mūsa (the springs of Moses), where we lunched, and watched the reloading of the camels after watering, from 1 to 2.15. The springs here are brackish and dirty pools, which, though good enough for camels, should not be reckoned on instead of the good water at Esh Shatt. The water is now used for considerable-sized gardens; there are four large enclosures, each holding from fifty to a hundred palm-trees, and a great quantity of tamarisk, which is a favourite food for camels. The spring to the south of the plantations is remarkable for the manner in which the dead water-fleas have gradually dammed it round, as described by Fraas, so that, with blown sand and calcareous accretions, a mound has been raised about 20 ft. above the plain, with the spring on the top of it. This implies that the strata are watertight around for a distance of perhaps a mile back towards the plateau, otherwise the water would not thus rise here to overflowing. It was rather below the top when we passed, but had overflowed a day or two before, owing to heavy rain-storms during the past week.

AYŪN MŪSA

The road to this place, which has been described, seems to have led to a fort of Roman age. On the north of Ayūn Mūsa is a mound of ruins about 15 ft. high and 120 ft. across. It is nearly all covered with Arab pottery, but there is some of late Roman age on the surface. The large quantity of slag from the burning of lime, which is mixed with this mound, shows that some large limestone building has been destroyed in Arab times. Hence it seems that a Roman station of some consequence existed here; and the cleared road which we had noticed led down to it. But no trace of a road or any fixed stations was met with farther south. There were great quantities of broken shells about, on the ground and in the mound, showing that the people depended much upon fishing for their food.

We walked on from 2.15 to 4.15, and the camels reached us and stopped at 4.30 in a small valley, where we pitched tents, just north of two flat-topped hills. Travelling in mid-winter is hindered by the short days; in the morning the tents are so wet with dew that they cannot be packed very early, and in the evening the early darkness cuts the journey shorter than it need be. Our system was that one of our party took charge of all the canteen and food, one took all the bedding in hand, and one superintended the tents to see that they were properly done up and no stray ropes or pegs were lost. Each morning we rolled up and roped our blankets inside the tents, and put out enough food for breakfast and lunch. Then, while the camel-men and our Egyptian packed the tents, we had breakfast in the open, and stowed our lunch ready to get it at midday without stopping. The rolls of blankets were always wrapped inside the tent to which they belonged, and this kept them from dirt and vermin. By keeping things in our own hands in this way we never had any insect plagues the whole time.

On December 5th we got everything off by 8.50.

At 10 we reached the fork of the roads,—one track going nearer the coast, and at last passing close below the cliffs of Gebel Hammám; the other track passing inland behind the sea cliffs. Our men took the inland road through the midst of the wide plain of old sea-bed. This plain has only been elevated from the sea in very recent geological times, since the pluvial period, and the valleys are not yet pronounced. Large discharges of water pour over it from the storms which pass up to the edge of the great Tīh plateau, which bounds it on the east. Yet the plain of twenty miles wide has scarcely anything that can be called a valley across it. The streams pour over wide spaces of half a mile to a mile and a half in width, seldom cutting more than two or three feet deep at any part. This is an interesting sight geologically, as it shows us the nature of a recently elevated land, on which denudation has not yet made any serious impress. Each land that we know has had this character when it was young, and had not long emerged from its formative sea; but the elevation has generally been so long ago that the vague wide sheets of flowing water, wandering over a spacious table-land, have cut out deep and decisive channels.

We rested from 12.30 to 1.40, but the camels went on till 4.45, when they halted in the Wady Werdán. The drivers wanted to stop for the night in the Wady Sŭdr at 2.15, quite regardless of food and water supply. But I insisted on pushing on, as we had only water for one night in our tanks, owing to the miserably weak water camel, which could not take a full load to start with. If we did not reach the Wady Werdán this night, we could not possibly have pushed on to water at Gharándel the next night; but of all this the camel-men seemed quite heedless, apparently accustomed to run short, and then make forced marches to get out of difficulties. The Wady Werdán is one of the widest of all these so-called valleys. It is only a slightly lower part of the plain, about a mile and a half across, covered with washed-down gravels and dotted with stunted bushes. The camping should always be made near such vegetation, as the camels slowly browse all night, and the dead stems serve for camp fires and cooking.

December 6th. We were off by 8.10 to walk, the camels following soon after. One of our party gave way in the feet; and as the water tanks were empty, one camel was lightly laden, and I insisted on our friend having a lift on it. As we had not bargained to have riding camels, M'teyr fought the change vehemently. He even said that no one ever could ride a water camel, though it turned out that he was only too anxious to put his own son on instead of one of us. Another of our party tried the camel in the afternoon, but soon gave it up. The brute always howled at every possible change, for better or for worse, and frequently waltzed about wildly, trying to throw its load. It could really take a far heavier load quite well, as we found on following days; but it objected on principle to taking any load at all. In short, the Conscientious Objector—as we named him—was so exceedingly troublesome that he got his own way pretty largely, and plagued us all.

In one place the road seemed to have been graded out, with a width of about 250 in.; but this was the only trace of any artificial track south of Ayūn Mūsa. At about six miles from Wady Gharándel there are great masses of gypsum rock, mostly crystallized, and large shining cleavage-faces appear on blocks of selenite met with in the marly earth. At about a mile and a half from Gharándel we passed patches of dark mud-soil, much like Nile mud; and these are cultivated when there is sufficient rain. It is difficult to see whence such a soil can have been washed down to this position; it might be merely a finely washed marl, which has accumulated humus by the decay of chance vegetation during thousands of years. From this we gradually wound down a side valley into the Wady Gharándel.

This valley is the most important of those in the limestone district. It is the largest valley, as it drains a large part of the foot of the Tih plateau, along which it runs as the Wady Wútah, making up an entire length of some forty miles. And it carries more water than any valley, except those fed by the snows of the granite highlands. When we passed early in December there had only been a few days of rain a week before; and when we repassed late in March, it was after a drier winter than usual, and without any rain having fallen for some weeks. Yet both times we found a good stream flowing down the valley; roughly it might be about a couple of cubic feet per second, and that below a point where much was lost by evaporation over some acres of shallows (figs. 2, 3).

Our permanent camp in Sinai lived regularly and continuously on one-quarter of a cubic foot per head daily, and so some hundreds of thousands of people might be watered in comfort by this stream. The water has only a suspicion of salt in it, much less than there is in that of some seaside places at home. The broad stretches of cool gleaming shoals dotted over with plants and bushes seem a paradise, after those dreary three days in the wilderness behind it. Long may this remain so, and not be seized on for some speculative settlement. A stray campment of Bedawyn here or there is all that breaks the wildness of unspoiled nature. It is the very image of peace and refreshing, after the inhuman waste around it. On the rises of sand above the water are some dozens of young palm-trees (fig. 4), and I heard that there were more farther down toward the sea. The most abundant tree is the tamarisk, beloved of camels; and a striking plant here is the broom-rape (fig. 5), of which I give a view at close quarters. It is well known to grow on the roots of other plants, and so to save its

IN WADY GHARÂNDEL, LOOKING NORTH.

IN WADY GHARÂNDEL (ELIM).

4   PALMS IN WADY GHARÂNDEL.

5   BROOM-RAPE IN WADY GHARÂNDEL.

energies for producing the lovely spikes of blossom. The same habit could be traced here, by the stems being distributed in long lines over the ground, evidently attached to the long roots of the tamarisk. Without thus acquiring its material ready for assimilation it could not have produced such a wealth of flowers from a desert of stone and sand. On the south side of the stream I saw some foundations of houses, made of the rolled stones of the valley; and there were some chips of pottery which were probably Roman, but there were no mounds or refuse from habitation. This points to only a short occupation of the place, probably in the Roman time, when Gurandela is said to have been a station on the road.

For the present I pass the connection with the Elim mentioned in the journey of the people of Israel, as the whole of that subject is considered in the fourteenth chapter of this book.

December 7th. We increased our caravan, as three of the party were more or less done up in the feet by the sixty miles of rough walking. We therefore hired from some Bedawyn three camels to finish the journey to Magháreh; but three of our party walked the whole way down. After crossing the Wady Salamín we came to the Mangáz, or small tributary valley, named Hisán Abu Zena on the map. The story goes that Abu Zena spurred his horse to death here, and the grave is marked by a heap of stones in the valley (fig. 6), to which every passer adds his pebble in hatred of the hard-hearted rider. Though our drivers did not throw anything on the heap, one of them spurned up the dust with his foot against it, and cried out "*Ikhs!*"—" For shame!" But a different story was told to our Egyptians on the road back, when the Arabs said that a Jew was murdered and buried there. If so, he must have been a pilgrim to Sinai, as there would be no chance of peddling any goods amid the native poverty of the folk.

We here began to enter on a more interesting and

hilly district, with outcrops of rock and cliffs. About half a mile farther there is a foot outlined upon a wayside rock, and holes for a game-board of apparently 5 × 5 places, the modern *sigah*. About a quarter of a mile farther is another foot, and a square similarly divided; also a game-board of 10 × 7 or 8 holes, the lines being confused in the middle. Some signs ⋋ and ⊢ ⊦ were also seen. Rather farther on is a game-board of 7 × 7 holes, the larger form of *sigah*.

By the roadside, on the east, was seen a heap of stones, about 3 ft. across and 1½ ft. high; and about 50 ft. farther on was a similar heap. Around each heap a trench had been scraped in the sand, and a long trench connected the two (fig. 7). The account given of these heaps was that a Bedawy had killed an enemy at one heap, and then ran on and succeeded in killing a second man at the other heap. This was said to have happened long ago; but the trenches in the sand round the heaps looked as if recently scraped out, and so some care is still shown for this memorial, whatever its origin may have been. Perhaps some similar arrangement may be found elsewhere to throw light upon this place.

Some small amount of pasturage is found here. The goats were browsing on the desert plants, and the men said they also had some sheep hereabouts. We met four kids being taken in saddle-bags, two and two, on the back of a donkey, with their heads looking out at the top. This region is a wild table-land of nummulitic limestone called El Qarqah, which is trenched up with many valleys and looks much like the desert east of Helwan, which is of the same stratum. It is comparatively frequented, as we passed two or three groups of camels, which were travelling northwards.

From this broken ground we went down (fig. 8) into the Wady Uséyt, which has a fair number of palm-trees and tamarisks fed by a brackish stream. On the opposite

5. THE HEAP OF ABU ZENA.

7. TWO STONE-HEAPS BY THE WAYSIDE.

8. ROAD NORTH-WEST OF WADY USÊYT.

9. FAULTED MARL STRATA IN WADY USÊYT.

side of the valley there is a fine series of faults in beds of brown and white marl (fig. 9). In one part there are drops of 3 or 4 ft. at about every 20 ft. of distance, the fall being towards the west. These faults in the marls do not extend up into the horizontal limestone beds above; and they are therefore due to movements before the Eocene limestone was deposited. The marl strata beneath the limestone appear to be exactly what may also be seen at Thebes, where many of the tombs and the chambers at Deir el Bahri are cut in soft grey marls. And some gigantic subsidences, or cliff falls, are to be seen at Qurneh, owing to the Nile having washed the marl bed away from under the limestone.

We next turned up a branch valley running south from the Wady Uséyt. This contained about five tall palms and some thirty young ones; the proportion suggests that the palm has been recently spreading (fig. 10). The tamarisk here is the last seen on this road, going eastwards, though some more grow in the Wady Tayibeh to the south. This branch valley has the strata dipping towards it for a quarter of a mile, more and more steeply as they approach it on the west, and finally edging the watercourse with a tilt of about 30°. In contrast to the horizontal limestones before seen, this scarcely seems to be due to extreme folding, but rather to the collapse of a subterranean channel or deep gorge, eroded through the marls below.

In the valley there is a thickness of about 20 ft. of river gravels; and these are cut through by a small streambed, for in recent times the rain-storms only form a narrow channel. The greater gravels apparently belong to the pluvial period, when the current filled the whole breadth of the valley. In these old gravels I found a flint scraper, which is certainly of human work; thus it is clear that man was here in the great pluvial age, and the same result was found elsewhere, as we shall note farther on.

We next crossed an open, high plain; and then

descended into the Wady Et-hál ; hence we went up the opposite side by a branch valley, and struck down the Wady Shebeikeh, into the head of the Wady Taýibeh, where we encamped.

On December 8th, we started down the Wady Taýibeh. In the upper part some strata dip into the valley at an angle of 45°. This seems almost too much for a line of folding, in a district which is not crushed or contorted to anything like this amount in general. It seems rather that there has been the collapse of a subterranean channel, like those to be seen in the midst of the perfectly level limestone of the Nile Valley.

The gravels here are very instructive. They fill the breadth of the valley, and have been cut through by later streams to a depth of 7 ft., the new channel not being half the breadth of the valley. The old gravels are very evenly stratified, the same beds of coarse sand, or of large flints, extending for hundreds of feet in length without any alteration, and being the same on both sides. This shows that these gravels were laid down by a wide stream, which filled the valley and rolled steadily for years together ; such beds cannot have been produced by casual shifting shoals of a small current, eating away in one place and shoaling up in another. Now in the bed of large rolled flints I found an excellent long thin flake of skilled neolithic work (fig. 162, no. 6), and another with parallel flaking (fig. 162, no. 5). The pluvial age, in which these gravels were rolled down by a strong and wide current, must, then, be contemporary with well-developed neolithic man. The same result is shown by a well-marked flake of flint which was found by Mr. Porch at 15 ft. deep in the old filling of Wady Magháreh, which is composed of granite sand and blocks. The later stream has cut through this filling, and so exposed a section of it. The flake is shown in fig. 162, no. 3. Others were found 2 ft. down in the gravel of Seih Sídreh, shown in fig. 162, nos. 2 and 4. All these agree with the flaked flints which

I found in the old high gravels of the Nile Valley (*Naqada*, p. 50, pls. lxix., lxxvi.), though these are perhaps mainly of an older type. The sides of the valley Tayibeh are worn with cascades of rainfall which have poured into it from the plateau above (fig. 11).

In the valley was a straggling stream, too brackish to drink; but it maintained some seventy palm-trees, beside tamarisks, tall rushes, and other plants, which formed a tangle of undergrowth. After a mile or two, however, the stream sank into the floor of the valley, and was no more seen down the rest of the barren track. In the lower part of the valley the whole of the limestone strata dip seawards at about 30°, and I traced about 600 ft. of vertical fall. Next a level part appears; and after that a renewed fall seawards, amounting to about 600 ft. more, until it tilts into the Red Sea. Thus, what has been the plateau, 400 ft. above the sea, must dip down to about 800 ft. below the sea within a couple of miles. On looking back northward, however, to the great mass of Gebel Uséyt, which forms a high cliff over the sea, the tilt is in the reverse direction, running about 6° down inland. The rocks near the sea are of hard black marl overlying red marl; and in the fissures of the black rock are films of green copper salts.

At the mouth of the Wady Tayibeh we came out upon the shore of the Red Sea, along which we walked for eight miles before turning inland again. First we passed the ruined tomb of Abu Zenýmeh, from which the headland is named; this stands out on a low, bare shore close to the sea. Beyond that the road cannot pass below the cliffs, as they come down into the water; and a passage is found over a low foot-cliff of about 60 ft. high, while above it towers a glaring white face of limestone sheer up for about 600 ft. These cliffs of El Murkheiyeh are noticeable for the extraordinary regularity of the strata. The alternations of harder and softer stone in the part which we crossed are so uniform that it appears exactly like a ruined building. There is much calcite in the limestone, some of it with good rhombic fracture, but not transparent; this is like the calcite so abundant on the plateau at Tell el Amarna and elsewhere. On rounding the headland of Gebel el Markha the sand is much of it black, being largely composed of magnetic oxide of iron and some garnets. This is evidently the final washing from the denudation of the igneous rocks inland; and the amount of such that come down the Wady Bába to the sea is seen by the blocks so thickly strewn on the plain of El Markha, to the south of this.

We next crossed the plain of El Markha diagonally, about five miles, to the Seih Bába. This raised sea-bed is almost a level stretch, about three to four miles wide and ten miles long. It is covered with blocks of grey granite, red granite, pink felspar, black quartzose rock, and basalt, which have been swept down from the inland mountains in the pluvial age.

On the south side of the mouth of the Seih Bába the rounded limestone flank was marked by a large black patch. On going up to it this is seen to be the "slag heaps" marked on the ordnance map. The furnace stood at the foot of the hill. It is a heap of calcined and crumbled granite blocks, about 15 ft. across and 5 ft. high. I intended to have cleared and examined it, but other work occupied all our time. Strange to say, there was no slag whatever around the furnace on the plain, but it had been all carried up on to the spurs of the hill. I searched the hill-top above, but there was no trace of a furnace or source of slag up there; and the heaping of the slag was not as if thrown over the edge above, but was greatest at some distance out upon the spur. On one spur an area of about 80 ft. by 60 ft. was covered with the black lumps, and a smaller part of the next spur; but there was none in the little hollow between the spurs. Among this slag are some pieces which contain a large proportion of copper, by their weight and by the green carbonation on the surfaces; also some

10 PALM-TREES IN WADY USEYT.

11 CLIFFS IN WADY TAYIBEH.

12 HEAD OF THE SEIH BÁBA.

SLAG HEAPS AT SEIH BÁBA

smaller pieces appear to be nearly pure metal. This site for smelting was evidently used in order to be near the fuel supply of desert plants, which grow scattered over the wide sea-plain of El Markha. The ore was doubtless brought down the Wady Bába, perhaps from the Wady Nasb. The lower part of the Wady Bába is known as the Seih Bába, a term for a broad valley in contrast to a gorge. We went up and camped for the night at the Mawaqf. The sharp bend in the valley just above this shows an interesting unconformity, tilted limestone strata being capped with horizontal strata above, probably of marls. The tilting, however, hardly shows in the photograph (fig. 12).

On December 9th I started on before the camels, and walked up a side turn from the valley, which is scarcely shown in the map, but which opens out into a wide upland valley, with enough resemblance to the Wady Shellál to be rather deceptive. After going a mile up it on a track, I rejoined the camels. A couple of miles up the Seih Bába the way appears to be blocked by a vast cliff of dark grey schist. The rock has fallen away along the planes of large faults, leaving enormous smooth surfaces which shine in the sun. Two valleys turn off sharply to either hand, and we left the Wady Bába on the left and turned to the right up the Wady Shellál. No waterfalls or steep watercourses were seen to justify this name; but there was enough underground moisture to grow several fine acacias.

We crossed the higher branches of this valley, along a plateau where the road follows the straight edge of a highly tilted bed of red sandstone (fig. 14). As we wound farther up we came to the pass of Naqb el Budérah, or "pass of the sword's point," which is 1,263 ft. above the sea. At the valley head there rises a steep blank end of rock, which seems to shut it in; but a winding track has been made, twining half a dozen times zigzag between the blocks, up which the laden camels can slowly toil. In the photograph (fig. 15) three camels have already made one turn and are passing away, while the foremost has made the second turn, and is coming up towards the camera, which is on the higher part of the road. The present track, and the banking up of it with retaining walls, seems entirely modern, due to Major Macdonald, in 1863. There is no trace of an older track, which is asserted in Baedeker to have been here; but that may have been entirely restored beyond recognition. At the head of the pass there is a fine view back, with a glimpse of the sea in the distance (fig. 13).

From the top of the pass we came into a wide, shallow valley, which slopes down into the Seih Sídreh, and from which we see a mass of red granite mountains before us. Descending toward these we come into the Seih Sídreh, a valley which sharply twists about, hemmed in on both sides with granite cliffs hundreds of feet high. At one point a great dyke of red porphyry, about 5 ft. thick, has filled an immense fissure in the granite. The whole of these granite hills had evidently been disintegrated and denuded into valleys, long before the Carboniferous sandstone was deposited; and the stripping away of the sandstone has merely revealed the older hill surfaces. In one place the sandstone is seen bedded against a great cliff face of granite. The sea-worn islands of granite are seen very clearly in the Wady Umm Themám, which branches to the left before reaching Magháreh. Turning up the Wady Iqneh we found ourselves at our goal, the mines of Wady Magháreh. This name means "the valley of caves," so called from the many ancient mines which occupy its side. There may not seem much in common with the name Trafalgar, which has, however, the same word in it. Terf el Ghor, "the end of the hollow," or deep valley, is the Moorish name for that great Spanish headland, which is at the side of a mountain ravine; and Ma-gháreh means "the hollowed-out place," or region of caves.

13 NORTH FROM BUDÊRAH PASS.   14 SANDSTONE RIDGE, WADY SHELLÂL.

15 CAMELS CLIMBING THE NAQB BUDÊRAH PASS.

CHAPTER II

THE BEDAWY AND THE DESERT

ON reaching Wady Magháreh we found some little difficulty. Our contract was ended, as I had been told at the Consulate that there would be no difficulty in making a fresh contract for camels on the spot. This might have been true enough if we could have waited to negotiate; but one of our two boxes sent as provisions, had proved to be other stores, so our reserve had vanished and we were on very short rations, even the last day down to Magháreh. Our boat of stores was duly ready at Burdéys, but we needed to hire camels to bring up supplies. Even water was two miles away, and a camel was necessary to fetch it. The pushful Khallýl organized a ring, and tried to force us to pay permanently as much as the greedy Abu Qudéyl had charged for camels on the way down. This was 20 piastres (4s.) a day, though he only paid the men 12 piastres a day. The claim was enforced by the argument that a certain young official from England had been charged as much all the time he was in Sinai. Not a single camel-man present would work except under a sealed contract with a head man, and Khallýl tried hard to force the price. However, I stood out until he came down to 16 piastres a day; and then next morning by candle-light I drew up an Arabic contract with Khallýl, guarding against the chances of further imposition. After duly sealing it, we got our camels off for water and stores. Even though we were thus in a hole, yet the whole difference between what we paid for the season, and the lowest rates we might have obtained, was not as much as the cost and losses of waiting a few days at an hotel, to get sheykhs up and contracts made beforehand in the usual way. Any one with a few days' supplies in hand could easily go on, and settle terms as they went, with much less loss than is caused by the usual delays. Of course, Arabic is essential, and enough to write a contract when needful, as no scribe can be found in the wilderness. Our whole account for the journey down, camels, supplies, and everything, only came to a quarter of the usual charges of a dragoman for such a party.

Subsequently, finding that Abu Ghanéym was the rightful sheykh of the district, and that he had gone off again to Suez, I sent his son after him with a letter to the Consulate, asking that a contract should be made with him for camels. This matter was handed over to Mr. Bush to arrange, and some ten days later the old sheykh turned up with his contract for camels and guarding duly signed. Khallýl had half suspected that I was negotiating over his head and dealing with some one else, and he remarked to my Egyptians vigorously, "If so, by Allah! I will slay him with a sword." When, however, a fortnight of his contract was completed, I walked up to him, in the presence of several other Arabs, as witnesses, and told him that I there ended our contract. Finding that Abu Ghanéym had us in hand, he gracefully disappeared; only to turn up again as a camel-man for our Suez post later on, and to cheat our men badly over their commission for tobacco. He managed also to completely get hold of the Abady sheykh's son, Yusuf, when he was on the road going up to Suez to meet my wife and Miss Eckenstein, and thus pushed himself into their employment without my knowing anything of it.

A constant difficulty in our arrangements was the tribal system of every one having a claim to profit by the stranger within their domain. However good a camel and driver you had secured for the post, or for water, so soon as his week was up he never could come again, because it was some one else's turn to get a share of patronage. There was no such thing as a personal service of a definite man; the service was that of the tribe, contracted for by the sheykh, and every man of the tribe had his equal right to get a share of the benefit, if only you stayed long enough. The system of incessant shifting caused by a man disappearing so soon as he had learned what to do, and a new man having to be taught in his place, makes little worries and difficulties almost daily. Even if a camel-man agrees to take you over a given country, you may find that at some point he enters the ground of another sheykh, to whom he has to transfer you and your affairs.

The account of Magháreh will be given in the next chapter; but, as we are here dealing with the Sinai road, we may continue with some account of the fresh parts that we traversed on our way back.

From Magháreh on our way to Serabít, later on, we went across the wide, open plain of the Seih Sídreh (see Map 1), and then turned into the narrow valley of the Wady Sídreh. The enormous red granite headlands of Gebel el Leben tower up some 800 ft. above the valley, and the magnificent gorge is the finest that we saw. A very curious feature is the number of caves a yard or two across, hollowed out naturally in the red granite. At first sight I could not believe but that some soft sandstone came in here; but it was sheer hard granite, weathered out in rounded caves, which run in deeper than their external width. These certainly seem as if they were due rather to sea-action than to aerial weathering.

The names of the valleys here are erratic, as will be seen on the outline of the valley system, Map 1. The Wady Sídreh turns off up a minor branch, while the main valley takes the name of Wady Umm Agráf, or "the mother of banks." And similarly, after a few miles, the Wady Umm Agráf turns up a minor branch, and the main valley is called the Wady Siq. Some miles farther the Wady Siq is a minor branch, and the main valley becomes the Wady Khamíleh. Thus the same main valley has four names within eight or ten miles' length. On the ordnance map the valley Umm Agráf should turn up northwards at the letter " A " of Agráf; above that point the Wady Siq begins.

In the Wady Umm Agráf we entered on grey gneiss, and then, turning off the main valley, we gradually wound up higher and higher into the sandstone region. This valley is not marked at all on the ordnance map; and on the Egyptian Government map (unpublished) only the lower half of it is shown. It runs north-north-west, until it turns west for a mile or so, at about a mile south of the temple of Serabít. The upper end of this valley, where we camped, gives by far the best access to the temple, and is well known to Sheykh Abu Ghanéym, though never noticed yet by Europeans. The description of Serabít will be given in Chapter V.; here we are only dealing with the roads.

The afternoon that I left the temple of Serabít for the last time, on March 18th, the copying had kept me as late as was safe for getting over the unknown ground, to our new camp on the return road; the rest of the party had gone on from our permanent camp by a long detour of the valleys. With one Egyptian who was up with me, I then set off down the desert valley to the north-west of the temple, the Wady Dhába. We worked around the sides of one precipice after another, and at a point where a fall of 30 ft. seemed quite impassable, we found a slight track, turning up over the hill into another branch of the valley, that could be scrambled over. The views of the cliffs, and the great tabular mass of sandstone that has fallen over (fig. 18), will give some faint

16, 17, 18.   VIEWS IN THE WADY DHÂBA, NORTH OF TEMPLE.

DESCENT TO THE WADY SUWÍQ

idea of the gorges. Often we had to drop 5 to 8 ft. down the smooth-worn cliffs.

At last we saw the open mouth clear into the great Wady Suwíq, and thought we had a plain way before us. Suddenly the valley-floor dropped about 50 ft. at a crescent-shaped overhanging precipice. We tried the east side, but in vain—the fall was still too great for us. Then we skirted over steep slopes of the west headland, which ended in a vertical fall; and at the extreme point of the spur there was such a slope of the lower detritus that it almost banked up the cliff's face below, and previous passers had piled up stones so that it was possible to scramble over the cliff edge, and thus descend. A long tramp over steep slopes of rotten red schist brought us at last to the track in the Wady Suwíq, after an hour of incessant steep descent from the temple plateau. What the plateau edge is in other places may be seen by the frontispiece, which shows a cliff with 700 ft. sheer fall, the nearest to the temple.

We then hurried on, as sunset was not far off and we knew nothing of the country or of our party. As we went down the valley our former guard, Selameh, overtook us, riding a camel at full trot, and said that our people had started before him; but as he, not being laden, could take a shorter road, they were still behind, though we did not know it. He turned up the Wady Zebéyr, where he lived, and we tramped on and reached the Wady Nasb at sunset. A peak of sandstone (fig. 19) stands opposite the entrance to the valley. We had arranged to camp at the Wady Nasb, where there is a good water supply; but there was no trace of the party. Seeing camel-tracks, we went up the valley about two miles to the well, but our people had not come. We found one man living there, and getting a subsistence from a small garden which he cultivates. He sees some society, as camels have to come up for water when any one is in the neighbourhood. He then trotted back with us by moonlight down to the entrance of the valley. There was not a sound to be heard. He shouted "Mersán," in a loud, hoarse voice, and there sounded back from distant cliffs a clear, bell-like echo to the note D, but no answer. After a time again he shouted "Mersán," and again the cliffs echoed clear, to the note E, but no man answered; yet again he shouted "Mersán," and again the cliffs echoed, to the note F, but no other human sound could be heard. It was strange how calls which seemed so rough and so similar close at hand, echoed on such clear and different notes from the distant hills. He then searched the sandy floor of the valley for tracks, and concluded that our large party of camels could not yet have passed. So I lay down on the smooth sands and rested, looking at the brilliant full moon overhead. It was a perfect night, warm and still, and bright with the clearness of a transparent air. The native and my Egyptian moved a little way off, collected some sticks, and lit a small fire, purely for the sake of variety, as there was no chill.

After an hour or so we heard the faint clank of our water-tanks, and soon our train of camels began to file out of the valley into the wide ground. There were thirteen camels of our own, and five of other Bedawyn, hanging on, as they were not employed; there were also eight others behind with more boxes of antiquities, so that accounted for nearly all of the thirty camels which I had seen crowding our peaceful little valley at Serabít in the morning. They all shed their baggage anyhow, and we had some trouble to get them to move off and keep quiet enough for the night. The proper course when travelling with a train of camels is to call a halt of the main body for pitching, and then move on the camels with tents and provisions 200 or 300 yds. farther; as soon as they have dropped their loads, they and their men can be sent back to the main body for the night. In this way they can be kept at a distance from the tents.

19   HILL AT MOUTH OF THE WADY NASB.

20   EAST SIDE OF WADY NASB. +, TABLET OF AMENEMHAT IV.

21   WADY LAHYAN, FROM + IN VIEW 20.

The next morning, March 19th, I went up the Wady Nasb, or rather Naseb, as it is pronounced, to see it by daylight. A mining prospector who had been there, Mr. Lintorn Simmons, had kindly sent me an exact note of the position of an inscription, and I easily found it. On the east side of the valley opposite the palm garden there is a pass over the cliffs, and at the spot with a cross + over it in the photograph (fig. 20), I found a rock tablet on the north side of the pass. It is much weathered, but shows three lines and parts of five columns of hieroglyphics, dated in the twentieth year of the reign of Amenemhat III (3300 B.C.). The view from here down into the Wady Lahyan is shown in fig. 21. (For the geology and minerals of this district see H. BAUERMAN, in *Quart. Jour. Geol. Soc.*, xxv., 26.)

In the Wady Nasb is an enormous mass of slag from copper smelting, about 6 or 8 ft. high, and extending apparently over about 500 ft. along the valley, and 300 ft. wide, but Bauerman puts it at 250 yds. by 200 yds. It has been dug about in recent times, and the man here stated that there had been found four bars like gold, of the size of his arm; he agreed, however, that they were copper. These were probably the leakings from one of the furnaces, of which the remains of several are to be seen amid the slag. Besides this mass of slag, which may amount to about 100,000 tons, I saw much scattered slag all the way up the path to the tablet, though it as difficult to account for its being thus moved, as for the piling up of the slag on the hill at the mouth of the Wady Bába. The man also said that large beads (*kháraz*) were found there, and that he had some; but on producing them they proved to be only a natural pebble and a concretion. I regretted that I had not a few hours to spare in order to go and examine the mines; but each day was planned till I left Egypt to keep an appointment elsewhere, and I had required all the time possible for finishing the inscriptions of Serabít.

The garden in Wady Nasb (fig. 22) contains many young trees, so that it will be more important a few years hence, when these replace the three or four full-grown palms that are there now. Some tomatoes and other herbs are also grown by the man. My wife asked him, when at our camp, if there was a village (*beled*) up the valley. He replied, "Yes." "And how many people are there?" "One," said he. This is on a par with a young Bedawy who, from the heights of Serabít, pointed out four black tents in the far-off valley, and exclaimed with dignity, " Behold the city (*medineh*) of the 'Aleyqat " —his own tribe. Such is population in Sinai.

There being a water supply in the Wady Nasb, natives make it a centre for camping, and hence there is a cemetery. The graves are curious, as the ordinary heap is piled over with slabs of stone, and often has stones set at the head and feet (fig. 23). The more important graves have an enclosure wall; and one photographed here (fig. 24) has a regular doorway, with jambs and sill, inside which is seen the pillar of stone at the head of the grave.

I then rejoined our camp and we went up a long gradual sand-slope for many miles, the Debbet el Qeray, rising about 400 ft. to a water-shed plateau, and then descending into the wide, flat-bottomed Wady Homr, where we passed from sandstone to limestone. We had on this journey the smallest camel-owner I ever saw (fig. 27). He had been left an orphan as an infant; but his father's property in one camel was scrupulously regarded, and the child-owner made his living by travelling with it. Generally, out of compassion, he was hoisted on to the top of the baggage, where he sat in silent dignity. He was never seen to laugh or to cry, and would hardly accept a sweet mouthful when offered to him. Solemnly and seriously he took the tiring world; let us hope he will find it brighter as he grows up more capable of bearing it.

22 GARDEN IN THE WADY NASB.

23 ARAB GRAVE IN THE WADY NASB.

24 ARAB GRAVE IN ENCLOSURE, WITH DOORWAY.

25, 26, 27. CAMELS ON THE ROAD.

THE RETURN JOURNEY

On March 20th we went on and rejoined our old route in the Wady Shebeikeh, reaching Wady Gharándel that night. The *retem* bushes were in full flower (fig. 30), covered with small white blossoms; the plant is a white broom, and is very bitter. The various protections of vegetation from the hunger of animals in this wilderness are notable. The *retem* has become so bitter that camels will not eat it, and I only saw it attacked by groups of kids, standing on end around it and eating the flowering branches. The more general defence is thorns, and the acacia, or *seyyál*, grows thorns like spike-nails, which might be thought to defy attack. But the camel has grown a mouth to correspond, and browses placidly on the thorns without hindrance (fig. 28). Indeed, our fire of dead thorn-bushes needed to be protected, and we had to drive away a camel who walked up to the smouldering heap and dragged off the dry branches to eat them.

On March 21st we went over the flat desert to Wady Werdán. In the afternoon a violent storm of wind came up; the sand drifted so that it was almost impossible to open our eyes, and we could hardly make way against the gale. How the top-heavy camels kept on was a puzzle, for with so wide a hold on the wind they seemed as if they must go over. We struggled up to the shelter of some sand-hills, in the lee of which there was less wind but more sand. To pitch tents was a hard matter; the pegs dragged out at once, and I had to dig holes and bury them a foot under the sand-heaps. By sunset the gale went down, and we had a peaceful evening.

March 22nd was a long day up to north of the Wady Khurdiyeh; but all hastened along (fig. 25) to the journey's end. Next morning, the 23rd, we repacked and arranged all our baggage, and a short way took us down to Esh Shatt, whence we and our stuff were ferried over to Suez.

To a town-dwelling Westerner no doubt the life of

these Bedawyn must seem bare of the attractions, and even of the comforts, that make existence worth living. Undoubtedly theirs is a highly specialised life, and they are a type as peculiarly fitted to the barren desert as are their own camels. It would probably kill a Bedawy if he were put into our life, as surely as it would kill a City magnate if he lived in the open, by day and night, rain and frost, and fed on unleavened dough half-baked. What, then, may be taken as the main advantages of Bedawy life, as countervailing the different kinds of benefits of our own life?

In health, the advantages are that the desert air is so pure that even coddled house-dwellers, like ourselves, could sit for hours with limbs insensible owing to the cold of the frosty winds, without once having sore throats or catarrh, which would be a certain result at home. The dryness and daily amount of hill-climbing quickly reduce the body to a minimum weight, and though some of us became a painful exposition of bones, yet we were never fitter for work. Such is undoubtedly the type of perfect health for that country. But our civilised laxities clung to memory in a fond craving for a land where it should be always afternoon tea. How much the Bedawy can bear we were astonished to find from our old sheykh, Abu Ghanéym. At Serabít he came and lived by us to see to our safety, in consideration of £4 a month; he sat down under a bush near by, and lit a fire. There he slept in the open; in hard frosts night after night, with thick rime upon the ground, the old man lay rolled in his *'abayeh* overall. Close by him were three tents of our Egyptian workmen, with whom he was on good terms; yet he never once availed himself of such shelter. Then we had one day and night of continuous heavy showers, about 2 in. of rain, which made a water-fall pour over the cliffs in our valley; but the old sheykh needed nothing; he only took off most of his clothes, rolled them up to save wetting them, and lay

28, 29. CAMELS IN THE DESERT.

30. WHITE BROOM, RETAMEH.

all night with only a shirt on in the cold rain. Here was an old man—as Arabs go—shrunken, thin, and showing age in his movements and physique, the most important man for twenty miles around ; yet not caring for shelter, sleeping out in all weathers, and preferring to live just like any animal in the open. Such health would certainly be bitterly missed, though exchanged for much that we value.

The unfettered sense of living in an open country, free to go in any direction, is also a boon of nature which is sorely lost at any price. Even though we have been without it for centuries, it is one of the sweetest pleasures to regain. The open down or moor is the nearest approach to freedom that we know at home ; but that is nothing in comparison with the desert. The limitless freedom, the absence of all barrier or bound, the wide stretch of plain, the range beyond range of hills, all your own as you will, is an intoxicating joy, even to those who have learned to live without it. And to the native it must be as the very breath of life—the enjoyment of it as unconscious, the restraint of it as bitter.

And the other great bondage of our life, that of time as well as space, is also unknown. What is not done to-day can be done to-morrow ; if a journey is wearisome, stop and rest; if it will be pleasanter to spread a day's employment over a week, then do so. "Quickness is from the devil," and if you have no fixed points in your future actions, life will space out as is best. To give up this liberty is a grievous bondage, and wears out the soul of man. Where no one leaves any mark on nature or on his fellows, there can be no ambition to do more than is pleasant and wholesome, and necessary for the moment; and that is the way of peace, which we have bartered for striving and ambition and competition, so that we can scarcely ever know its blessedness, or realise the misery of those who have suddenly to abandon it. Deal with them tenderly, therefore, and expect not that which is contrary to nature.

We pity the dulness of a people without art or literature; for such as their race may have, they have not the knowledge to enjoy. But conversation is their pleasure and constant delight. The steady stream of words which I have heard pouring out hour after hour from a group of Bedawyn, the excitement, the passion, the layer over layer, two or three deep going on at once, is an artistic activity of which we have but a faint reflection left in our lives. It is the same with most nomads, whether the wilds be in Asia, Africa, or America; the use of rhetoric and oratory is one of their greatest powers and pleasures. This is their fine art, this is their literature, this is their politics. And a dreary and clumsy thing the printed page must be when thrust upon such a people, who scarcely need it, as their memories have not been atrophied by its use. Even still the spoken word is more effective than the printed, to all lower types of intelligence among ourselves. They have not learned to distrust its fallacies of feeling, of inattention, and of artifice, nor to prefer a diagram of argument to a flow of heart.

In his family, also, the Bedawy has his advantages. He does not denaturalise his children by putting them into a distant cramming machine, and finding them nuisances in the few weeks he ever sees them. The girl or boy takes charge of the family herds, guides and cares for them, and knows them closely. Without fear they spend their days in the remotest places. Once I nearly stumbled over a little goat-herd of perhaps ten years old, sitting high up on the desert, almost indistinguishable from the stones around. He never moved, and would not condescend to notice me except with his eyes. The children grow up in all the work of the family —quiet, dignified, reserved, and occupied with what their age can do. The close and integral family affection which this joint life produces is certainly a large part of an Oriental's happiness.

The position of women is curiously independent in

view of the law of Islam, which has hardly out-rooted the older life. The tent belongs only to the women and their infants. The men we found sleeping out under the bushes, while only the women were in the tents at night. The open-air life of our old sheykh, despising all shelter in the worst weather, is the type of the man's life among the Bedawyn. The only women we met in the desert were going about alone in charge of their herds of goats, which seem to belong to them as the camel belongs to the man. The woman, in short, appears in the same light as in Egypt, where in early times she was always the property-owner, the "mistress of the house"; and where, even down to the middle ages, a Copt, when selling anything in the market, added the formula, "With my wife's permission." On the coinage of the Nabathaean chiefs of Petra and North-west Arabia, we see Aretas with his queen Sykaminith, Malkhos with his queen Seqilath, Zabel with his queen Gemilath; this custom of placing the queen's head on one side of the coinage is unknown in any other land. And matriarchy has even survived the power of Islam.

CHAPTER III

WADY MAGHÁREH AND ITS SCULPTURES

The sandstone district of Wady Magháreh is about three miles wide between the granite of the Wady Sídreh on the south and the mountains of the Tartír ed Dhami on the north. The name Tartír means "a conical cap," and is applied elsewhere also to hills. The general appearance of this great central mass of mountain, in the midst of the rhomb of valleys (Map 1), may be seen from the figures 31-4. The upper view in each page shows a part of the ridge seen below, enlarged by the telephotographic lens. In the lower views the ridge in fig. 32 just joins to the ridge in fig. 34, showing a continuous line of mountain, as may be seen by the overlapping view, fig. 35. The mountain rises over 2,000 ft. precipitously. The level of the flat valley in the foreground is 1,000 ft. above the sea; the ground rises a few hundred feet, back to the mountains, and then the peak is at 3,531 ft., about the height of Snowdon. The ridge runs from north-west to south-east, and the form of the mountain is best seen about noon, when the sun lights the successive edges, as in the views. But to see its internal structure it should be examined near sunset, when the light is behind Magháreh and there are no shadows on the Tartír. Then it is seen to have been sheared through, again and again, across and across, age after age, by successive faults, each filled up and solidified with porphyries and other fused rocks. The whole face is striped with straight dark lines from top to bottom of

31. EL TARTÎR ED DHAMI, BASALT HILL IN FRONT. TOP OF LOWER VIEW.

32. EL TARTÎR ED DHAMI, FROM MAGHÂREH.

33. TOP OF LOWER VIEW.

34. MOUNTAINS NORTH-EAST OF MAGHÁREH.

MAP 1.—THE SINAI PENINSULA

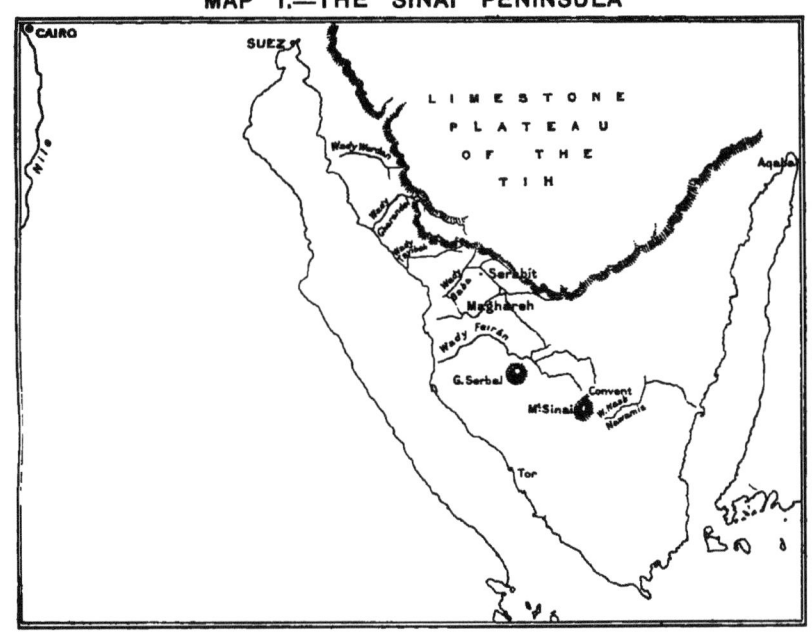

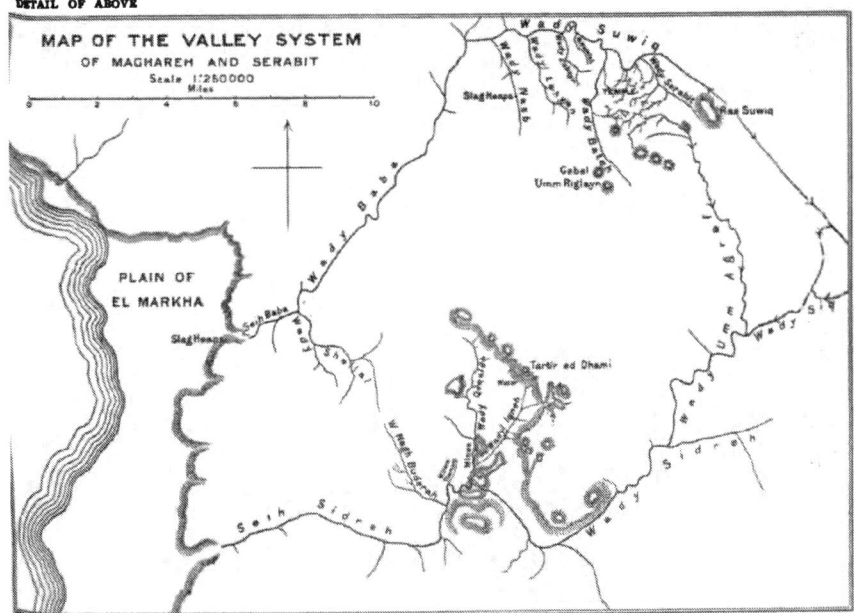

DETAIL OF ABOVE

MAP OF THE VALLEY SYSTEM
OF MAGHAREH AND SERABIT
Scale 1:250000
Miles

the mass, crossing one over the other at all angles. It is an impressive spectacle of a long history, while as yet there were thousands of feet more of granite covering the present core that is left; this alone could make all these fusion fissures possible, through what is now a rugged row of broken buttresses. Later on, a wide, deep space was ploughed out between this mass and the high cliffs of the Wady Sídreh, and a great depth of granite was removed by denudation. Probably an area of sea washed the foot of the Tartír; and the Sídreh cliffs, worn and rounded, rose as islets off that coast.

The next step in its history was that the whole region sank into the sea of the Carboniferous age, and sandstone was deposited hundreds of feet in thickness over the granite. In fig. 31 will be seen a pyramidal peak as the highest point, which must be about 60 ft. high. This appears to be dark brown and stratified, as seen through the telescope, and is of sandstone overlying the highest part of the granite. Many more sandstone peaks cap this granite plateau farther back (see H. BAUERMAN, *Quart. Jour. Geol. Soc.*, xxv., pl. 1). These show that a great upthrow of the central table of granite, amounting to about 1,500 ft., has taken place since the Carboniferous sandstone was deposited; and indeed, probably since the basalt flow in the Tertiary age, which caps these beds at both the high and low levels. The Carboniferous sandstone was carved out into the valleys by rapid water denudation; this is shown by the very smooth outline over its harder and better-preserved parts, quite different to the cavernous hollows of aerial denudation which eat into it along the softer strata. The general appearance of it is shown very clearly in the foregrounds of figs. 32 and 34.

The next stratum is a ferruginous bed, which varies from dark brown sandstone at Magháreh to pure fibrous haematite occasionally at Serabít. The depth of sandstone below it varies from 150 ft. (HULL, *Mem.*, p. 45) to certainly over 800 ft. at the great cliffs of Serabít (see frontispiece). This variation is probably due to the different levels of the older strata over which it is deposited. At Maghâreh the lower sandstone is 170 ft. thick over the valley floor, and also of an unknown depth below that. The thin ferruginous stratum must clearly be taken as deposited at one level anciently, though it is at the level of about 1,170 ft. at Maghâreh and 2,650 ft. at Serabít. It doubtless originated during a long cessation of the laying down of sand, when decaying organisms reduced the iron to oxide, and produced a mass of ferruginous deposits on the sea-floor.

It is only just beneath this iron bed that turquoise is found. The Bedawyn specially search the purply-brown bands of the sandstone as the most profitable. The turquoise is usually in hard nodules, which are picked out after crushing the mass, and are rubbed down to test if they have a turquoise centre. Sometimes the veins of turquoise, or small patches, occupy cracks in the rock. As the turquoise is a hydrous phosphate of alumina, stained with phosphates of iron (blue) and copper (green) in mixed proportions, it was probably derived from the phosphorus of the same organisms that caused the deposit of the iron stratum.

Above the iron at Maghâreh is a stratum of 430 ft. of sandstone rather lighter in colour. At Serabít this upper sandstone appears to be the Nubian sandstone (HULL, *Mem.*, p. 46), as it forms the upper part of the twin mountains of Gebel Umm Riglayn, which rise far above the general plateau about the Wady Nasb. The age of this is Cenomanian, about coeval with the Gault of England.

On the top of this Nubian sandstone is a flow of basalt, which has been nearly all denuded off the country, but yet caps the hills at Maghâreh and the tops of the peaks of Umm Riglayn and those to the east of Serabít. Its level is based at about 1,600 ft. at Maghâreh, and

35. MOUNTAINS NORTH-EAST OF MAGHÂREH, AND WADY IQNEH.

36. CAMEL'S SKULL ON "FORT" HILL, WADY IQNEH BELOW.

37 THE EASTERN MOUNTAINS, FROM MAGHÂREH.

38 THE SOUTHERN MOUNTAINS AND SERBAL, FROM MAGHÂREH.

IRON AND BASALT BEDS

certainly over 3,000 ft. to the north-west of Serabít—a difference of level which is also seen in the sandstones and the iron bed, and is therefore due to elevation. The volcanic eruption in Palestine is put down as Pliocene (HULL, *Mem.*, p. 98); but it is not certain that the Sinaitic basalt is of the same age. On the west of the Wady Umm Themám the basalt is overlaid by a stratum which appeared to be limestone, as seen from a distance; but its position might have been due to a basalt sill working in between two strata, and floating up the upper stratum.

In the views 37 and 38 are the mountains to the east and south-east of Magháreh. The crest to the left of the top view is that seen on the right in fig. 34; and the right of the top view is repeated in the lower view, where it gives way to a distant view of Gebel Serbál, twenty-five miles away, south-east of Magháreh. The foreground shows the faulted beds of sandstone at the side of the Wady Iqneh.

The wide valley, Wady Iqneh, is best seen in fig. 35, with scattered acacia-trees in the flat bed of granite sand. On ascending the hill immediately to the left we have the view of the lower part of Wady Iqneh, which is seen in fig. 36 looking down from the hill. The camel's skull in the foreground was placed on the hill-top by the Bedawyn.

Turning now to the ancient remains, the positions of the tablets connected with the mines are shown in fig. 39, which is a view of the west side of the Wady Qenayeh, or otherwise Wady Magháreh. No. 3 is the tablet of Semerkhet, 400 ft. above the valley floor. The others are all at the 170 ft. level of the iron stratum; 4 is Sahura, 5 Sneferu, 6 Men·kau·hor, 7 Zeser, 8 Sa·nekht, 9 Tahutmes III, and slightly nearer is the second tablet of Sneferu. The hill in the middle rises to 616 ft. above the valley floor; the view is taken from our camp. To follow the general positions, Map 2, of Magháreh, should be compared. All these tablets, except that of Semerkhet, are now in the Cairo Museum, see p. 46.

The approach to Wady Magháreh is shown in the photograph, fig. 40. The great boulder on the left is a fallen block with several inscriptions of the XIIth dynasty, the largest of which is given in fig. 55. This block is marked in Map 2 as "Amenemhat III." Looking here up the broad Wady Iqneh, there is seen a pointed hill in the middle. This has miners' huts around the top of it, a settlement of the Old Kingdom commonly miscalled the "Fort." The Wady Iqneh turns to the right, and the Wady Magháreh branches to the left. The hills to the right are part of the distant granite range of Tartír ed Dhami.

On ascending to the top of the "Fort" hill we look down into the Magháreh Valley, as in fig. 41. This shows the spur of the hill with the Zeser and Sa·nekht tablets on the left, and the XIIth dynasty mine on the right, see Map 2. Down the edge of the spur a wall of loose blocks of sandstone was piled, as seen in the photograph. This wall crossed the valley and ran up to the "Fort" hill. Immediately south of it, to the left in the view, are the huts of the miners; the excavations of these are here seen, at the foot of the spur.

The miners' huts consisted of five chambers, roughly square, and built of the rounded stones of the valley. The walls were about 2 to 2½ ft. thick. On clearing out the rooms five pits were found in the floors, three of which contained pottery jars, the forms of which show that they were of the XIIth dynasty. These pots are shown as they lay, before being moved, in figs. 61 and 62. The plan of this place, and the drawings of the forms of the pottery, will be published in the Exploration Fund volume, *The Egyptians in Sinai.* The contents of the chambers are described farther on.

The position of these rooms shows that the wall across the valley was still used in the XIIth dynasty. And as it

39. NAGHÁREH, NUMBERED POSITIONS OF INSCRIPTIONS.

40. INSCRIBED BLOCK IN VALLEY APPROACHING NAGHÁREH.

41   MAGHÂREH.   HUTS OF XII DYNASTY.   WALL.   MINE OF XII DYNASTY.

42   MAGHÂREH VALLEY.   HUTS OF IV DYNASTY ON HILL IN FOREGROUND.

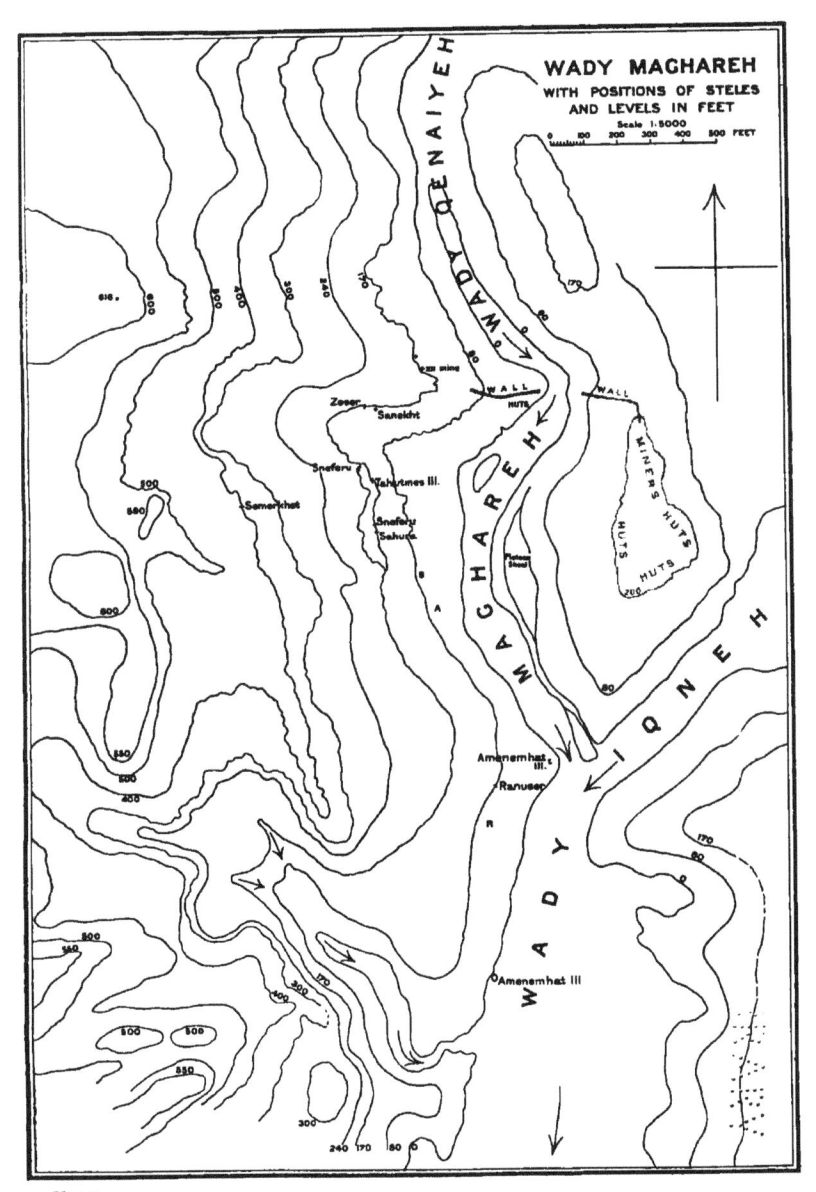

MAP 2

THE MINERS' DWELLINGS

runs up to the settlement of shelters on the top of the hill, which is of the IVth dynasty, it was probably built at that date. It will be seen in fig. 41 that at the bottom of the valley the wall has been washed away, up to a height of about 10 ft. This shows the level of the highest flood that has happened in the last six thousand years, a stream of about 80 by 10 ft. coming from a catchment basin of about eight square miles. Supposing 4 in. of rain to actually flow off from the valley (beside soakage) within twelve hours, which is the probable maximum, that would imply a flow of less than a foot a second at this point, which would scarcely shift the blocks away. The storm must therefore have been remarkably sudden to wash out the wall in this manner.

The view in fig. 42 is from a point on the hill to the left of fig. 41. It shows the same spur and valley, and in the foreground are some of the shelters, which are built all round a platform near the top of the "Fort" hill. This platform is triangular (see Map 2), about 400 ft. long and 200 across at the widest part. Altogether there are 125 of such shelters. Some of these have perhaps been high enough to be roofed, but most of them are mere shelters or wind-breaks, a foot or two high, of rough piled stones.

The question naturally arises why the miners' habitations should have been placed around a hill 200 ft. high, while their work lay nearly as high up on the opposite side of the valley. The approach to the hill was defended by putting the huts just over a cliff-scarp, and building up the only road which led to this by a defence of blocks of stone which left but a narrow entrance.

That all this was done to form a "fort," as it has commonly been termed, is quite absurd. The place could not stand a siege of even a day or two, for it is not possible to get any water under two miles' distance, and there is no means of storage to any useful extent. Moreover, if a fort, why should the better-built houses be put on the shoal at the foot of the hill? Certainly it is not a place for protection against actual fighting and violence.

Is it, then, arranged as a protection against night thieving and marauders? If so, there would be no point in the poorest men, who only made the most miserable shelters of a few stones, living up on the plateau, and climbing up so far every day.

Rather should we look to this being a defence against wild animals. The solid houses of the chief men were proof against any animals, and could be put in the valley; but the poorer people, with very little to shelter them, needed to perch themselves in a less accessible position. One valley in Sinai has been named from the lioness (*labwa*), and the hyaena still haunts camps at night. Seeing how greatly wild animals have disappeared since early days in Egypt, it is not too much to suppose that when the Egyptians first sent parties to Sinai there were enough ferocious animals to make men need the protection of an isolated position, or else of solid houses in the valley. Further details are given below in describing the contents of the huts, and also of those at the foot of the hill, marked "plateau shoal" in the plan. These latter houses had thick walls remaining, but they have been levelled down by the mining company, and can now only be traced under the surface.

The general appearance of the sculptures on the rocks is shown in fig. 43. The large tablet to the right is that of Sneferu; just below it is the small broken tablet of Men-kau-hor; and farther on is the tablet of Sahura, half broken away. The best example of ancient mine-cutting is shown in fig. 44. A trench has been prepared for opening a mine, and the chiselling on the side of it still shows very clearly. This cutting was done with a copper chisel; and much of the mining shows traces of the same tool. But stone picks and mauls were also commonly in use, as we shall see in Chapter XI.

43 MACHÂREH. TABLETS OF SAHURA AND SNEFERU.

44 MACHÂREH. CHISEL-CUTTINGS ON ANCIENT MINE.

45 MAGHÂREH. SCENE OF SEMERKHET AND GENERAL. I DYNASTY.

46 GENERAL OF SEMERKHET.

FIRST DYNASTY TABLETS

The earliest signs in Egypt of intercourse with Sinai are the beads of turquoise, rarely found in the prehistoric graves. And even these must not be taken as conclusive proof; for lazuli is much more often found, and yet the nearest source of that is Persia. Hence the rarer turquoise may have also been from Persia. But when we reach the beginning of the Ist dynasty we find it more freely used, as in all the four bracelets from the tomb of King Zer. And in the tale of Sneferu and the magician Zazamankh, it is a jewel of *mafkat* that was lost; and we now know that *mafkat* was turquoise.

The beginning of the monuments of Sinai is in the Ist dynasty, about 5300 B.C. The seventh king of that dynasty is here written as Semerkhet; and this is doubtless the true form of the name, though it is usually inverted in Egypt as Mersekha. On a smooth natural face of the upper sandstone rock, at 394 ft. above the valley-floor, the scene of this king has been engraved, by sinking the ground and leaving the figures in relief (figs. 45, 46). The surfaces of the figures are left of the natural fractured face of the stone, without any rounding or dressing. The stone does not appear in the least weathered since it was cut, except in the title, and part of the figure of the general; the original face does not seem to have lost even a single coat of sand-grains. The position is rather difficult to reach, and requires some climbing towards the end. A fallen block lies in front of the scene, and there is no footing outside of it, except at a lower level. The flat view in fig. 45 could not have been obtained without my swing-lens camera, which was turned up to a steep angle.

It will be seen that there are three figures of the king. First as king of Upper Egypt, with his *ka*-name, or name of the hawk, with the crown of Lower Egypt; second as king of Lower Egypt, unnamed; and third as king of Upper Egypt, with the hawk-name, uncrowned, smiting a chief of the Bedawyn, whom he has seized.

42 WADY MAGHÁREH AND ITS SCULPTURES

The face of the Bedawy, roughly indicated here, is very like that of the present chief of the same district, Abu Ghanéym. The upright object which is seized by the king is clearly distinguishable here, though it is quite unintelligible in later examples. It is the Bedawy spear, with a very long blade, the projection at the base of the blade showing just over the hand. It has been seized at the tassel, which hangs just below the blade as in the modern spears; and this tassel is shown projecting above the arm. The spear is shown as being also still held by the Bedawy, along with what seems to be an ostrich feather, judging by the outline and the slight ribbing on it. Possibly taking the plume off the head was the emblem of submission. The king is armed with the mace, as in all such scenes, and with the dagger in his girdle, also shown in the other figure with the Upper crown. Both of the standing figures hold a mace in the right hand, and a short pike in the left. These are the oldest examples of rock-carvings, or figures on a large scale. The general of the expedition is figured also here, a little in advance of the group of the king, and on the same scale. The figure is shown squarely on the whole scene; but when closer to it I could not get any but a very skew position, which could hardly be overcome by the swing-lens, as in the lower figure, 46. He has no distinctive dress, but holds a bow in his left hand, of the doubly curved type usual in early Egypt; with it are two objects which may possibly be intended for arrows, but they are so much curved on the outer sides that this seems unlikely. The parting line is too straight for it to represent a flexible object, such as a sling.

The work of this earliest sculpture is summary; no finish is put into it, but it is excellent in the technical qualities and knowledge shown. The action is free and true, without any stiffness or exaggeration. The muscles are admirably rendered, every curve of the outline being

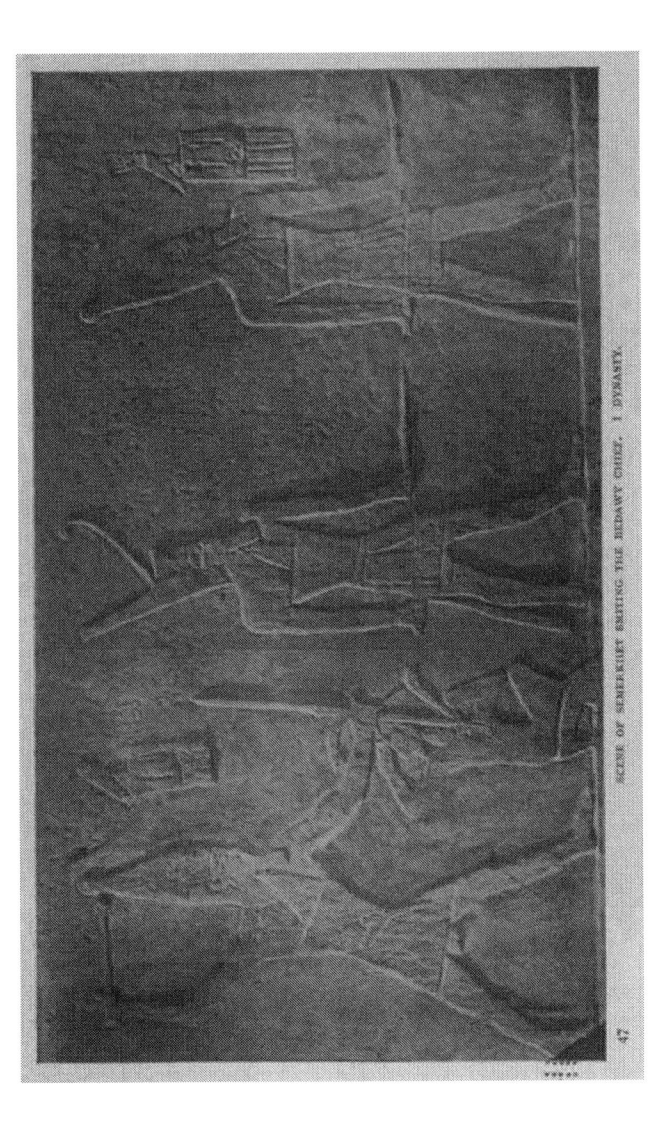

SCENE OF SEMERKHET SMITING THE BEDAWY CHIEF. I DYNASTY.

MAGHÂNEH. HEAD OF SA-NEKHT. III DYNASTY.

full of correct character, though simply cut, without any elaboration. It has the fine qualities of an early art—the very antithesis of clumsy over-elaboration, which is the mark of decadence. The strange thing is that it should have been put in so inaccessible a spot. It is entirely invisible from below, owing to its distance, and even the place of it can hardly be kept in the eye. It cannot be said to demonstrate itself at more than ten yards off, and yet it is more than a hundred yards from any spot where a man would readily pass. Why the record of conquest of the district should be thus put out of sight it is difficult to understand. This is the only monument left at Maghâreh, the others being now in the Cairo Museum.

The next monument carved was that of King Sa·nekht, the founder of the IIIrd dynasty, about 4950 B.C. This is the first inscription directly connected with the mining industry, as it was placed over an early mine. Later mining had brought down the face of the rock, and destroyed part of this tablet (fig. 49), and also another tablet of Sa·nekht showing inferior work; a piece of the latter was found by us in the banks of chips below, and is now in the British Museum. By this mining the place was rendered quite inaccessible. On a ledge of rock I could get a very clear view, which was rectified as far as possible by the swing-lens; but the face was so important that we examined it from about fifty feet distance with a powerful telescope. The drawing of the whole thus made will be given in *The Egyptians in Sinai*, and Mr. Currelly also made a large drawing of the head alone, which is here reproduced (fig. 48). It will be seen how strongly Ethiopian is the character of it, even more so than Shabaka, who was the most marked of the Ethiopian dynasty, the XXVth. The type is one with which we are very familiar among the Sudánys of the Egyptian army and police; it goes with a dark brown skin and a very truculent character. From this sculpture, then, it may be inferred that the declining civilisation of the IInd dynasty was overthrown by an Ethiopian invasion; and the great art of the IVth and Vth dynasties arose out of this mixture. This sculpture has never been copied or published before.

After this, the following king, Zeser, carved a scene lower down to the left. It shows the regular group of the king smiting a Bedawy, and several figures of officials also accompany it. But the work is very rudely and slightly cut, and will not photograph intelligibly.

The next sculptures are those of Sneferu, the last king of the IIIrd dynasty, about 4750 B.C. One scene is finely carved with well-formed hieroglyphs and careful marking of the forms of the limbs (fig. 50). The king wears the pleated kilt and a collar, with an unusual head-dress of two tall plumes and a pair of horns. The inscription along the top contains several names of his, enclosed in one long cartouche. Below is, "Sneferu, the great god, giving power, firmness, and life, all health and all satisfaction of heart for ever, smiting the countries." This is one of the best known of these sculptures, and until the discoveries in recent years of those above described, it was for long the oldest known here.

A short way to the north, in a recess of rock and facing south, was another tablet (fig. 51), cut in the older style of Semerkhet. The natural cloven face of the rock is retained for the figures, without any smoothing; and the ground is dressed away around it. Sneferu is smiting the Bedawy; his *horus*-name is in relief before him, and incised behind him, with the inscription, "Giving power, firmness, and satisfaction of heart." Below are two smaller figures of the king, with the crowns of Upper and of Lower Egypt. The work is very summary, but the large figure is fairly good in action and proportion.

The next sculpture is that of Sahura, of the Vth dynasty, of which a third part was destroyed by recent blasting (fig. 52). Here there have been the three regular

49. MAGHÂREH. SA-NEKHT. III DYNASTY.

50. MAGHÂREH. TABLET OF SNEFERU. III DYNASTY.

GROUP OF FIGURES OF SNEFERU. III DYNASTY.

52. MAGHÂREH. TABLET OF SAHURA. V DYNASTY.

53. MAGHÂREH. TABLET OF RA-N-USER. V DYNASTY.

FIFTH DYNASTY TABLETS

figures of the king, but the standing ones hold a staff in the left hand, and a mace in the right. The standard of the jackal-god, Up-uat, is in front of the king, as on the tablet of Sa-nekht. The whole scene is bordered with the two sceptres down the sides, supporting the heaven, covered with stars, along the top. The work is very coarse and poor compared with that of the earlier times; the forms are clumsy, and the anatomy of the figure is disregarded.

A little later is the tablet of Ra-n-user (fig. 53), which was at the corner of the hill over the entrance to the valley. It is the largest of all the sculptures here, being 63 by 102 in.; but it is on a bad piece of rock, and is but poorly cut. A curious feature is the large vase figured at the side of it, on a stand supported by three *ankh* signs. The work is deep, but coarse; the reliefs have long sloping sides, roughly cut, and the whole is inferior to the earlier work.

A yet poorer carving is that of King Men-kau-hor (fig. 54), also of the Vth dynasty, which was just below that of Sneferu. Part on the left hand had been cut away anciently, and the hawk-name on the right hand has been blasted away recently. This is about the poorest level of work here; as in the XIIth dynasty, the carving was neater in execution, though far weaker in design. This may be seen in the tablet, fig. 55, which was carved high up on the large boulder-block shown in fig. 40. It is dated in the second year of Amenemhat III.

CHAPTER IV

THE MINERS OF WADY MAGHÁREH

HAVING now described the sculptures which were still remaining at Maghâreh, we must turn to the statement of what has unhappily been lost. When we reached the valley we found that most of the monuments previously known had been destroyed or injured about three years before. A company had been formed which had taken out of the hands of the natives their ancient resource of turquoise hunting, in order to "develop" it for the benefit of English shareholders. Everything gave way to the greed for dividends, with the result that the promoters lost their money, the natives lost their turquoises, and the world lost many of its most ancient monuments. No care seems to have been taken by the department which gave the concession to prevent injury to the monuments; no inspector or guardian took charge of the historical remains; and ignorant engineers destroyed what was, in the European market of museums, worth far more than all the turquoises which they extracted. The Khufu sculptures were smashed up. The half-dozen Assa inscriptions were all destroyed or buried. The Pepy inscriptions were annihilated. The whole of the Amenemhat inscriptions at the mines have likewise disappeared. The Sneferu scene has been brutally bashed about with a hammer, and the only portrait of Sneferu has been destroyed. The Sahura scene and the Men·kau·hor tablet have both been partly blasted away.

54 MAGHÂREH. TABLET OF MEN-KAU-HOR. V DYNASTY.

55 MAGHÂREH. TABLET OF AMENEMHAT III. XII DYNASTY.

The Ra-n-user tablet has had pieces knocked off it. Only the Semerkhet scene, high up above the quarries, the second Sneferu scene, and the tablet of Tahutmes III have escaped the wanton mischief done by the ignorant savagery of so-called educated man. The Goths, who protected and preserved the monuments of Rome, were cultivated in comparison with the dividend-hunting Englishman. To find a parallel to the destruction by speculating companies and engineering we must look to the Turkish destruction on the Acropolis of Athens, or Mehemet Aly's wrecking of temples to build factories and magazines. In all these cases a little extra proportion of cost or labour would have attained exactly the same benefits without doing any injury. But the destroyers had not that education which would enable them to understand or value what they unluckily had the inclination to waste. Thus perishes year by year what might so easily be preserved by a little foresight and care. Had any one proposed to carefully transfer these sculptures—the oldest scenes in the world—to a European museum, he would have met with reprobation for appropriating what had stood in position for six thousand years, unaltered and unharmed; and certainly onerous terms would have been demanded of him by the Government. But to abandon the whole to mere savage destruction was the easy course of neglect which befell them.

When we came to the place, we found that the natives had been stimulated to imitate the methods of the defunct company. Blasting was continually going on, and the nearness of sculptures made no difference to the operations. A large block with an inscription of Sahura was being broken up, and we just saved the inscription, now in Brussels. While we were in course of copying the minor inscriptions of the XIIth dynasty, a native came and effaced them with a hammer during the dinner-hour. Nothing was safe, and the only possible course was to remove the remaining carvings bodily from the rocks. I represented the matter with full details to Sir William Garstin, who, in the absence of Professor Maspero up the Nile, at once asked for an estimate of the cost of removal, and made a grant for the purpose. Mr. Currelly undertook the task; and, so soon as our excavating was over, and the workmen could be dismissed, he returned to Maghàreh and successfully cut out all the inscriptions, except that of Semerkhet, which is high above the quarries, on the upper rocks. In spite of many difficulties, and all but shipwreck in a storm in the Red Sea, the whole of the sculptures were safely taken to the Cairo Museum. I do not dwell on the details of this work further, as I trust that Mr. Currelly will give an adequate account of it himself.

Beside the great royal tablets on the rocks, which had caught the eye of every native and every traveller, there were other results of the Egyptian occupation of Sinai to be looked for.

The mines had been nearly all re-worked by the company, and by the natives, who had continued the destruction. All the faces of the rock which had borne the royal inscriptions at the sides of the excavations had been blasted away; and the old galleries had been so widened and destroyed that the roof had at last fallen in immense blocks, and all the rock front over the mines was a fresh surface of broken stone. A few galleries remained, however, which held the greater part of the original working untouched. The oldest mine was that beneath the inscription of Sa·nekht, of the IIIrd dynasty, about 4950 B.C. This was a wide, irregular chamber, only about 5 ft. high and 20 ft. or more across. The sides were entirely cut by the chisel, the marks of which showed everywhere on the surfaces. In some places the chisel-cut ran round in a circle, three or four inches across; and this suggests that the workmen were familiar with tube drills, and reckoned on cutting round lumps out

56 STONE POUNDERS FOR CRUSHING SANDSTONE.

57 STONE PICKS (1, 2). STONE VASE GRINDER (3). 1:3

58   STONE MAULS AND HAMMERS FOR CRUSHING SANDSTONE.

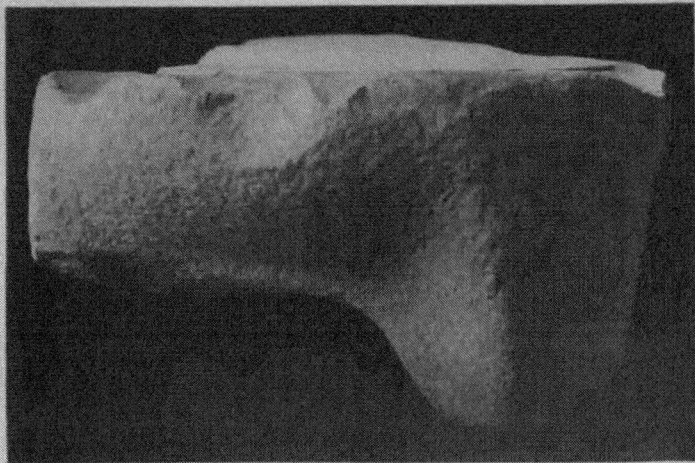

59   SERABÎT. BLACK STONE TRIPOD, ONE LEG REMAINING.

of the stone. But I did not see any holes which had been worked by drilling. The sides of the chamber were not flat in any direction, but ran in irregular curves, scolloping inwards in lengths three or four feet in each sweep. They were not upright, but curved inward at the floor and roof. In fact, a seam had been cut out in a rambling sort of manner, without making use of any fissures to help the work. The rubbish from this mine had been thrown out in a heap, running down the face of the cliff below it. Most of this was turned over by my men, and they found hundreds of turquoise fragments in it, the colour of which was spoilt by exposure. But they did not find a single flint or stone tool, nor any trace of copper ore. Probably, therefore, this was solely a turquoise mine; and it was worked entirely with metal chisels, which were too valuable to be thrown aside, as the stone tools were when broken or worn.

Another mine also showed the ancient work. This was the mine of Tahutmes III and Hatshepsut, with their inscription on the rock-face just outside the gallery. This was worked in a different way to the others. The natural fissures were fully used, and the stone was cut through with metal chisels. But there were no circular holes for breaking the stone; nor any curved surfaces in the cutting out. Wherever the natural fissure was not used the surface was rough-broken, with just as few chisel-cuts as would flake away the stone in large pieces. The gallery was about 24 ft. long, 60 to 70 in. wide, and 100 in. or more in height.

The rubbish heap of this ancient work was searched, and large numbers of discoloured turquoises were found in it, but no traces of copper ore. A very few flint flakes were found, but no stone tools.

Another site which we searched was the cliff below the Ra·n·user inscription. There is a mine now worked just above that tablet, to the south of it; and this may have been the mine of Ra·n·user in the Vth dynasty. All down the ledges of the cliff there were hundreds of flint flakes, and many pieces of the basalt pounders which were largely used to break up the rock. At first it seemed as if they might have been pieces of stone chisels used for cutting into the rock; but we never found there a cutting edge or point (though pointed stones occur at Serabít), and it seems that they were only pounders and hammers for breaking up the sandstone in search of the turquoises (figs. 56, 57).

Two large waste heaps lay on the valley side, about half-way up to the main mines, A and B on Map 2. These we turned over, and found hundreds of flint flakes in them, many of which had been much used. The commonest were long, stout flakes, which were entirely rounded at the edges and point, evidently from having been used for grubbing in the sandstone. A common type with these was a flake chipped in at both sides of the end, so as to give a point. These were seldom or never worn down by grubbing, and hence were probably for some other purpose than for working on the sandstone. The principal types of these flakes are given in fig. 60.

The great rarity or absence of any such flakes in the waste-heaps of the Egyptian galleries shows that we cannot attribute this abundance of flakes to the regular Egyptian work. Probably they were the tools of the native Bedawyn, who extracted the turquoises in various ages since prehistoric times, when they supplied them to the neolithic Egyptians, down through any period when the mines were not worked by more civilised people.

These mines required a considerable amount of labour, and we read in one inscription of 734 men coming in a single party. Such men needed some sort of settlement to live in; for although the natives of Sinai will now live day and night in the open, even under the winter frost, yet the Egyptians from the Nile Valley

60 FLINT TOOLS USED FOR WORK IN SANDSTONE, AND OTHERWISE.

would require some shelter. Accordingly, we find various groups of huts, and walls to break the wind, about the mining region. The wide shoal opposite to the mines seems to have been the most important of these places. The company had levelled the ground for their own purposes, but beneath the surface there are well-built stone walls of houses, with flat faces and straight sides. In these houses we found a small quantity of turquoise, and a great amount of copper slag and waste scraps from smelting; also some chips of copper ore, many broken crucibles, and part of a mould for an ingot. Evidently, copper smelting or refining was done here. The age of this settlement is shown, by the pottery, to be mainly of the Old Kingdom, but partly also of the Middle Kingdom. Hammer-stones for crushing ore were frequent (fig. 58), but none were of the cylindrical form found so commonly on the cliffs opposite.

Another settlement was on the ledges of rock just above this shoal, which were strewn with pottery of the Old Kingdom. On going up to the top of this hill we found, at 200 ft. above the valley, a plateau, with a central peak rising still higher, as I have before described. On this plateau were 125 huts, nearly all grouped together in lines along the edges of the cliff. The forms are in some cases fairly regular, and from the quantity of stones it is clear that a few have been high enough to carry a roof. From this kind of hut they vary down to rudely oval lines of stone, added one against another, and of so few blocks that they can only have been mere windbreaks. The purpose of putting them close to the edge of the cliff is strange. We do not perceive that there was any object in the miners being able to look over the edge of the hill from the huts, and for purposes of defence it would be very awkward to have the edge encumbered in this way. Certainly this hill is not a "fort," as commonly stated. Possibly close to the edge there may be less driving in a high wind, as the upthrow

52 THE MINERS OF WADY MAGHÁREH

of air from the cliff below may make a quieter eddy just inside the edge. No other purpose seems apparent in this arrangement.

In all these huts there was a great quantity of wood-ashes, and scraps of pottery of the Old Kingdom; but no trace of pottery of earlier or later dates. One copper borer was the only piece of metal found, and there was no slag or sign of smelting.

Just within the wall across the valley, on a shoal on the west side, was another settlement, as we have mentioned, which was entirely of the Middle Kingdom, dated by the pottery. The walls were of rough boulder-stones from the shoal, in some parts large and well laid, in others only small and scrappy. In the middle of each room was usually a pit, and in three of these pits the property of the last occupants was left buried (see figs. 61 and 62). Evidently, when they returned to Egypt, after a season at the mines, the things which were not worth carrying about were carefully buried, in order to be preserved for another season. The large corn-grinders, or mealing-stones, were put in round the sides of the hole; then the pottery jars were stacked together upside down, and the small bowls piled one on the other, with a large jar, mouth down, over them. So careful was the placing that they had survived mostly without a crack or flaw, though some suffered from scaling, owing to salt drying in them near the surface. There is much salt in the rock at Magháreh; after rain, all the lower beds come out white with efflorescence, and thick veins of salt are collected from the rocks and used by the natives. In this settlement, also, there was a great quantity of copper slag, scraps from smelting, pieces of crucibles, charcoal, and, in one case, part of a crucible-charge of crushed ore not yet reduced. The tips of two copper chisels or picks were found, broken anciently; also many hammer-stones, food shells of various kinds, and spines of echini. Here, again, copper-smelting and refining was done, probably

61. NAGHÂREH. POTTERY, XII DYNASTY, BURIED UNDER HUT.

62. NAGHÂREH. POTTERY AND CORN-GRINDERS, XII DYNASTY.

for making tools, as there is no trace of copper ore in the rock here.

Turning to modern times, the most curious personality connected with Sinai is that of Major Macdonald. After visiting the place in 1845, he returned and settled here with his wife in 1854, to search for turquoise. His house was built on the east of the "Fort" hill, and many Bedawyn came to work for him, and settled near by, learning to build stone huts from his example. The walls of his settlement yet remain, and Abu Ghanéym still uses the principal building. The appearance of this touching relic of a disappointed hope is seen in fig. 63. He lived, vainly trying to succeed in turquoise mining, until 1866. Then he left, and lived at Serabít for a year, after which he retreated to Cairo, where he died in 1870. Sheykh Abu Ghanéym remembers him well, and is always ready to talk about " Mazhur" and his boy " Willem": that memory is the main pivot of Abu Ghanéym's boyish recollections, and the ways and doings of " Mazhur " are always appealed to as an authority. He at least set the best example of a mining explorer, for he was always diligent to take paper squeezes of the inscriptions, to search out fresh ones, and to carefully preserve all that he could find. The great collection of squeezes at the British Museum is mainly due to his care.

In the Wady Sídreh, at the junction of the Wady Iqneh, there is a large Arab cemetery, of which fig. 64 is a view, taken from above. These recent tombs are noticeable for their variety. There is the simple heap of two or three slabs of sandstone; there is the larger heap or mound of stones; there is the stone circle without any central mound; and there is the stone circle with a central burial mound, though none are completed with doorways as at Wady Nasb (fig. 24). Now all these are being made at the same time, and this serves as a warning against distinguishing differences of burial custom as indicating different periods or peoples.

The simple kitchen of our workmen, on the shoal at Magháreh, is shown in fig. 65. At the left side is the bread-maker, who had to mix, roll, and bake forty pounds of flour every day for the camp; and on the right is the cook, who used to come off work an hour before sunset to stew the three big pots of lentils for supper, and rice for next day's breakfast. The mines of the IIIrd dynasty are seen just over his head.

63   MAJOR MACDONALD'S HOUSE AT MAGHÁREH.

64   TYPES OF GRAVES IN ARAB CEMETERY.

65   THE CAMP KITCHEN, MAGHÁREH.

VALLEYS OF SERABÍT EL KHADEM

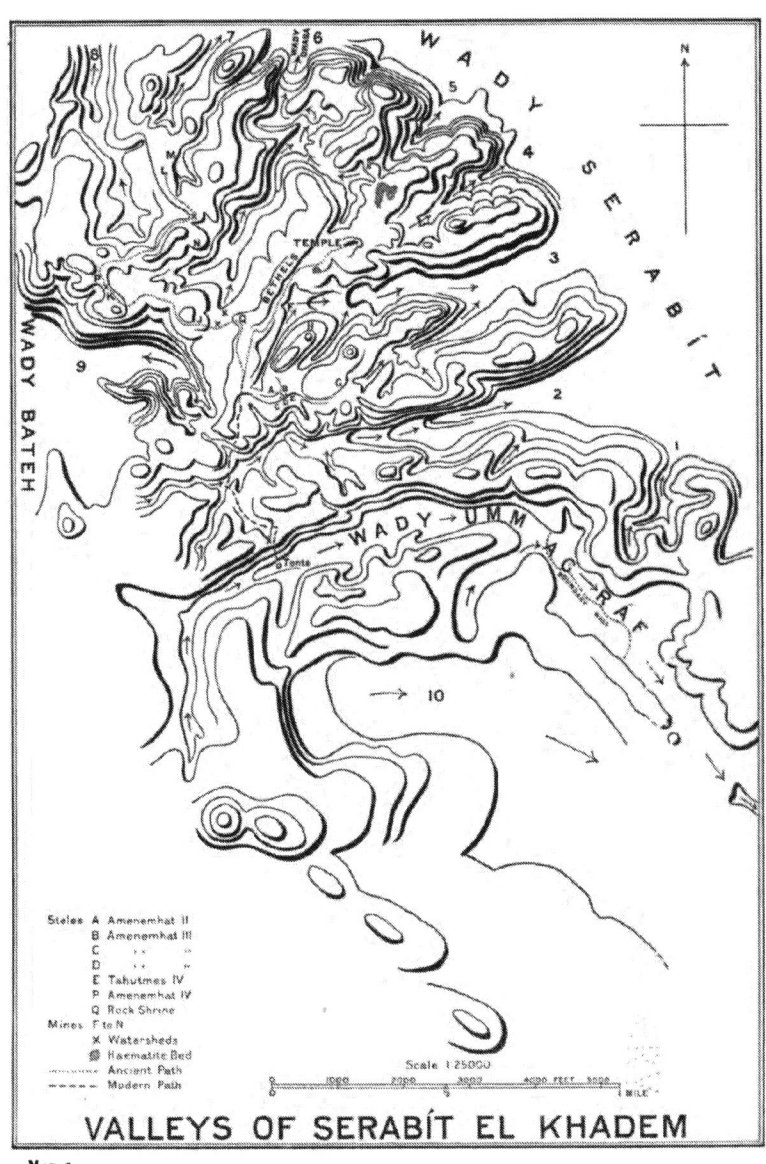

MAP 3

CHAPTER V

SERABÍT EL KHÁDEM AND THE BETHELS

THE rocky ravines around the temple of Serabít have never been planned until now; nor have the positions of the mines been mapped, or even described in relation to the temple. Such work was, therefore, one of the matters which claimed two or three days' attention. I measured a base of about 150 ft.; extended another from that of about a quarter of a mile in length; and then triangulated with box-sextant all the hill-tops around. The positions of these hills, when calculated out and plotted, served as fixed points for observing on with the prismatic compass; and from two to four bearings were taken for each natural feature as I went on. I plotted these features while on the ground, and immediately sketched in the valley lines which are shown in Map 3. This map is, therefore, more accurate as to the hill-tops and high features than it is to the valleys. As the mines are all in the top-level, this is what was needed. The valleys might have more detail shown in the bottoms, more especially at the various cascades and the lower edges opening into the Wady Serabít. But such detail would be of no practical value, so far as we can see, there being no ancient remains at the lower levels. The lines drawn here represent the cliff-escarpments in most cases, and are not, therefore, at equal distances apart or at precise levels. In showing ravines, the sides of which are mainly in vertical stages like steps, with a single stage often some hundreds of feet high, it is impractical to attempt the level contours at equal distances, as the cliffs are the essential features.

As the detail is so close and confused, it was scarcely intelligible when drawn with uniform lines. I have, therefore, drawn it as if it were a model of the ravines, seen in a high left-hand light. One side of each valley is therefore in shadow, and each cliff on that side casts a broad shadow in proportion to its height; on the opposite side of the valley the cliffs are mere lines, casting no shadows. With this shading, and arrows to show the fall of the stream-beds, it is easy to realise the structure.

The connection of the detailed Map 3 with the main Map 1 is not so satisfactory. The ordnance map, produced with care and cost by the Palestine Exploration Fund, is very detailed for such a large piece of work quickly done; but it does not give much around the temple, and the temple is certainly entered in a wrong place, nearly a mile too far south. The Egyptian Government survey is yet unfinished; but I was permitted to order a tracing through the kindness of Captain Lyons, R.E., the Director of the Survey. Unfortunately, it did not include the valleys about Serabít, and the accuracy of the topography of it scarcely advances beyond that of the ordnance survey, on which it is based, the real work of it being geological. Map 1 here is accordingly taken from the ordnance survey, with such additions as I could make. The valley lines only are shown, except where some hill detail was needed. The valleys round Serabít were connected by me with the main fixed points of my plan, which were the two peaks of Gebel Umm Riglayn, the two peaks of Ras Suwíq, and some minor hills. The points that I have named, and the mouth of the Wady Dhába, served to connect it with the ordnance map. But I found that the azimuth needed to be twisted back some 14° to fit the ordnance map—that is to say, I had to take the magnetic declination at 18° instead of 4° W., which is a difference beyond local variations. The

66. WADY DHABA, LOOKING NORTH FROM ANCIENT ROAD TO TEMPLE.

67. SERABIT, HEAD OF VALLEY 2, SOUTH OF TEMPLE.

MAPPING. SUCCESSIVE DENUDATIONS

general azimuth of this part of the ordnance map, therefore, requires checking. The Wady Umm Agráf, which turns northward, I sketched by sun-direction as I walked, and timed the distances. It was then fitted between the two termini, and the lower third agrees closely with the part which is shown in the Egyptian survey.

The structure of this district suggests some curious problems. For the sake of reference I have on Map 3 numbered all the valleys: 1 to 8 draining into the Wady Serabít, which runs round the east and north; 9 draining into the Wady Bátah, on the west; and 10 and Wady Umm Agráf draining southward. There have been three or four different systems of drainage, one after the other, each successively cutting out and destroying the earlier one. The oldest valley here is 10, as at the head of it is a dry bed of an immense waterfall, a grand concave cliff nearly a quarter of a mile wide and between 100 and 200 ft. high. This must be part of a very large drainage valley, much larger than any shown here; and it can only have been fed before Wady Bátah was excavated back, and when it got the whole flow from Gebel Umm Riglayn. That the first drainage lines should run southward is to be expected, as the strata are about 1,500 ft. higher at Serabít than at Magháreh. The next change was that Wady Bátah cut its way southward and tapped this region, running the previous valley dry; but the grand precipices at the head of 9, a branch of Wady Bátah, are in their turn hopelessly dry at present, being entirely cut off by the valleys running into Wady Serabít. The precipices are 300 or 400 ft. deep, and almost vertical, at the head of this valley 9; and it must have been fed by all the region of Umm Agráf and valleys 2 to 6. The third stage was the deepening of Wady Serabít, and the drainage of the plateau all being captured by valleys 1 to 8. Lastly, Wady Umm Agráf has worked back, but is later than

58 SERABÍT EL KHÁDEM AND THE BETHELS

valley 2, as it has not received any drainage from that side.

The geology of the district is like that of Magháreh, only all the beds are at a higher level above the sea. The levels in feet are as follows:—

	Magháreh.	diff. about	Serabít.	
Tertiary.—Basalt floor	1610	2200	3800?	{Umm Riglayn. Ras Suwíq.
Carbonif.—Iron bed	1170	1400	2600	
Igneous.—Base of sandstone	900?	900	1800?	

The basalt flow having probably emerged at different dykes, there is no necessity that it should be at the same level when formed; though, from the thickness, it might be supposed to have run over a wide extent and to have equalised. The iron bed was probably at one level of formation, as it was a uniform sea deposit. The base of the sandstone was on metamorphic and earlier rocks, probably eroded and shifted to very different positions; and, indeed, on the central table-land at Tartír ed Dhami it is at 3,500 ft. level, due to later elevation.

Turning now to the actual appearance of the district, the great plateau of sandstone is shorn off vertically by the Wady Suwíq on the north, as shown in the frontispiece. The cliff here is 400 ft. from the level of the point of view down to the beginning of the slope of rotten schist below, so it is therefore about 700 ft. in all. This view is taken where a drainage valley has been cut through by the cliff face, between valleys 5 and 6.

The general appearance of the plateau valleys is shown in fig. 66, which is taken from the temple looking down the east branch of the Wady Dhába, no. 6, seeing the dark promontory in the course of it and the right flank of the valley mouth beyond. The distant range is the Tíh plateau of limestone.

The deep ravines cut through the plateau make it only accessible by winding round the heads of the valleys. Such a valley, no. 2, we daily crossed, in its shallow

68. MINE BANKS AT F. STELE OF BETY IN DISTANCE.

69. GORGE OF VALLEY 3, FROM F. RAS SUWÎQ IN DISTANCE.

70   GEBEL UMM RIGLAYN AND BRANCH OF WADY BÂTAH.

71   CAMP AT TOP OF WADY UMM AGRÂY.

VALLEYS AROUND THE TEMPLE

upper part, on our road to the temple, and looked down the course of it (fig. 67), raking the successive headlands of its side branches.

The mines nearest to the temple are at F (Map 3), and onwards towards the temple. The upper part of this valley south of F is shown in fig. 68, where the banks of chips from the mines are in the foreground to the left; above the slope of these is a peak of black haematite, shown on the map by the shaded patch north-east of F. A little to the right of this is seen the stele of Sety I, outside the temple.

Passing further to F, the view down ravine 3 is shown in fig. 69, taken from the pathway. This shows the precipitous sides and weathering of these ravines. The two highest hills over the ravine are the Ras Suwíq and its fellow, lying to the east, which are of sandstone capped with black basalt, the only remains of the great flow which must have covered a large extent at that level. The whole depth of sandstone below that has been denuded since this Tertiary outflow.

Looking south, instead of east, we see the other two peaks of the Gebel Umm Riglayn, or "mother of two feet," as in fig. 70. This view is taken at the head of the deep ravine 9, which runs to the right hand into the Wady Bátah. These peaks also have the remains of the basalt sheet upon them, at a level of about 3,800 feet.

Coming now to the head of the Wady Umm Agráf, and standing just north of our tents, the view looking toward the double peak, three-quarters of a mile to the south, is shown in fig. 71. This gives a good idea of the general denudation of the sides of the Umm Agráf, which are not so precipitous as those of the other ravines. The upper end of this valley turns round to the right, and starts just below the pointed peak, which is some hundreds of yards in front of the flat-topped peak behind it.

We may now consider the positions of the mines, which have been the only cause of man ever visiting this region.

60 SERABÍT EL KHÁDEM AND THE BETHELS

The most important group of mines is in the ridge between the heads of valleys 2 and 3 (see Map 3). On the face of the rock at the head of valley 3, at A, are two inscriptions of Amenemhat II. A good deal of cutting has been made below them, and near by is a tunnel in the rock following the turquoise vein; this tunnel runs into various workings in the hill, and opens out on the other side of the ridge at D, cutting through about 220 ft. of rock. The length of these workings seemed to demand a direct opening on the hill-top, so a square shaft was sunk down about 10 ft. to open up the mine from the top. Most absurdly this has been called a "reservoir"; but as it is on a ridge, and the banks of chips are piled up around it, no water could flow into it; and as it opens below into extensive workings with exits, no water could ever be retained in it. On the west face of the pit is a long inscription engraved by Sebek-her-heb, who was the leader of the expedition in the forty-fourth year of Amenemhat III. The mine had already been developed on the south side, as at C is an inscription of the thirty-fifth year of Amenemhat III. At D is another inscription and a scene of Amenemhat III, put up by the general Iuka. And at E is a scene of the fourth year of Tahutmes IV.

At F is a long range of irregular workings in the west side of the valley, but no inscriptions remain to show the date. At G is a large work about 35 ft. square; much of the roof of it has fallen in, so that it is partly open to the sun. At H is a mine in the north face of the hill; a tablet has been cut inside of it, but has so powdered away that nothing can be read. At J is a large shallow working, of which the roof has partly fallen, and it has also been reworked and cut to pieces in modern times. At K is a mine in the north-east face of the hill, but without any inscription. At L is a mine which has been worked by square galleries (see fig. 72). It has been cut through the ridge and opens out on the western side

72   QUARRYING IN MINE AT L.   XVIII DYNASTY.

73   INTERIOR OF MINE AT M.

THE ANCIENT MINES

into valley 8. In order to maintain good access, three square shafts have been sunk down from the top of the hill. The main part of it is about 50 ft. long and 25 ft. wide; and the usual form of the galleries is about 70 in. high and 30 to 40 in. wide. Lower galleries have, however, been cut in parts to follow a particular bed, as in the view given. The cutting was all done with metal chisels or picks, in the usual Egyptian style, as shown in the upper face of the view. The chisel was $\frac{4}{10}$ in. wide. In the chips of the rock I found a piece of pottery with red and black lines, characteristic of the age of Tahutmes III; and the work and chisel-marks are like those of the mine of that reign at Magháreh. Over the north-east openings of this mine were several tablets roughly engraved in the new alphabet, which will be described in Chapter IX.

A little farther on, at M, and lower down, is the largest hall that I have seen in these mines (fig. 73). It is about fifty feet across without any support, and opens into galleries on all sides beyond that. No inscription or pottery shows the date. At N is a large mine, which is very visible from the ridge leading up to the temple. It opens in the south face of a turn of the valley. The main hollow is about 50 ft. wide, and goes in about 25 ft. It has been cut in two levels, following particular red strata in the yellow sandstone, and these have been mostly broken into one hollow. At the base is 20 in. of a red stratum, then 25 in. of yellow, then 55 in. of red, 20 in. of yellow, and 10 in. of red on the top. The mode of cutting seems of an earlier kind, more like that of the third dynasty at Magháreh. There were galleries of about 70 in. wide, and pillars of about 20 to 30 in. between, which have been cut away later. The details of the working will be stated in Chapter XI.

It will thus be seen how the remains of the turquoise stratum on the hill-tops between the valleys have been worked in all the places which the Egyptians thought promising. Eight separate localities have been attacked, and a large amount of labour has been spent upon each of them.

One question that has long been a difficulty is the original way of access to these mines and to the temple. The way that most travellers have reached the temple is by the Wady Dhába, or "hyaena valley"; but it seems certain that this cannot have been the Egyptian way, as there is no trace of cutting or of building up at the many points of difficulty. The access to the lowest shelf of rock, at the side of the great waterfall, is barely practicable; the path from that has never been flattened, but is on a dangerous slope; and the many steep falls above are a matter of climbing which a very little rock-cutting would have made far easier. When we had to transport stones down to the Wady Suwíq, our men found that the most practicable way was by valley 3. It was possible to let blocks down the slopes of débris at the sides, until they could reach the highest point in the valley to which camels could ascend. There is, therefore, some practicable passage this way, but scarcely a likely one for frequent use. We went to the temple every day from our tents in the Wady Umm Agráf; but the path at the south part was mostly made by us, and what traces there were had been only camel-tracks, for grazing purposes. The Arabs carefully make ascents for their camels to get on to the plateau, in order to feed on the scanty bushes, like those seen in fig. 90; and such a track is not at all like that which an Egyptian would make, for it winds round all the easiest contours; the distance is no object, as there are occasional herbs for the camel to pick up all the way along. As there were no traces of huts or of occupation in the valley near our tents, it does not seem that the Egyptians ever settled there. I also carefully searched to see that there was no track leading down into the Wady Bátah, south or west of Q.

The most direct clue is the ancient path which I

THE ANCIENT ROAD

traced joining the mines. This is marked by a dotted line on the map, while the new track of our own making is a broken line. On this path there is a sharp ascent at Q, and here a small shrine has been made (see fig. 74). A recess has been cut in the rock, and at the side of it a tablet has been let in. All of this has been much broken and destroyed, and the tablets are much weathered. One, however, has borne a scene of a king adoring Ptah, and a figure of the official who set it up, probably of the late XVIIIth or XIXth dynasty.

Farther on this road, at P, was a tablet of the 6th year of Amenemhat IV, set up by an official, Sebek-hotep. It had apparently stood on a rise of rock at the side of the road. Now, were this road only the track to some mines, it is not likely that tablets and a shrine would be set up here on the wayside, rather than at the temple or the mines themselves. But if it were the main way to the temple it would be very possible for wayside devotions to be in favour here. It seems, therefore, more likely that the road to the temple from the plain below led over this plateau top, winding between the valley heads; and this would be all the more reason for the series of shelters and stones, erected along the ridge between Q and the temple. That was the approach to the holy place, and a site of devotion. It is, therefore, somewhere down the hill between valleys 7 and 8, or more probably on the western side of valley 8, which falls away in easy slopes, that further search ought to be made for the Egyptian approach to the plateau, its mines and temple.

We now turn to another class of remains which are scattered over this district. Above some of the mines, particularly those at L and M, many slabs of the sandstone have been set upright. The pieces are from only a few inches to a couple of feet high, and they are propped by other stones, if needful, to make them stand on end. This same system of upright stones is also seen along ridges of the hills, or an edge of a precipice, or any other striking position. One such row of single stones and piled stones is shown in fig. 75, which is on the hill near P. Similar lots of stones and piles are on the edge of the hills between valleys 5 and 6, and on the hill at H. But they are not found in places out of sight of the temple ground, such as around the Wady Umm Agráf and south of that. The custom is not, however, restricted to this district. Mr. Currelly found large numbers of stones set upright on the most striking hills and passes of the mountains nearer Mount Sinai. And on looking at fig. 34, stones can be seen on two or three of the hills, and in the enlarged view, fig. 33, the stone on the top of the conical peak to the left is clear; this example must be about 12 ft. high, probably piled up from two or more stones. It is evident that this is part of the well-known system of sacred stones set upright in adoration, or in token of pilgrimage, a system familiar in many parts of the East, in Syria, India, and other lands.

Another type is the grouping of such stones, which occurs near P. In fig. 76 the dark ground is a cloak, laid down to show more clearly the points of three or four stones which stand upright. Other upright stones are standing nearer to the camera, forming altogether a very rude rectangular enclosure. The ground is all hard rock, so that this group cannot be around a grave; nor was it a shelter of any kind, as the stones stand singly and are pointed. It is clearly an independent memorial of a visit, presumably devotional. We cannot dissociate this from the devotional use of stones in Palestine, which has been so finely illustrated by Macalister's discovery of the row of great monoliths in the high place at Gezer.

Though the origin of this custom cannot be attributed to the Egyptians (as it is seen all over Sinai and is a part of the religious customs of Palestine), yet it was adopted by them here directly, and influenced

74 ROCK SHRINE ON ANCIENT ROAD TO TEMPLE.

75 UPRIGHT MEMORIAL STONES AND HEAPS, SERABÎT.

76 GROUP OF UPRIGHT STONES.

77 ENCLOSURE AND STELE OF SENUSERT I.

their other monuments indirectly. On the ridge which bordered the path to the temple, from Q onwards, there are a dozen steles, varying from 5 to 12 ft. in height. Though we carefully cleared the ground around them, no graves were found, and they are clearly devotional and not sepulchral.

The earliest of these steles is of Senusert I, and is shown in fig. 77. The two peaks of Gebel Umm Riglayn are in the distance; the conical hill at the left hand of the stele is the peak marked on the south side of valley 9; to the right hand is valley 9, running into the Wady Bátah, the ridge of which is along the horizon. Now steles of this kind are entirely unknown in Egypt; by far the greater part of the Egyptian steles are sepulchral, attached to tombs; some are religious and placed in temples; but none are known as monuments of devotion in a place which is neither a temple nor a tomb. The treatment of the stone is also different to general usage in Egypt. There it is rare to find a stone inscribed on more than one face; here it is rare to find a stone that is not inscribed on all four sides. The reason is that in Egypt the stele is descended from the false-door panel of the tomb, as Maspero has shown; in Sinai the stele is descended from the memorial stone of devotion.

These stones are nearly all connected here with rough rings of stones piled upon the ground. The stele with the name of Senusert on it (fig. 77) is at the side of a ring 15 to 20 ft. across, which is approached by a roughly hewn flight of four steps, rising from the lower ground on the north-west. A small ring joins this at the side, and three other small rings of 4 or 5 ft. wide inside are near by.

The most complete example is that of one of the smallest steles, which had been early overthrown and buried, and is hence perfect. This is connected with a slight enclosure of stones, and has an altar in front of it. After clearing the ground, and replacing the stele upright, the views were taken. In fig. 78, looking south-west, the peaks of Gebel Umm Riglayn are in the distance. To the right on the horizon is seen the last-described stele of fig. 77. The enclosure of stones has on the east a straight side of about 14 ft. long, in the middle of which is the stele; to the north is another straight side of about 10 ft., and the rest is an irregular curve. In front of the stele lay the flat altar on the ground. The other view, fig. 79, is looking rather north of west; it shows the tumbled stones of some structure in front of the stele. The stele and its altar are also shown in fig. 80. It is dated as an afterthought at the top, naming the 44th year; and this is of the reign of Amenemhat III, as the same official carved another stele in the 40th year of his reign. It reads: "A royal offering to Hat-hor, Lady of Turquoise, for the *ka* of the chief chamberlain Sebek-her-heb, for the *ka* of the seal-bearer, deputy of the overseer of the seal-bearers, Kemnaa, born of Ka-hotep." The formula of the royal offering is that of all Egyptian acts of devotion, but it is rarely that they made a stele for unrelated persons. Evidently this is the adoration by the principal people of the expedition; and it shows how the custom of pillar-stones in Sinai was adapted to hold the usual pious formula of Egyptian devotion.

It might be considered that these enclosures with the steles were connected with offerings or with consecration of the ground. But on the rest of the hill we find many other such enclosures, without any steles or upright stones; and clearly we must consider the meaning of these simple enclosures, in connection with those above described with steles. In fig. 81 we see a small enclosure of a square outline opening to the south-west. It is only about $2\frac{1}{2}$ ft. wide and 4 ft. long. In the middle distance is another such enclosure; to the right hand is the temple, and the path leading to it; behind all is the plateau of the Tîh. In fig. 82 is another small ruined enclosure, with two others behind it. This is

78. ENCLOSURE AND STELE OF SEBEK-HER-HEB, LOOKING WEST. XII DYNASTY.

79. ENCLOSURE AND STELE OF SEBEK-HER-HEB, LOOKING NORTH.

ALTAR AND STELE OF SEBEK-HER-HEB; AMENEMHAT III.

ENCLOSURES OF STONE

looking down into the head of valley 3; the middle-distance hill is the south-west end of that on which H is, and the distant hill is the one shown in fig. 71. A double enclosure is shown in fig. 83, which is about 8 ft. long inside, and four or five feet wide in each division. The most complete and considerable of these enclosures is that in fig. 84, which was a circular enclosure about 12 ft. across outside and 5 ft. inside. The mountain at the back is the ridge of Ras Suwíq, and the hill in the middle distance is marked H in the map.

Now most of these enclosures have no steles, and therefore the enclosure has a separate use and meaning, and is not merely an accompaniment of a memorial stone where they occur together. The enclosures are not at all of the system of the miners' huts at Wady Maghåreh. These are always joined in groups and lines, so as to save material in their erection. But these are usually single, sometimes with a second ring at the side, rarely with two or three lesser ones. When we look at the sizes we are led to the conclusion that they were for sleeping in; four feet to six feet is the usual inside size, with some larger, up to ten or twelve feet, like the dwellings at Maghåreh. Though most of them were mere wind-breaks, and not huts, yet, so were a large part of the miners' shelters at Wady Maghåreh. The isolated nature of these, however, prevents our taking them as the huts of miners in a settlement. No people would lay out a couple of dozen huts, straggling over a quarter of a mile, as being parts of one establishment. They seem, then, to be for sleeping-shelters, but built separately at various times. And many of them have well-cut Egyptian steles, belonging to different expeditions.

Now the only explanation of this would be the well-known custom of sleeping at or near a sacred place in order to obtain some vision from the deity. The Greeks did so in later times in Egypt, as at the Serapeum of Memphis, the Serapeum of Kanobos, and the temple of

Abydos; though in early times this custom was rarely, if at all, known in Egypt. It was, however, a favourite custom in Syria and Greece. The fullest accounts that we have of it are those of the shrine of Asklepios, at Epidauros, where the sick went to sleep in order to seek indications for their treatment and cure. A shrine of Poseidon the Healer, in Tenos, was similarly visited to obtain dreams in aid of the sick; and the custom is maintained in the vaults of the church there to this day. Seeking dreams in sleep was also practised at the shrine of Mopsos, at Mallos, in Cilicia. The worship of Sarpedon, at Seleucia, in Syria, was supplanted by that of Thekla, with the same intention of seeking indications for the relief of the sick. And similarly, the sleeping in the cave of Matrona [Magna Mater?] at Daphne, in order to get an answer to a question, was kept up by Christians, to the scandal of Chrysostom. Attention has lately been called to these survivals by Dr. Odgers, in a lecture at Manchester College, Oxford; also by Professor Dill, in *Roman Society from Nero to Marcus Aurelius*. We have happily preserved to us an example of the connection between the dreams and the steles in the story of Jacob. We read that he journeyed from Beersheba, which is just north of Sinai, and at a time only a few centuries after these steles were set up at Serabít. "And he lighted upon a certain place, and tarried there all night, because the sun was set; and he took of the stones of that place, and put them for his pillows, and lay down in that place to sleep. And he dreamed. . . . And Jacob awaked out of his sleep, and he said, Surely the Lord is in this place; and I knew it not. . . . And Jacob rose up early in the morning, and took the stone that he had put for his pillows, and set it up for a pillar, and poured oil upon the top of it. And he called the name of that place Beth-el" (Gen. xxviii. 10-19).

Now this account teaches us some points in the

81   SHELTERS OF STONES ON HILL BEFORE TEMPLE.

82   SHELTER OF STONES ON HILL BEFORE TEMPLE.

religious customs of this age and country. The immediate result of having a striking religious dream was to conclude that the place was sacred, for such dreams could only be associated with sacred sites. The next step was to set up a pillar-stone as a memorial of the dream, and to associate it with a religious purpose by anointing it with oil. Such a stone cannot have been large, for it was only one of those which he had arranged for his convenience the night before; and if literally a pillow, it cannot have been more than a few inches thick and a foot or two long. Therefore, comparatively small stones might be used for Bethel marks and memorials, and there is no need to expect that only great blocks and tall pillars would have this meaning.

We have, then, the custom of dreaming in sacred places, of setting up on end stones of portable size as memorials of such dreams and as tokens of a sacred place, and the custom of consecrating them with oil. All this belongs to the same age and region as that we are studying. And it is the earlier stage of that custom of sleeping for oracular quests in sacred caves and temples, which flourished in Syria and Greece in later times, and has survived through Christianity until the present day.

All of this applies closely to the remains at Serabít. The enclosures in front of the sacred cave, along the road leading to it, are apparently for a person to sleep in, occasionally for two or three persons. There are about thirty such shelters, and among them are a dozen steles. These memorial-stones are dated in kings' reigns, and the only perfect one contains a prayer for the benefit of the principal people of an expedition. Such a formula for a living person is not the usual form in Egypt.

The purpose of dreaming at the sacred place is obvious. The whole object of coming to the district was to mine for turquoise, hidden in the hard rock; and there was always much uncertainty in finding enough to recompense the great loss and labour of such a search. There would be no more likely subject on which to seek for some external guidance and help. The divinity of the place was always called the " Mistress of Turquoise," and to propitiate her was the sole purpose of the temple and the offerings made here; the good-will and favour of the goddess were essential if success was to be obtained in the mining. The " Mistress of Turquoise " was besought to give her treasures from her stores to the worshippers who sought her favours by their gifts. And after the shrine was built and carved, the ceremonial courts provided, and offerings and sacrifices lavished upon the goddess, how was she to requite these devotions except by revealing the longed-for gems? And in what more likely way should this revelation be sought than by giving indications in dreams to those who prayed for her help thus at her shrine? There is no place where a demand for the help of oracular dreams was more certain than at a place where the help of the " Mistress of Turquoise " was so constantly sought.

Probably the earliest place for seeking dreams was in the sacred cave itself; as in the cave of Matrona, the Great Mother, near Antioch, where even Christians also slept for dreams. Then, when the cave of Serabít was built up and enclosed as a shrine, various shelters were put together along the road leading to the temple. Later on the Egyptian kings added a series of small chambers in front of the temple, cubicles just large enough for men to lie in. And these cubicles were heaped over with stones and sand, so as to make them subterranean, and thus a substitute for the sacred cave itself.

That Egyptians should follow these customs of worship, different to their own, is a surprise to those who have not considered the polytheist point of view. The gods of a country were looked on as supreme in that country; and in order to obtain success it was necessary to consider the local god, and to propitiate him with the local rites. How a district belonged to a

83 SHELTERS OF STONES ON HILL BEFORE TEMPLE.

84 THE BEST-BUILT STONE SHELTER BEFORE TEMPLE. RAS SUWIQ IN DISTANCE.

special god is shown when "the servants of the king of Syria said unto him, Their gods are gods of the hills; therefore they were stronger than we; but let us fight against them in the plain, and surely we shall be stronger than they" (1 Kings xx. 23). And thus the divinity of Sinai and of turquoise must be worshipped for success when in that district and on that quest.

And the rites of worship must be those of the country also. This is clear from the account that "they spake to the king of Assyria, saying, The nations which thou hast removed, and placed in the cities of Samaria, know not the manner of the God of the land: therefore he hath sent lions among them, and, behold, they slay them, because they know not the manner of the God of the land. Then the king of Assyria commanded, saying, Carry thither one of the priests whom ye brought from thence; and let them go and dwell there, and let him teach them the manner of the God of the land. Then one of the priests whom they had carried away from Samaria came and dwelt in Beth-el, and taught them how they should fear the Lord. Howbeit every nation made gods of their own, and put them in the houses of the high places which the Samaritans had made. . . . So they feared the Lord, . . . and served their own gods, after the manner of the nations whom they carried away from thence. . . . So these nations feared the Lord, and served their graven images" (2 Kings xvii. 26-41).

Here we have a complete parallel to the Egyptian worship in Sinai. The goddess of the place was the main object of adoration, and—as we shall see—her worship was on a Semitic and not on an Egyptian system. But the other gods of the Egyptians were also brought in, and Ptah, Sopdu, and even Amen, appear upon the monuments. They feared the goddess of the land, and served their own gods after their manner.

CHAPTER VI

THE TEMPLE OF SERABÍT

THE earliest shrine here was doubtless the sacred cave in the highest point of rock toward the front of the plateau, apparently as early as the reign of Sneferu, 4750 B.C. From this the Temple grew outward between 3450 and 1150 B.C., until it reached a total length of two hundred and thirty feet (see Map 4). It will be the more intelligible to first describe the Temple topographically from different points of view; then, following the plan from the entrance to the cave, to deal with the architecture and decoration of it, in this chapter. For the unarchitectural reader it will be more useful to follow the account in historical order from the cave to the entrance, describing the purpose and use of the parts, which is the subject of Chapter VII.

We have already shown the appearance of the neighbourhood, and the view along the approach up to the stele of Sety I, which stands out as a signal of the sacred site (fig. 68). On approaching nearer we see the great knoll of black haematite at the side of the path, which had originally upon it a high stele of Senusert III. The fragments of that stele I collected from around the knoll, where it had been scattered, and so succeeded in finding enough to restore the height of it, about 7½ ft. Coming nearer, we have the view in fig. 85, where the Sety stele is to the right, the knoll of the sacred cave in the middle, and the steles at the entrance to the temple on the left. It should be said here, once for all, that the

85 APPROACH TO TEMPLE FROM WEST. STELE OF SETY I.

86 NORTH-EAST SIDE OF TEMPLE.

87. TEMPLE OF SERABÎT, FROM WESTERN QUARRY.

88. TEMPLE OF SERABÎT, LOOKING UP AXIS.

VIEWS OF THE TEMPLE

whole building and monuments are made of the local sandstone, quarried just below the temple.

The general view of the outside of the temple from the other end is seen in fig. 86. Here the Bethel stele still standing on the hill (see fig. 77) is seen in the far distance on the right. Then there are the steles inside and outside of the temple up to the tumbled masses of the pylon. Next stand up the two old steles reused by Tahutmes III east of the Hat·hor *hanafiyeh*. The remaining wall of the Sanctuary is seen where a workman is standing. To the left are the great steles of the Portico Court, and at the end the rocky masses of the knoll of the Sacred Cave. The blocks lying in the foreground were monuments that we had moved out of the temple, ready for transporting to Cairo and England.

On approaching the front of the temple, a telephotograph from the heaps of ancient quarry chips gives the view in fig. 87. Here we see on the right the pylon ruins and the doorway through the pylon ; nearer are the two steles of Amenhotep III, and the broken stele of Ramessu II at the entrance. To the left is the large stele of Hor·ur·ra, and beyond that the other steles of the XIIth dynasty expeditions. Above them in the middle distance is a hill of black haematite (marked with diagonal shade in Map 3), overlooking the deep valley around this plateau ; and the horizon is the plateau of the Tih Desert. This view shows the appearance before our excavations began. On standing exactly in the axis of the temple, we see in fig. 88 the same parts somewhat differently. Nearest is the broken stele of Ramessu II, then the large, round-topped stele of Amenhotep III, and beyond is the doorway of the pylon. The stele of Hor·ur·ra and the same distant points are also seen here.

Now going on to the top of the knoll over the sacred cave, we see in fig. 89 the deep valley Wady Dhába on the right. The remaining wall of the Sanctuary is in the middle, next are the steles of the Portico Court and those of the Hat-hor *hanafiyeh*, and the length of the temple stretching away into the distance. Turning a little to the left, we continue the view in fig. 90, where the enclosure walls of the temple are in the foreground, with scattered bushes, which were growing over the ground before we excavated the area. Beyond the end of the wall are the mine-heaps, and on the horizon is the Bethel stele of fig. 77. To the left is the stele of Sety I, and in the distance the great mass of Gebel Umm Riglayn.

In order to understand these walls better, we come off the knoll, and look back at it, in fig. 91. Here we see the main enclosure-wall running up to the top of the knoll, and a later branch from it passing round the knoll lower down, as an outer fence. The steles of the Portico Court before the Sacred Cave are seen to the left, and above them the haematite hill. Next, passing around the inner wall, we see the best-preserved part of the outer wall in fig. 92, and the space between the walls after we had cleared it. The haematite hill is in the distance. These fencing walls around the temple are built of loose blocks of sandstone piled together. These are quite rough, and are probably the waste blocks of quarrying, as they are not of the same size or weathering as those that lie on the natural surface. The stones become stained a dark bistre-brown by this exposure. I could not succeed in finding anywhere a definite and regular face to the walls; and they do not seem to have been well fitted and afterwards ruined, but rather the stones were heaped together as closely as they would well lie, and left in a rough line. This work was done under Amenhotep III.

We may now turn to the details of the Temple itself. The general appearance of it, as restored, but without the roofing, is best grasped from the model. Fig. 93 shows the view from near the entrance, the scattered steles of the XIIth dynasty in the foreground, the cubicles behind them; to the left the pylon and the chambers up to the

89   THE TEMPLE, LOOKING WEST, FROM TOP OF THE KNOLL OVER THE SACRED CAVE.

90   ENCLOSURE WALLS OF TEMPLE, FROM SAME POINT AS 89.

91. ENCLOSURE WALLS OF TEMPLE, LOOKING UP TO KNOLL OVER THE SACRED CAVE.

92. ENCLOSURE WALL AROUND THE KNOLL. HAEMATITE HILL BEHIND.

Kurll over cave.   Sanctuary.   Hatsepsut.   Pylon.   Shrine of Kings.   Cubicles for sleepers.

93   MODEL OF TEMPLE OF SERABIT, FROM THE NORTH.

Sacred cave.   Hatsepsut.   Pylon.   Cubicles for sleepers.
Sanctuary.   Shrine of Kings.   Approach of XIIth dynasty.

94   MODEL OF TEMPLE OF SERABIT, FROM THE NORTH-WEST.

THE ENTRANCE

cave, which is shown by removing the side of the knoll to uncover the chambers. Fig. 94 shows the view nearer to the cave, with the actual form of the knoll above it. These views will give reality to the plan, in Map 4, which we now proceed to follow in this description.

At the ENTRANCE there formerly stood two tall steles, the northern one of Ramessu II, 1300-1234 B.C., the southern one of Set-nekht, 1203 B.C. The former was complete, though cracked from top to base, when the Palestine Fund expedition took photographs here; since then nearly all the south half had been overthrown, and we replaced a portion of it as seen in fig. 88. The Set-nekht stele has been overthrown, and is lying, face up, a few yards before the entrance. The base-block of it, 40 × 29 in., is all that remains in place; and that is higher than the Ramesside base in order to equalise the heights of the stele tops. The Ramesside stele is 97 to 103 high (that is, at shoulder and at top) × 26 × 10 in.; that of Set-nekht is 88 to 93 high × 27 to 28 (at top and base) × 10 in. The doorway has perished, except a piece of the reveal shown in the plan, and a block of the jamb with a figure.

In the chamber A were four pillars, 70 in. high, with heads of Hat-hor on the sides next the axis. These stood on bases 6 in. high, which were wider than the pillars from north to south. On the east side are fragments of a true wall, independent of that of the next chamber; and two blocks of paving, which probably supported steles, one at either side of the door, before chamber A was added on. In this chamber is a beam of stone 71 × 12 × 12 in., which is too long for any position except across the axis. If the passage, then, were roofed, doubtless the whole chamber was roofed. One roof slab $35 + x \times 35 \times 8$ in., probably spanned the passage, resting on other stones at the side, as we shall see farther on. The insides of the walls are in good alignment, while the outer sides are rough, and have no finish or sculpture. As the entire outside was found heaped up with blocks of stone and sand, it seems that it was never seen, but that the chamber was treated as subterranean, and only the roof was left visible outside. The same is true of all the chambers up to the pylon. In the walls are stones of the XVIIIth dynasty reused, and on the south side is a scene of Sety I offering to Ptah. In the south-west corner stood a stele of Ramessu III, of coarse work and in bad condition.

The doorway of chamber B had a lintel 70 × 10 to 14 × 8 in., with a door-recess 33 in. wide in it. This doubtless spanned the door, which is at present 35 in. wide, measured into the reveal where the door turned. It is clearly seen in the plan how this wall was the temple front at one time, as the chamber A is out of alignment with it on the north, and was evidently a later addition. There is the lower part of a pillar, and the base of another opposite to it. But their architraves probably did not go over the steles; the chambers here are all between 80 and 90 in. high inside, while the north stele is 81 to 93 high (shoulder and top), and the southern is 72 to 83 in. high. There must, therefore, have been a portico roof only over the western side of the chamber, but no beams or roofing remained. The two steles are of Amenhotep III, and evidently stood before chamber C as the front of the temple of that age. The walls of chamber B are not in line with those of C, and are much inferior to the front walls of C, showing that they are a later addition.

The doorway of chamber C has a lintel 50 × 12 × 10 in., with a door-recess of 32 in., or 29 in. wide from the pivot centre. As the present doorway is 31 in. between the reveals, this agrees with it. The north end of the west side is the best-preserved piece of wall; its courses are at pavement 0, joints 20, 52, and 73 in., measuring upwards. These courses are evidently a cubit, a cubit and a half, and a cubit high. One pillar-base and the stump of its pillar remain, but there is no trace of

THE SLEEPING CHAMBERS

the other. Some pieces of stone beams 12 × 20 in., and portions of the roofing, also remain.

In chamber D a large lintel remains, but of which door is uncertain. It was originally of Senusert I, 90 × 17 in., but was cut down to 69 × 14 in. Two Hat·hor pillars stood here, but they had been overthrown, and there was no trace of any bases, so their positions are uncertain. We re-erected them and took the view given in fig. 95; in this the tall stele of Amenhotep III is seen at the left. These pillars are 76 in. high, × 18 × 12 on north, or 17 × 10 on south. They were inscribed by Amenhotep III. There is a beam 56 × 12 × 9 in., which could only go across from the east or west wall to the pillar, the half-room being 52½ in. wide. There was also a block of roofing 62 × 26 × 5 in. As the whole chamber is 194 in. from north to south, this block would not span a third of it; and from being so thin it was probably one of the covers of the passage, 62 long and 26 in. wide across the axis.

In chamber E there was also a Hat·hor pillar, 76 × 15 × 10 in., of Amenhotep III, and some fragments of roofing. The pillar was shifted, and no base remained, so its position is uncertain on the plan. The roof was probably only over the north side, as on the south side is the lower part of a stele of an official, Pa·nehesi, 28 × 14 in., on a base. By the uniform alignment it seems that chambers D and E were built together, but that C was later, as shown by the double wall between C and D. The stele of Pa·nehesi probably belongs to the time when chamber F was the front, as the face is only 12 in. from the west wall, so that it could hardly have been read in its present surroundings.

Chamber F had a regular front, as being the temple entrance; the wall is well built, plain below, and inscribed along the front above. There was a beam $35+x \times 10 \times 10$ in., a reused stone of Amenemhat III; also some pieces of roof slabs, $56+x \times 23$ in.

Apparently chamber G was built at the same time as F. There was a fragment of a Hat-hor pillar in it, 17 × 10 in., and two beams of stone which had been cut from a XIIth dynasty slab, 58 × 13 × 11 in. As these are not long enough to be of any use in this chamber, they were probably turned over from chamber H, which is 57 in. wide at base, and may have been narrowed slightly to give the beams a hold. In this chamber was a whole roofing-slab, which explains a good deal. It is 71 × 40 × 7 to 10 in. thick. Now a block 71 in. long from each side, north and south, if there was a bearing of 4 in. on the walls, would leave 14 in. clear along the axis. And the end of the slab is rebated nearly half its thickness to support another slab, as if a slab covering over the axis had rested on the ends of the roofing slabs at each side. Now we find thin slabs of 5 in. through, with breadths of 18, 21, 23 and 25 in., in the adjoining chambers; and as the clear space was 14 in., and the rebate 6 in. on each side, there was a seat 26 in. wide for the roofing of the axis, agreeing to the breadths of 18 to 25 in. found on the thin slabs. The two flat slabs by the door were probably bases for statues.

In chamber H there were no pillars, and probably the beams reached across it. There were thin roof slabs 32 × 21 × 5, 71 × 18 to 21 × 5, and 37 × 25 × 4 in.

Chamber J had a well-built front wall, which was evidently the front of the temple at one time. The door had been repaired by Merenptah, who inscribed the northern jamb. The lintel has a regular cavetto cornice to it, which has been probably a cubit high. In the chamber is one Hat-hor pillar in place on the north side, of the same flat type as in fig. 95; it is 82 × 16 × 10 in., and a fragment of one like it is on the other side. It appears to be inscribed by Tahutmes IV, and stands on a belt of paving.

Chamber K had been a regular front to the temple, with a footing to the well-built wall, and a cavetto cornice

THE PYLON

19 in. high over the door. The northern jamb was inscribed by Tahutmes III or IV, doubtless the latter, as there are Hat·hor pillars of Amenhotep II in the chamber, and his name is on the wall. These pillars are 80 × 13 × 10 in.; they are thus more square than the later columns, and they have the curved outline and curling wig, like those of Tahutmes III, fig. 104. It is, therefore, between Amenhotep II and Tahutmes IV that the change of type took place.

We now come to still better masonry and thicker walls of Tahutmes III, in chamber L and its temple front. The pillars in this chamber are plain: that on the north, 70 × 22 × 17; on the south, 24 × 22 in., and broken above. Two lines shown across the south wall mark the gap cut out to receive the end of the beam stretching from the pillar. On the walls are cartouches of Tahutmes III, and one of Tahutmes IV, added later.

Over the doorway to the court M was a lintel 23 in. high, with two lines of inscription of Tahutmes III. The shaded spaces are two great steles, which at first stood free in front of the pylon, but were later built in with the wall of the court M. That on the north, now overthrown and broken, is dated in the 5th year of Tahutmes III; that on the south, in the 5th year of a Tahutmes, doubtless the IIIrd. They differ much in height, however; the northern is 87 in. high, the southern is 126 in.; as the north foot-block was raised 5 in., this yet leaves 34 in. difference between the tops. These steles were only inscribed on the east faces.

We now came to the PYLON, which was the original front of the temple of Tahutmes III, the two steles just named standing clear before it. The size of it was 26¼ ft. wide, 13 ft. high, and 68 in. thick. The northern half is so much ruined that nothing can be traced of its sculptures; but the southern half still retains even the lower part of the cornice, and shows the original scenes and the additions. The masonry was never good—

merely an outer wall retaining a rubble core. And the decay of some of the sandstone blocks of the lower part has led to a partial collapse of the work, the upper parts having tipped inwards, and most of the stones being shifted. In the lower part of the west front there are four stones belonging to some earlier wall here; we learn their age from there being irregular gaps over them before beginning the continuous masonry of a rather different stone built by Tahutmes III. This points to an earlier building having extended as far as this. Now such a building of Amenhotep I would not have been ruined and rebuilt so soon as the reign of Tahutmes III; and hence it seems that the XIIth dynasty had some building here. The original batter of the end is 1 in 16, and that of the sides was probably the same. The scene on the pylon was of Tahutmes III offering to Hat-hor; behind him are the *ha* Prince Sen-nefer and the *mer per* (*major-domo*) Kenuna. Other scenes of Sety II and his officials have been roughly cut, partly below this and partly trespassing upon the earlier scene. The doorway through the pylon bears figures of Tahutmes III and Hat-hor in relief on the sides of it; these are the only relief sculptures in the temple.

The chamber N was complete before the pylon was built against it, yet it was strangely unsymmetrical. We cannot see why such lop-sided rooms as N and O should have been built. The line of the doorways is blocked by the pillars, but so that light could pass on either side of the pillars. That there was a roof is clearly shown by the pillar whose stump is yet in place, and the other pillar which was overthrown. These are Hat-hor pillars of the curling-hair type. The roof-slab still lying against the pylon in the south-east corner shows that the architraves ran north to south, and the length of the roof-slab east to west. The cut in the south wall for the stone beam also shows this. The roof-slabs are 96 × 32 to 25 × 6 in. thick; with a rebate along

95. HATHOR PILLARS OF AMENHOTEP III. XVIII DYNASTY.

96. WEST FRONT OF PYLON, CARVED BY TAHUTMES III AND SETY II.

the long side 2 in. wide; also 81 + x × 40 × 8 in.; also 71 × 30 × 10 in. As the distance from the pillar to the east wall is 59 in., the latter roof-slab would easily cover that. In this chamber is a lintel 52 × 11 wide × 10 in. high, which must be that of the west door. This is proved by the lintel in chamber O, which belonged to the door N-O, being 24 in. wide, which would not leave room for 11 in. more on a wall only 23 to 30 in. thick. The base-block which is still in place belonged to a stele of Tahutmes III, dated in his 25th year, which is still lying there. The fellow stele has gone, and its base is shifted. This second base is 38 × 32 in., with a socket 26 × 15 in. for the stele; and as the wall south of the door is only 42 in. long, the base must have been put close in the corner.

The chamber O was complete before N was built, as each has an independent wall, and the sides do not run through. But rebuilding by the Ramessides has modified this, and single blocks take in all the thickness on the south of the door. Of the four pillars (see fig. 112), only one, the north-eastern, is in its original place. The others we replaced; and the positions are, therefore, not certain here, and the north to south position of the fixed column was not measured, and so is not certain in the plan. A great lintel-beam remains here, near the west door; as it is 24 in. thick it was doubtless made to fit the double wall, which is 23 to 30 in. thick. The length of the lintel is 73 in., and height 15 in. It was originally cut by Tahutmes III with fine, thin hieroglyphs; but later, Ramessu IV re-inscribed it in coarse, large signs. The recess in the lintel for the door is 43 in. wide, and has only one pivot-hole; but this is too narrow to fit this doorway as it stands, and the lintel cannot have gone over any other door, as the other walls are not thick enough. The doorway has, therefore, been widened in the Ramesside rebuilding. A stone beam is 63 × 14 × 13 in.; these beams lay from east to west, as there are no recesses for the ends at the top of the south wall. A roof-slab is $42 + x \times 36 \times 5$ in.; by its thinness this probably covered the middle passage. Of the east door the traces of the door-jambs are visible on the sill, and they are here drawn from this mark; the north jamb lies broken.

The OUTER STELES on the north should now be considered, before dealing with the complicated region to the east. The dozen steles outside the temple proper are all of the XIIth dynasty, and of Amenemhat III (3300 B.C.), so far as we can trace, excepting one of his successor. No passage-way can be found now through the rough stone walling around these steles, and this is a later condition of affairs. The rough wall was built by Amenhotep III (1400 B.C.), and only after the temple buildings had established a different line of approach to the cave. In the XIIth dynasty, when these steles were set up, the site of the later temple was covered with burnt sacrifices; and the line of approach to the sacred cave seems to have been along the edge of the hill past the steles. These were then erected, bordering the way, which probably ran along the broken line here marked. There was already a bed of sand and chips on the ground before the wall was built; the first walling (of the XVIIIth dynasty) was of straight stones, unhewn, but evenly laid; that was patched at a higher level with a rubbly mass of blocks irregularly laid, probably in a Ramesside restoration.

The first stele to the west is that of Hor·ur·ra (fig. 114), describing his expedition, which was in the hot summer weather. This—as we shall see—has a great chronological value. Around the foot of the stele, except on the west, is a pavement of stone slabs. Next there are three steles, one of which is still in position, and the other two overthrown; the original positions can be identified by the sockets, which were cut into the rock for the foot of each stele. At the side of these is a

STELES IN THE APPROACH

piece of rough stone walling, which appears to have been the retaining-wall for the mass of stones and sand which were banked up against the temple. The fallen steles have been weathered through and so divided, after which the parts have been shifted. Most of the steles have suffered much on their north faces; the decay is from the ground-level upward for a foot or two. This is not due to sand-blast borne by high winds, as that would be mainly from the south-west, and very little sand could be blown up from the bare rock to the south. The injury must be due to wet rotting the stone, especially water splashing up against the foot; and to evaporation of wet from the stone, aided by frost attacking the damp parts. Beyond these is a rock-socket with two channels at the sides to allow of levering the stele into place. In this stood the longest list of workmen, the inscription of 100 miners, of which the upper part is in fig. 118.

At the side of chamber J a square opening is seen in the rock. This was covered by two stone slabs when found, beneath the rough stone blocks that were banked over it, against the wall of the temple. It originally opened into a recess 41 by 30 in. to the south, of the same breadth as the pit (see the inner outline, dotted). This recess had been cut out larger, to 63 by 62 in., as shown by the outer broken line. The recesses were 27 in. high. On the side were traces of colouring, and of the painted hieroglyphs reading . . . . *y r neter seh*. The original recess seems too small for a burial in any case, and even in its enlarged form can hardly have held a coffin. When cut in the rock this part was a rough rise, covered with ashes of sacrifices; but the pit was hardly connected with sacrifices, as it was finely smoothed and decorated.

Farther north is the socket of a stele, shaded across here, which fits the size of the broken stele of the 23rd year of Amenemhat III, lying near by (see fig. 113). This socket was cut down on the north side, in making a large, levelled space, the outlines of which are here marked, called on the plan the SHRINE OF KINGS. This space is about 26 ft. long, or 313 to 314 in. × 204 to 206 in.; this is 15 × 10 cubits. There was a roof covering the southern half of the area, but probably not more than this; for the fluted columns are not in the middle of the breadth, being 73 in. from the south and 131 in. from the north wall, and the north wall of rough stone does not seem as if intended to carry the weight of a roof. We must look on this as a portico, tetra-style, between pilasters. The outline here is the limit of the cutting into the rock, which amounts to about 30 in. deep along the south. The double line at the south shows the top and base of the wall, which has a batter.

The sides were carried up by building to about 55 in.; portions of a projecting course, apparently a corbelling to the roof, remain over this. The fluted columns were 12 in. in diameter at the bottom, on bases 23 in. in diameter. The lines projecting in the middle of the south side show the rock-cutting for the base of an altar, about 30 in. square. The whole appearance of the shrine is shown in fig. 97. Here the rock-cutting and the course above it are seen on the left, capped with the corbel course. The slope down of rock on the west side is seen, and the stump of the pilaster. The column in the foreground is only of loose fragments, placed on the base to show the position of the portico front. The early stele fills the right-hand side.

The carvings of this shrine are much injured; most of the top course is lost, and the rock has suffered from scaling. The subjects are the early kings Sneferu and Amenemhat III (see fig. 98), Hatshepsut, and the divinities Sopdu and Hathor. The inscriptions mention the honouring of Sneferu by Hatshepsut, and give a long account of the founding of the shrine by that queen; also a long recital of all the offerings that were to be made. There is no other such monument known, which

97 HATSHEPSUT'S SHRINE OF KINGS, ON NORTH OF TEMPLE.

98 FIGURES OF SOPDU AND AMENEMHAT III, SHRINE OF KINGS.

99 NORTH DOORWAY OF TEMPLE, HAT-HOR HANAFIYEH BEHIND.

100 HAT-HOR HANAFIYEH, FROM EAST SIDE.

THE SHRINE OF KINGS

makes us regret the more that it is not in better preservation. The whole of it was buried, and no one had any knowledge of it until we cleared the site. The original entrance to the enclosure seems to have been on the east, where there is some pavement around an old XIIth dynasty stele; this stele was built into the wall, and served as a door-jamb. The door-socket is clearly seen, and the groove by which the lower pin of the door was passed into the socket; the door shut at right angles to the groove, and was 36 in. wide. There was evidently an aversion to meddling with the old steles, and this one was not even shifted so as to be square with the building, but the wall was accommodated to its direction.

A few feet farther to the east there was another wall, which absorbed two steles in its course. No trace of the wall remains; but the sill of a doorway plainly implies a double door, 42 in. across, and therefore a continuous wall through which the door opened. This wall must have shut off the whole region of the XIIth dynasty steles; and the Shrine of the Kings was in that enclosure. Some way farther to the east is a very thick and short stele, with names of officials in the reign of Amenemhat III.

We now reach the SIDE DOOR of the Temple, of which the lower courses remain; the view in fig. 99 should be studied in connection with the plan. The doorway is in the foreground, the left jamb remaining vertical; of the right wall four courses are standing. On the extreme right are two of the pillars of chamber O, and the south wall of that chamber. The architrave against the sky is that in the Hat-hor *hanafiyeh*, of which two of the pillars are seen. To the left are the two steles re-inscribed by Tahutmes III, which bound the east of the *hanafiyeh*. On the plan will be seen, at the side of the doorway, a tank (59 x 26 in.), which is shown in fig. 143, no. 16. This tank was cut out of an earlier stele (about 25 to 26 x 14 in.) of the XIIth dynasty, which had been much defaced by weathering. It was broken into two pieces, which were found close to the position here shown. The size of it so nearly agrees with the recess in the outer wall that it almost certainly stood there.

The door opened into a long COURT, which was probably divided originally into an outer and inner portion, as there was a stele standing at one side, just opposite to the change in the wall at the other side. That a cross wall might disappear altogether is not impossible, as the outer wall of this court was ruined to within two courses of the ground, and was never seen until we cleared it; and of the south wall of the court only one course of stone remains, while of the corner of chamber O there is not a block left. There were no traces of a roof; though one Hat-hor pillar with curling hair was found, whose shaft was $10\frac{1}{2} \times 9$ in., like those of Amenhotep II. The large size of the court, however, makes it unlikely that it was covered in, especially as only the top of one pillar was found in it.

To the south of this is the largest covered chamber, the HAT-HOR HANAFIYEH. The pillars are the finest in the temple, and the heads of Hat-hor on them have often been published (see figs. 100-104 and 111). The south-west pillar has never been shifted; of the north-west pillar only a stump remains in place, and the head lies apart (fig. 104). The north-east pillar had been overthrown, but we replaced it on its base, which remained; the block is in good state, and it taxed our men to set up fourteen hundredweight entirely by sheer lifting power, as we had no tackle. Of the south-east pillar only the base and the head were left, but it was set up in place for photographing (see fig. 101). One of the architraves that was perfect was also lifted up to its old level, and blocked in position. The size of the pillars was 84 high, 16 or 17 wide, and 12 to 14 in. thick. The complete roof-beams were $84 \times 17 \times 15$, $84 \times 13 \times 13$, and $67 \times 13 \times 13$ in. The longer ones lay from the pillars to the walls, and the

101. HAT-HOR HATHETPE, FROM SOUTH-WEST.

102. HAT-HOR HATHETPE, FROM NORTH.

HEADS OF PILLARS IN THE HATHOR SHRINE OF TAHUTMES III.

THE HATHOR HANAFIYEH

shorter ones between the pillars. The beams lay from east to west, as there is a recess for the beam-end in the lintel of the door to the east, and in another block on the east side, shown in fig. 110. The remaining roofing-slabs are 62 × 31 × 8 and 58 × 22 × 10 in. As the intervals in the clear are 47 to 55 in. wide, these slabs would cover them safely.

On the east side are two steles of the XIIth dynasty, which had been much weathered, and were then re-inscribed by Tahutmes III; the southern one is fixed in a high block as a base, which block is trimmed into shape as part of the later door-jamb. These two steles are seen from the outside in fig. 100, looking into the *hanafiyeh*.

In the centre of the *hanafiyeh* is a circular basin of stone, 31 in. across, with a hollow 25 in. across. This was broken into two parts, but I replaced them together, and it will be seen best in figs. 101 (looking down upon it), 102, and 111. In the corner of the *hanafiyeh* is another stone tank, 44 × 30 in. These tanks for ablutions are similar to those in the *hanafiyeh* court of a mosque, and hence the name adopted here for this part of the temple. To the west there was a continuous mass of broken stones and sand up to the pylon. A few scarabs of the XVIIIth dynasty were found in this.

To the east, the Hathor *hanafiyeh* opened into a triangular space, which contained nothing definite. There was a mass of broken stone backing of the southern walls, which projected forward to an irregular extent; certainly no actual wall remained to limit this space on the south. It is possible that there was merely a passage between the two *hanafiyehs*. Up to this part the axis of the passage has been 20° to 22° south of west; beyond this the sanctuary is 38° north of west; we, therefore, continue to write of the axis as being east to west throughout.

The LESSER HANAFIYEH was reworked by Ramessu II

whose names are on the pillars; but these are cut over older inscriptions, so the whole may well be as old as the Hat-hor *hanafiyeh*; and, indeed, from the positions it would be difficult to suppose that the lesser *hanafiyeh* was the later of the two. The western wall is ruined down to one course, except just at the south corner; and as the doorway has entirely disappeared, it is possible that walls connecting it with the other *hanafiyeh* door have also been removed. The two northern pillars stood intact; of the south-western, half remained in place, and we replaced the upper part; the south-eastern had disappeared entirely. The appearance of these is shown in figs. 105 and 106. The architrave was lifted up on to the pillars by us, to give somewhat of the original effect, and to get it safe out of the way in clearing the closely-packed blocks which filled the place. As this beam is 86 × 13 × 13 in., it is too long to have lain in any position here except from the north-east pillar to the east wall. A roofing-slab was found 73 × 38 × 10 in., which belonged to the south part of the roof.

Between the pillars lies another stone tank, which by its form was doubtless cut from an old stele; it is 54 × 23 in., with a hollow 37 × 17 in. This is seen in both the views, 105 and 106, between the pillars. In fig. 106 are seen the steles in front of the cave, and over the broken pillar is the walling between the Portico of Hat-hor and the Hall of Sopdu. In the corner is a stele, the upper part of which has perished; the lower part has the figure and titles of a Ramesside official.

East of this is a court which is marked on the plan as the APPROACH OF SOPDU. It gave access to the Hall of Sopdu on the east, and to the Portico of Hat-hor on the north. That the passage was regarded as going northward, and not as coming southward, is indicated by a sphinx of Tahutmes III, which faces to the south. This sphinx lies along the west side of the passage, facing south; and fragments of a fellow were found, which

105. LESSER HANAFIYEH, LOOKING EAST.

106. LESSER HANAFIYEH, LOOKING NORTH.

THE SHRINE OF SOPDU

doubtless had been on the opposite side of the doorway to the Hathor shrine. The face of it is quite perfect, and it is a fine piece of work, but we were not able to remove it with the means of our present transport. After a day or two I found that the Bedawyn were looking after it, and inquiring to see it; and, fearing that they might damage the face, I had it at once covered over deeply with sand and stones.

The HALL OF SOPDU is next reached, a chamber with two pillars. It was entirely roofed originally, as a part of the roof reaching to the west wall was yet in place. This showed that it was not a portico like that of Hathor. The ends of slabs remaining are 30, 32, and 40 in. wide. The architraves lay from north to south. Only the stumps of the pillars remained, bearing inscriptions and figures of the scribe Nekht, and of Hatshepsut and Hathor embracing each other. The mention of the god Sopdu on these columns is the authority for attributing this lesser shrine to that god. On the north wall are portions of an inscription concerning the offerings and building of the shrine by Hatshepsut. On the west wall, south of the door, are figures of officials drawn in red, but not yet sculptured. At the back of the wall is the CAVE in the rock, which contains three steps leading up to a round-headed recess. This seems to have contained a tablet in honour of the god; but no trace of such a tablet was found here, nor would any of the tablets found agree with the size of the recess.

We now turn back to the open court. At the east end of this, turned askew about 35°, is the SANCTUARY, leading to the shrine behind it. The successive changes of this building are difficult to trace. The highest part remaining is the north wall, and the adjacent part of the front up to the door. This half of the front wall retains its sculptures inside and outside, as shown in figs. 107 and 108. On the outside, 107, the subject is clear enough; one complete scene of Ramessu IV receiving a falchion from Amen, with the king's name on a band below, and the god's name in a column before him. The heads of the figures are lost, and these, with their head-dresses, must have occupied a large space above. At present the courses are at 0 footing, 9, 19, 28, 40, 50, 60, 71, 83 in. high. And in proportion to similar scenes of Merenptah and Ramessu III (L., D., iii, 211, and Israel stele), we must recognise that 31 in. have been removed, and the total height was 110 in. over the footing of the wall, or 70 from the feet of the figures.

But when we look closer at this wall there is a different scene. Across the feet of Amen is the basis of a divine figure, whose foot is also visible. This was undoubtedly of a goddess, probably Hat-hor. Several other traces of earlier sculpture are also found upon the wall, and it is clear that a scene of an earlier king adoring Hat-hor has been removed, to make way for the present one. The limits of the older scene appear to have been the same as those of the present.

On the inner face, fig. 108, the whole sculpture visible is of Ramessu IV. But only the figure of Hat-hor remains; and of the king, who was offering to her, there is but the arm bearing the offering, and the foremost foot. The whole body of the king was on a part of the wall which is removed. On comparing this with a similar scene (of Sety I, in photograph), it appears that at least 17 in. of wall have been cut away. The present door-jamb is therefore later than that of Ramessu IV, and was probably made by Ramessu VI, while the door of Ramessu IV must have been at least 17 in. more to the south. Thereby the entrance to the sanctuary was in a direct line between the door of chamber O and the porch; and thus it was parallel to the south side of the court, which bounds the triangular space. In the foundations of the sanctuary wall are pieces of sculpture of Tahutmes III, so what buildings may have been here in his time we cannot now trace.

107. OUTSIDE OF SANCTUARY WALL, RAMESSU IV AND AMEN.

108. INSIDE OF SANCTUARY WALL, ALTAR AND HATHOR.

THE SANCTUARY

Along the south side of the Sanctuary was a roofed space built by Ramessu IV. The lower parts of two pillars remain on their bases, and before our clearance four of the five roofing-slabs lay fallen, just below their proper places. I measured them, and then turned them on edge in order to clear the ground below. Their forms are shown by the broken outlines in the plan; their thickness was 11 in. The architraves of this roofing remain, marking a span of 40 in., with 13 in. built into the wall, which space is shown as white on the plan. The inscriptions are of Ramessu IV, reading symmetrically from the middle to each end of the architrave, and also on the pillars. At the east end a stele was cut down flat on the top to receive the other end of the architrave.

The PORCH in the sanctuary, leading to the shrine, was built by Ramessu IV, whose cartouche is on the stump of the front jamb to the south of the door. The north jamb was built up of steles of the XIIth dynasty, which we removed in order to copy their inscriptions. The cornice over the porch was very unusual. The block was 73 in. long, 18 high, and 36 deep through. On the sides and front it had the usual cavetto, but no roll below, as that probably came on a lower block. The palm-leaf pattern of the cavetto is outlined on the front, except for a space of 21 in. in the middle, which has never been carved. In this space is a round-headed passage-way 17 in. wide, cut out to a height of 8 in. There is no other instance of an arching top to a doorway cut through a lintel; and that this was not due to heightening the doorway as a later change is seen by the cornice pattern stopping short, and not being continued past the archway.

It is possible, though hardly likely, that there was a roof over the rest of the sanctuary. The reasons against a further roof are that no traces of other pillars were found here; that it is unlikely that the architrave of the roof on the south side would be inscribed unless it were a front line; and that the east roof-stone is notched out to fit the steles against the east of it, so that its front edge would project a little beyond the architrave, and leave no room for any other roof to rest there. On the other hand, there was a piece of the edge of a roof-slab 14 in. thick, with a rebate along the edge 4 in. deep and 7 in. wide for the support of a thin slab; and there was a thin slab, 35 × 22 × 5 in. These point to a roof of thick slabs, with thinner ones resting on rebates, as in the chambers A to L. But we do not see where any roof of this construction would occur near here.

The east side of the Sanctuary is fenced with an irregular line of steles, which formed a barrier before the portico court. Of these fourteen steles, six are of Amenemhat III; five are probably so, but the date has decayed; one is of Amenemhat IV, and two are of Tahutmes III. We shall note the evidence of changes in dealing with the history of the shrine. Four of these steles of the XIIth dynasty have flat slabs in front of them, outlined in the plan; and these show that the steles were not shifted later, to be utilised in forming walls or barriers. Almost in the axis of the shrine it will be seen that there is a gap in the line of steles, with two lines here drawn across it. In this space a stone walling has been inserted; it seems probable that it was left as the entrance to the shrine originally, and that later it was blocked with building, and the latest stele of Tahutmes III was set up against that old doorway on the inner side. This grouping is shown in fig. 120, where are seen the bases of the steles side by side, and the Tahutmes stele before them. Of these steles, only four of the line in front of the portico are standing; four others have been weathered through, and it was with difficulty that I identified the fallen portions, by means of the variations in size. The two of Tahutmes III are of dark red sandstone, which is very weak: one is the latest of all the steles, and is almost rotted through and only held up by leaning against another;

the other had entirely broken away, and parts were found lying to the east of it.

The PORTICO COURT was formed by a stele of Amenemhat III on the north side of it, and one of Amenemhat IV at the south. It was, therefore, an original feature. There is no trace of any roofing to it; and as the roof of the portico has a cornice-edge, and over-rides its architrave, a further roof could not have been placed here.

The PORTICO roof was supported by two fluted columns of Amenemhat IV; the stump of one yet remains. The pieces of these columns taper from 12·0 to 9·3 in a height of 86 in.; there are fourteen flutings of 1·8 to 1·9, and a flat band of 3·7 in. wide to receive the inscription. Thus these were 16-sided columns, with two sides merged together. The architrave upon them is 11½ in. thick, and the roof above is 11½ in. thick. The roof-slabs ran from back to front; one that remained was 96 long × 48 in. wide, or over 2 tons in weight. At the south end of the architrave it rests upon a stele, which is cut flat on the top to receive it. The sides of the portico are all of red sandstone slabs, and many of them have fallen out or are decayed. The view of the north-east corner is shown in fig. 109. This shows the stele on the left hand; then the portico wall; the corner, with the butt of a roof-slab over it; a fallen roof-slab leaning against the back wall; the cornice-edge of a roof-slab in place near the right hand; and below it the stele, trimmed into a portion of the wall. The subjects of the portico walls can scarcely be traced; they are alike on both sides, the goddess seated and the king offering to her, followed by a long row of officials whose names are now illegible. The doorway to the cave is broken away on both sides, but the south side bears the names of Amenemhat IV. Part of a flat lintel-slab 16 in. high, of an Amenemhat, was found here; and just in front of the door lies a perfect lintel-slab of Amenhotep I, 22 in. high, with cavetto cornice, and 50 in. long. Another piece of a cornice of Amenhotep I is 19 in. high; and it is difficult to see where this can have been placed. Though the sides of the doorway have been removed, we can trace from the lintel that the doorway was 29 in. wide.

The CAVE OF HAT-HOR is entirely cut in the natural rock, without any lining or piecing. The sides of the entrance are rough, and have lost a lining of about 12 in. thick on the north side. The sides of the chamber have been carefully smoothed; they were flat and regular, the length being the same on both sides, the width 3 in. more at the back than at the front. But most of the sides have scaled off a thickness of 1 to 4 in., and thus the inscriptions are lost excepting the top edge. We found several pieces of the fallen inscriptions, but not nearly all; the loose pieces I was able to fit into place through the variation in the breadths of the columns, and then they could be transferred to the copy. Probably the cause of finding a part, but not all, of the fallen pieces, is that some had been removed in the restorations of the cave by later kings; and all that we found were pieces that had fallen since the XXth dynasty. It is difficult to see what has been the cause of this scaling, because the pillar of rock left *in situ* in the midst has not scaled at all in the same way, though the strata are the same. One large slice has fallen from the north side of it, but the other faces are perfect. It cannot, therefore, be pressure from above, nor can it be wet, as the rain that ran in must have soaked the pillar quite as much as the walls. It is possible that the accumulation of soluble salts, crystallizing out of the rock behind into cracks and fissures near the face, has induced the falling away of the outer two or three inches. The subjects on the walls are prayers for the officials who made the shrine and for their families. The pillar has figures of Amenemhat III, the chief chamberlain Khenemsu, and the chief seal-bearer Ameny-senb, adoring Hat-hor.

109. NORTH-EAST CORNER OF PORTICO BEFORE SACRED CAVE.

110. HAT-HOR AND KHNUMU, EAST SIDE OF HANAFIYEH.

THE SACRED CAVE

The recesses of the cave are three. A large one high up at the back was probably for the sacred emblem of Hathor, most likely a sistrum of valuable material. This recess is 35 in. back, 38 in. wide, and from 57 over the floor up to the roof at 82 in. At its side is a small recess 9 in. wide and 14 in. deep, with a shallow rebate round the edges as if for fixing a door to it. On the south side is a recess 29 in. wide and the same deep, and from 12 to 34 in. over the floor. Nothing was found in any of these recesses.

In the north-west part of the cave was found an altar to Hathor, which from its size had probably stood in that corner. It is 40 × 26 in., and 14 in. thick, of the reign of Amenemhat III, dedicated by Ameny. On the other side of the cave were fragments of a curiously formed altar, about 41 × 33 in. and 26 in. high, with the names of Amenemhat II and III; and small circular altars of incense were also found here, which are described farther on (see figs. 142 and 143).

CHAPTER VII

THE HISTORY AND PURPOSE OF THE TEMPLE

HAVING now described the actual remains and architectural facts of the temple, we will turn to describe its history and purpose.

The oldest trace of occupation here is the hawk of Sneferu, the last king of the IIIrd dynasty, about 4750 B.C.; this is shown in fig. 126, and the workmanship of the hieroglyphs marks it as a contemporary carving. Certainly such forms of signs, and the thin, severe style of them, would not be paralleled in the XIIth or XVIIIth to XXth dynasties; nothing else here at all resembles it. That the later knowledge and traditions about the place agreed with this is evident from the other remains. The throne of a statuette of Sneferu (fig. 129) was dedicated by Senusert I. In the XIIth dynasty group of four kings seated at a table, made by Senusert I (fig. 128), we see his father, Amenemhat I, of the XIIth dynasty, next to him; then Mentuhotep Neb·hapu·ra, of the XIth dynasty; and then another king earlier than the XIth dynasty, which is probably Sneferu. A stele of the 27th year of Amenemhat III says that he is beloved by the deceased King Sneferu. A stele of an official of the XIIth dynasty says that he had obtained more turquoise than any one since the time of Sneferu. In the XVIIIth dynasty Shrine of the Kings, carved by Hatshepsut, we see Sneferu as the only king figured earlier than the XIIth dynasty (see fig. 98). On the dark red sandstone stele before the portico, the upper part of which has fallen, the style and the figures are like those of the neighbouring stele of Tahutmes III, but it commemorates King Sneferu. Thus, from the history of the place known to later ages, and from the hawk found here, we must credit Sneferu with having opened these mines. That he should do so is only an enterprise to be expected of him, when for several centuries before his time the mines of Magháreh had been worked, and he had put two large tablets there himself.

How much of the shrine existed here in his time is not known. But we may conclude that probably the cave was begun then. The condition of the figure of the hawk, which is of limestone, and yet is not at all weathered, points to its having been in some permanent shelter.

The next trace of a date here is the honouring of King Mentuhotep Neb-hapu-ra of the XIth dynasty, about 3500 B.C., who is figured by Senusert I, as we have noticed above. Soon after him we find Amenemhat I, the founder of the XIIth dynasty, leaving the base of a statuette here, and having also a statuette for which a regular place was appropriated in the temple. But Senusert (or Usertesen) I was the first king (3400 B.C.) of whom any pieces of construction remain. His lintel is of fine limestone and unusually long; two or three other pieces of his sculpture were found, and a very interesting slab has come from the wall of his shrine, marking the places where the statuette of Senusert I was kept, the statuette of Amenemhat I, and the hawk of Senusert I. This hawk in sandstone, much weathered and broken, was actually found by us in the temple. The inscription mentions also Khent, the queen of Senusert, Sebat his daughter, and the overseer of the north land, Ankh-ab. This shows that Senusert I arranged the shrine, and left a permanent building of some solidity here. The first of the Egyptian Bethel-stones was also put up in his reign.

Of Senusert II there is the base of a kneeling statuette; of Senusert III there is a squatting figure, with the names of his officials who dedicated it, now in the British Museum. Of Amenemhat II there is one great Bethel stele and part of another, three mine and quarry inscriptions, a statuette of Hat-hor dedicated by his ship-master named Sneferu, and other remains. His name appears also on the altar in the cave. These show that the shrine was maintained all through the dynasty, and that each king worked here and honoured the "Mistress of Turquoise."

When we come to Amenemhat III we find incessant activity here all through his long reign, the first date being in his 4th year and the last in his 45th year. The cave was enlarged to its present size by him, as on the walls are the names of an official, Ameny, and his family; and the same official dedicated the altar in the cave in the name of Amenemhat III. The other altar in the cave was also inscribed by the same king. Some of the steles set up in front of the portico are of this reign, in the 8th, 13th, and 30th years. And it seems very probable, therefore, that the building of the portico was at least begun now, although inscribed under the next king. The essentials of the sacred cave of Hat-hor and its front were what constituted the shrine in this reign. The greater part of the steles of the mining expeditions also belong to this time.

The inscriptions on the portico, and a large stele at the side of it, are due to Amenemhat IV. He also showed continued activity here. The stele of Set found in the Shrine of the Kings (fig. 116), a Bethel stele, a stele of his 6th year on the road to the mines, and a private stele of the same year, all belong to this reign. No small offerings of this dynasty remain, such as dishes, vases, or ornaments; but the large number of statuettes of the kings and of the goddess show how much attention was given to the shrine.

AMENEMHAT III

Of this period a very interesting result was found beneath the later temple. Over a large area a bed of white wood-ashes is spread, of a considerable thickness. In the chamber O there is a mass, 18 in. in thickness, underlying the walls and pillars, and therefore before the time of Tahutmes III. In chamber N it varies from 4 to 15 in. thick; west of the pylon it is from 3 to 12 in.; and it is found extending as far as chamber E or F with a thickness of 18 in. Thus it extends for over a hundred feet in length. In breadth it was found wherever the surface was protected by building over it. All along the edge of the hill, bordering on the road of the XIIth dynasty past the steles, the ashes were found, all across the temple breadth, and out as far as the building of stone walls of chambers extends on the south, in all fully fifty feet in breadth. That none are found outside the built-over area is to be explained by the great denudation due to strong winds and occasional rain. That large quantities of glazed pottery have been entirely destroyed by these causes is certain; and a bed of light wood-ash would be swept away much more easily. We must, therefore, suppose a bed of ashes at least 100 × 50 ft., very probably much wider, and varying from 3 to 18 in. thick, in spite of all the denudation which took place before the XVIIIth dynasty. There must be now on the ground about fifty tons of ashes, and these are probably the residue of some hundreds of tons. The age of these ashes is certainly before the XVIIIth dynasty. And on carefully searching a part of this stratum for pottery embedded in it, I found pieces of thin, hemispherical cups, of thick, large, drop-shaped jars, and of rough white tube-pots, all of which belong to the XIIth dynasty. We have just seen that the XIIth dynasty was the most flourishing time in the early history of the place, and this agrees with the date of these remains.

What, then, is the meaning of this great bed of ashes? One suggestion was that it was the remains of smelting

100 HISTORY AND PURPOSE OF THE TEMPLE

works. But smelting elsewhere does not leave any such loose white ashes; on the contrary, it produces a dense black slag. Also, there is no supply of copper ore at that level, nor within some miles' distance, and the site is very inaccessible for bringing up materials. Moreover, there is no supply of fuel up on the plateau; whereas the ore has been elsewhere transported to valleys and plains where fuel could be obtained, as at the Wady Nasb, Wady Gharándel, and El Márkha. The statement of Lepsius and others that there are beds of slag near the temple is an entire mistake, due to ignorance of mineralogy; the black masses are natural strata of iron ore, and not artificial copper slag. Another suggestion was that they were like the beds of ashes near Jerusalem, which were supposed to have originated from the burning of plants to extract alkali. But, again, this is the most unlikely place for obtaining a supply of plants. Neither of these suggestions can be an explanation. Again, these ashes were supposed to be from workmen's fires; but if workmen continually burnt great fires in front of the shrine, we must suppose some religious motive for it.

The locality itself shows the meaning. In front of the sacred cave, on the high place above the valleys around, there was a great burning, continually repeated on thousands of occasions. The connection of this with the worship here is evident. This was a type of worship well known in later times as the popular worship of Palestine, which all the efforts of the priestly party could not suppress for centuries. Under Jehoash, "the high places were not taken away: the people still sacrificed and burnt incense in the high places" (2 Kings xii. 3). The same account is repeated reign after reign (xiv. 4; xv. 4, 35); and Ahaz "sacrificed and burnt incense in the high places, and on the hills" (xvi. 4). In Samaria, also, "they set them up images and Asherim in every high hill . . . and there they burnt incense in all the high places" (xvii. 10, 11). It was not till about

700 B.C. that this worship was overcome, even under Jewish rule (xviii. 4; xxiii. 13, 15). It is clear that there was in Palestine from early times a regular worship upon the high places, with sacrifices and burnt incense. On this hill we see great evidence of burnt sacrifices; and in the cave itself were many altars for burning incense, see figs. 142 and 143. The popular worship of Palestine is here before us.

What was sacrificed we do not know. The normal Semitic sacrifice was the libation of blood, which "was all that fell to the god's part" (R. SMITH, *Relig. of Semites*, 213), and "originally all sacrifices were eaten up by the worshippers" (p. 370). Though I carefully searched the ashes in various parts, and though my men would have preserved anything noticeable, we did not find aught but pottery. The absence of bones would not at all imply that there were no animals sacrificed, for the scarcity of food in this region brings hyaenas and dogs to devour every fragment that they can find. Although our men killed a goat or sheep every week, I never saw a single bone lying about our camp; every one was carried off and eaten. The same would be the case if animals were sacrificed in these burnt offerings, and we could not expect to find any bones left here. Further, we must bear in mind that the Amorites of Palestine were akin to the prehistoric Egyptians; and among the latter in Upper Egypt an immense burnt offering took place at funerals, the white ashes of which were laid by in jars placed in the tombs. Sometimes as much as a ton of ashes were so preserved. Though I carefully searched these ashes in dozens of instances, winnowing them in a breeze, I never found a fragment of bone, or anything beyond clean ash. These were not similar burnings to those before the sacred cave at Serabít, as they were entirely funerary, like the burnings for the Jewish kings (2 Chron. xvi. 14, xxi. 19; Jer. xxxiv. 5); but they show that it was common for a people, kindred to those of Palestine, to make great burnt sacrifices without leaving any trace of animal remains. We shall refer to this subject more fully in Chapter XIII.

We must, then, picture to ourselves the shrine of the XIIth dynasty as a cave in a knoll of rock, with a portico before it. Many tall steles stood in front of this, hedging in the portico from open view. The road to the shrine led past the head of a valley up to the cave, with a line of steles along the way ; while many shelters for visitors who came to dream at the holy place were scattered along the roadside farther off, with tall steles standing in them. At the side of the road, on the hill in front of the sacred cave, was the place of sacrifice, piled over with heaps of the ashes far and wide, where fires often smouldered with offerings to the great goddess.

After a long period of neglect, during which no expeditions were sent to Sinai, we find offerings made by Aahmes I, about 1570 B.C., of an alabaster vase with the name of his queen, Aahmes Nefertari (fig. 144, no. 2), *menats* of glazed pottery for that queen (fig. 148, no. 3), and for his daughter, Merytamen (no. 4), and a handle of a sistrum which was probably for Nefertari (fig. 151, no. 17). In the next reign we find that Amenhotep I, about 1550 B.C., repaired the sacred cave, the lintel and portico of which were broken down, and put in a fresh lintel, and a new architrave to the portico ; he also sent offerings to Hat·hor, of which we have parts of *menats* with his name (fig. 148, no. 1), and a sistrum-handle (fig. 151, no. 16). Tahutmes I, about 1520 B.C., continued to send offerings here ; his activity is shown by an alabaster vase (fig. 144, no. 3), glazed pottery vases (fig. 146, no. 1), *menats* of himself and his queen, Aahmes (fig. 148, nos. 5, 6), and wands (fig. 150, no. 1).

The greatest builder of the place was Queen Hatshepsut, associated with her nephew Tahutmes III. From the 5th to the 22nd year we find work done here in which the two rulers are always named in unison. In one case, even, we read, "*Suten bati Maat-ka-ra, Si-ra, Tahutimes,*" one cartouche of each ruler being put together to express their joint rule. There is not a single erasure of the name of either ruler, and no trace of that alternation of power which has been erroneously supposed. What changes they made in front of the portico we cannot now trace, as Ramessu II rebuilt the sanctuary, and Ramessu IV altered it. That the long walls of the court are due to them, or on their lines, is shown by the Hat-hor *hanafiyeh*, and the certainty that their work extended as far as the pylon, which is of the same date. The side-door of the temple seems to be a survival of the old line of approach, past the steles, up to the cave, a way which continued in use until the new buildings in the line of the pylon established another direction.

It may be asked why the great bend should have been made in the direction of the temple, and why the new buildings did not continue in line with the axis of the cave. The form of the ground prevents any building being carried much to the north of the sanctuary. The head of a branch of the Wady Dhába comes so close to the cave that any continuation along the axis would have run steeply down hill. The path led along a fairly level line, contouring the slope at the valley-head; and the new building was bound to follow that direction. No doubt some persons will seek for a meaning of these directions in astronomical settings of sun or stars. The axis of the cave was $308\frac{1}{4}°$ magnetic, in 1905, or probably $304\frac{1}{2}°$ true azimuth. This is beyond the range of sunset, which does not exceed $297°$ at this latitude. As the cave was the sole work at the time when its direction was established, its wide entry in proportion to its length is very unlikely to have a reference to any star setting. Regarding the new axis established by Tahutmes III, and rather irregularly continued to a greater length by his successors, the obvious fact that it is parallel to the

104 HISTORY AND PURPOSE OF THE TEMPLE

older path of approach is a sufficient cause to determine its direction. We may state, however, that its azimuth in the parts of 1500 B.C. may be $253\frac{1}{4}°$ magn., 250° true in ,, ,, 1200 ,, ,, ,, $252\frac{1}{4}°$,, 249° ,, extremes possible $\begin{cases} 253\frac{1}{2}° \\ 251\frac{1}{2}° \end{cases}$,, 250° ,, 248° ,, —and these directions would correspond to sunset between January 23rd and 31st, and between November 12th and 20th. But it would be very unlikely that there should be any meaning in a direction which was already fixed by natural causes centuries before the building was even anticipated.

The chambers O and N, the pylon, and the steles before it are all of Tahutmes III and Hatshepsut, and must all have been finished by the 5th year of his reign, as that is the date on the steles which were the final adornment of the pylon. Of this reign of Hatshepsut is also the Shrine of the Kings, which was constructed at the side of the pylon. In every part we see that so long as a stele was legible it was respected and left unmoved. The steles before the portico have many of them the altar-slabs of the XIIth dynasty still in place. The steles of the old approach have not had their old irregularities of position rectified; on the contrary, the new constructions have even been skewed to meet them. The steles that have been reused, for cutting into architraves or tanks, or for re-inscribing, were almost entirely obliterated by weathering before they were thus appropriated. There was far more careful conservation than we are accustomed to find in the merciless scourge of the thefts of Ramessu II in Egypt.

We now turn back to the east end, and see a fresh work of Hatshepsut and Tahutmes III. The old Sacred Cave belonged to the "Mistress of Turquoise," Hat·hor, and she alone was worshipped there. But later the devotion to other gods came forward, and Sopdu, the god of the East, had a cave-shrine carved for him, side by side with that of Hat-hor. How early this was done we cannot say, as the present construction is all of Hatshepsut; but the door from the portico court leading southward is inscribed by Ameny, who carved the cave of Hat-hor in the XIIth dynasty. No doorway would be required leading out against the rising hill-side, unless there were some other construction of importance on this side. So it seems as if there had been an earlier shrine of Sopdu, which was entirely remodelled during the XVIIIth dynasty. This god was worshipped in the Arabian nome —that is, the desert east of the middle of the Delta. His emblem was the zodiacal light, that great cone of brilliancy which in Egyptian skies rivals the Milky Way, and which rises in the East long before the sun.

The Cave of Sopdu, the Hall, and the Approach were all constructed in this reign; and the pair of sphinxes of Tahutmes III adorned the way thence to the shrine of Hat-hor. The lesser *hanafiyeh* must have also existed, as it lies between these works and the Hat-hor *hanafiyeh*. But there is only a private inscription on it earlier than that of Ramessu II.

The Hat-hor *hanafiyeh* is the most imposing part of the whole temple. Four great pillars with heads of Hat-hor stand around the central basin, as seen in the view in fig. 111. The faces of the great goddess are full of dignity and strength; and the wall-sculptures were among the best here, see fig. 110. Two great steles of the XIIth dynasty were incorporated in the eastern wall, serving to flank the jambs of the doorway. But they had been so weathered as to be mostly illegible; and Tahutmes inscribed the western face of the worst of them in the 27th year of his reign, after the death of Hatshepsut (see fig. 123).

In these courts of the Hat-hor *hanafiyeh* and the lesser *hanafiyeh* we see what great importance belonged to the ceremonial ablutions. At the north door of this temple stood a large tank, presumably for a preliminary cleansing. Then, crossing the court, the worshipper entered the Hathor *hanafiyeh*. There a circular basin in the midst was set for the next ablution. Yet a third tank stood by the door for another ablution before entering the lesser *hanafiyeh*; and there a fourth tank supplied the final cleansing before approaching the shrine. Such a series of ablutions must have belonged to a complex ritual; each applying to a different part of the body. We do not find this multiplication of washings defined in the early Jewish ritual, where it is only said that the priests were washed before the door of the tabernacle, at the laver (Exod. xl. 7, 11, 12), and that they always washed their hands and feet there (31), But the later Jewish ordinances are more detailed, and washing of the mouth and nose, of the arms to above the elbows, and other parts is obligatory. The Muslim washings are better defined. The Quran ordains washing the face, the hands to the elbows, and the feet. And the later customs are well given in the four hundred and fortieth night by the damsel Tawaddud, in her valuable outline of Muslim life. The *Wudu*, or minor ablution, includes (1) washing the face, (2) washing the hands to the elbow, (3) wiping part of the head (round the back of the crown, at present usual), and (4) washing the feet and heels; while the traditional statutes of the *Wudu* include (1) washing the hands (preliminary), (2) rinsing the mouth, (3) snuffing up water to rinse the air-passages, (4) wiping the whole head, (5) wetting the ears in and out, and (6) parting through the beard with wet fingers. Each of these actions is familiar to any one who has lived with present-day Muslims. The private ablutions, after excretion before prayers, are taken for granted in the ordinances, but are always performed. Which of these various ablutions were appropriated to the four tanks here provided we cannot now say; but it is clear that such a series of ablutions as we have mentioned might well be appropriated to the four successive tanks that are found here.

HATHOR HANAFIYEH, OF TAHUTMES III.

THE HANAFIYEHS

It is noticeable that only one of these tanks is before the outer door of the temple, while three of them are in the finest buildings of the temple, and belong evidently to its fixed ritual. The ablutions were not a preliminary cleansing before any religious ceremony could be worthily performed; but they were part and parcel of the acts of religion in the temple itself. This is parallel to the Jewish arrangements, where the laver stood before the door of the tabernacle, even nearer than the altar of burnt-offering. And there, inside the court of the tabernacle, close before the door of the sanctuary, the washings of the whole body before robing, or of the hands and feet at every ceremony, were constantly performed. The same observances were in the temple, where the great brasen sea for the priests to wash in stood in the court before the door of the holy place (2 Chron. iv. 6). The same Semitic system is seen in every mosque. The principal court of a mosque is that of the *hanafiyeh*, which is an octagonal basin in the midst of the court, usually surrounded with pillars. Here also the ablutions are a part of the religious service, performed in a court that may only be trodden by bare feet (or in side lavatories with water from the court), and following a very precise ritual, full of detail, which is essential to its efficacy. The system was evidently the same at Sinai in 1500 B.C., in the Jewish worship of 1000 B.C., and in the Muslim worship down to the present day.

The next stage of the building was that Tahutmes III added a court, M, along the line of the steles, and a chamber, L, in front of that. To this, Amenhotep II added chamber K. Tahutmes IV finished the door of this, and added chamber J. This formed a definite front to the temple, and it seems likely that his work stopped here; but it may have included the group G and F. These two chambers evidently were built at the same time, and had steles placed before the entrance, of which one remains. Next were added the fencing of the steles by means of court E, and the chamber D, which formed a front. After this Amenhotep III added the chamber C, placing two steles in front of it in the last year of his reign, the 36th. At the same time the rough stone wall was built around the whole temple, running to right and left on either side of the entrance. Lastly, the steles were enclosed in a court, B, and another chamber, A, was added by Sety I. This ended the growth of the temple.

Later kings made various reconstructions on this plan. Ramessu II rebuilt the sanctuary wall, and erected several steles, one on the north of the entrance. Merenptah inscribed the doorway to chamber J, and put in a stele. Sety II re-inscribed the pylon, adding his name across some of the carving of Tahutmes III. Ta·usert made many offerings of glazed pottery here. Set·nekht erected the last of the steles, on the south of the entrance. Ramessu III re-inscribed two steles of an older time, which were weathered. Ramessu IV built the porch, altered the door of the sanctuary, and built the roof over the south side of the sanctuary. Ramessu V left some offerings here of glazed bracelets. And lastly, Ramessu VI inscribed the pillars of chamber O, as shown in fig. 112. After that no trace of any later construction or offerings is found here; and only a piece of Roman pottery in the cave supplies a single point of history until we come to the *graffiti* of modern travellers.

112. PILLARS OF RAMESSU VI.

113. STELE OF AMENEMHAT III.

CHAPTER VIII

THE MINING EXPEDITIONS

THE Egyptian was in all ages a great organizer, and in that special ability of his lay the secret of the power of the nation. The bureaucracy of Egypt was a force from the days of the Ist dynasty; and it maintained the traditions and the national life with a persistency which enabled it to overcome many disasters. The native administrator under the Ptolemies, or the Copt under the Arabs, gave a vitality to the organization of the land, and a resisting power against entire dissolution, like that which the Diocletian system gave to the Byzantine Empire. And though, no doubt, a country always suffers dearly for having such a force living on it, yet this control tides over disasters which might otherwise root out all continuity, and saves a powerful people from being overthrown, as was the dominion of the Gaul, the Arab, or the Mongol. Any view which we can get into the working of a continuous organization is very enlightening; and a great study like that of Mommsen on the construction of the Roman Empire shows how much care, foresight, and restraint is involved in upholding such an instrument of civilisation.

The records of the mining expeditions have fortunately preserved some little insight into the organization of an expedition by the Egyptians. Unhappily, each record is more or less defective; but we may supplement one by another, so as to restore a general view of the varied grades and functions of the men who were employed. At first sight we might suppose that a gang of men, with a few overseers and a captain of the party, would be all that were needed. But the precise subdivision of labour was then, as in Egypt of the present day, the condition for obtaining great results from small minds. Each man has a very limited task, in touch with others on both sides of him; he must know exactly what he has to do, and be perfect in that, and then pass his work on to other hands in the next stage. This modern system, pursued by those who successfully organize the administration of Egypt to-day, was likewise the ancient system. Of the general officials, brought from regular official work in Egypt, we find no less than 25 different grades in Sinai. Of the local officials, who were concerned with the management of the special work of mining, there are 11 varied titles. Of the technical artisans who were employed there are 8 classes. And of the labourers, who formed the bulk of the party, there are 9 varieties.

The head of an expedition was always a high official who had experience in organizing. He usually combined three different titles, which belonged to different branches of administration. He was, before all, a "seal-bearer of the god," *neter sahu*. This title does not seem to imply any religious office, but goes back to the ideas of a time when the king was the divine descendant who represented divinity on earth. A title which was kept up till even the New Kingdom was that of the "excellent god," *neter nefer*. This title of "seal-bearer of the god" implies more than a mere official post; it refers to a relationship with the intrinsic nature of the king, much as our Lord Chancellor is "keeper of the king's conscience." Beside this intimate position, he had a high place in the trained official world, as "chief in the department of the interior," *mer akhenuti*. Whether the *akhenuti* refers to the interior of the palace, or the interior of the kingdom, is not proved. Probably it means the *diwan*, or inner office of administration in the

114   STELE OF HOR-UR-RA, IN XII DYNASTY APPROACH.

CHIEF OFFICERS

palace, as apart from the external offices of inspection and direction. And thirdly, this head was a "chief of the land of the north," *mer ta mehu*, one having experience of control in the management of the border people with whom he had to deal.

The next most important person was a "commander," *kherp*, whose charge is represented by what looks like a scorpion. In one case we find in a similarly important position a "commander of the palace gate," *kherp aha*. Whether the sign is really a scorpion, or no, cannot be settled until other examples are compared; the form proves nothing, as common signs of office were often much varied and corrupted by constant use, when the origin of them had been forgotten. There is, however, one great office, the most essential to such an expedition, the organizing of provisions, and yet we do not see any official identified with this alongside of the commander. From mere external presumption we might suppose that this title was that of head of the commissariat; and the appearance of a "commander of the palace gate" in place of him would not be unlikely, as the gate would be where all the provisions were tallied as tribute, or brought for sale.

The next most important office was that of "seal-bearer," *sahu* (?). Only once do we meet a "chief seal-bearer," *mer sahu*, and then he even takes precedence of the "seal-bearer of the god." It is not certain that he actually visited Sinai, as he only appears among the officials placed after the king in the adoration of Hathor, on the central pillar in the sacred cave. The usual official was a "seal-bearer, deputy of the chief seal-bearer," *sahu, khery ā mer sahu*. His office probably was to see that all orders and contracts were drawn up in due form, and to affix the royal seal to orders, agreements, and receipts, without which they would have no validity. This class of official is the one most commonly met with in the Middle Kingdom; and in a land where malversation, and oppression by the claim of government rights and priority, needed close control, as in the East at present, such power of sealing in the name of the king was very important. In the absence of currency the seal-bearer was the equivalent of paymaster. It is noticeable that we never find a seal-bearer along with a commander, *kherp*. Of 15 expeditions we have sufficient detail to judge of the status of the officials; in 6 there is a commander, in 7 there is a seal-bearer, but never both together. Now the seal-bearer would be mainly occupied in giving orders and receipts for supplies, as, in Sinai, there would be little other contact with the rest of the world; and hence he would probably have the commissariat in his charge on such an occasion. This agrees with his being the equivalent of the commander.

A high official, only twice named, is the "chief of transport," *mer qemāau*. He is mentioned where *ahau* boats are named, but no "chief of boats" is named as well. So he may have had the sea transport under him, though the presence of great trains of asses for the land transport may well have required a manager.

Another office, only once mentioned, is the "husband of the treasury," *tha en perui hez*. This is used in the same sense as our office of "ship's husband," the man who husbands or takes care of the providing of all that is wanted in the way of supplies and material. It was probably his task to act like the treasury clerk in a modern department, to see that the requisite orders were honoured, and that waste did not take place.

A somewhat similar "elder of the treasury," *āa en perui hez*, appears in another expedition.

The "scribe," *sesh*, or "sage scribe," *sab sesh*, of the expedition, is named in most cases. The combined title is constant in the Old Kingdom; but a plain scribe generally did the writing and account-keeping in the Middle Kingdom, perhaps owing to officials more frequently doing their own writing in later times. A

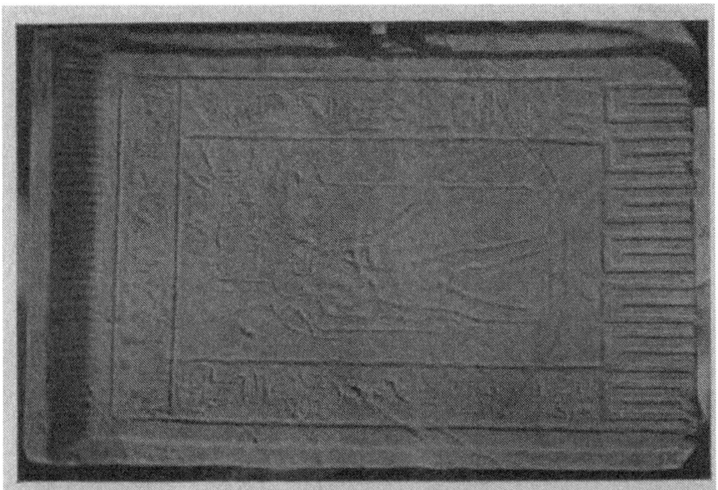

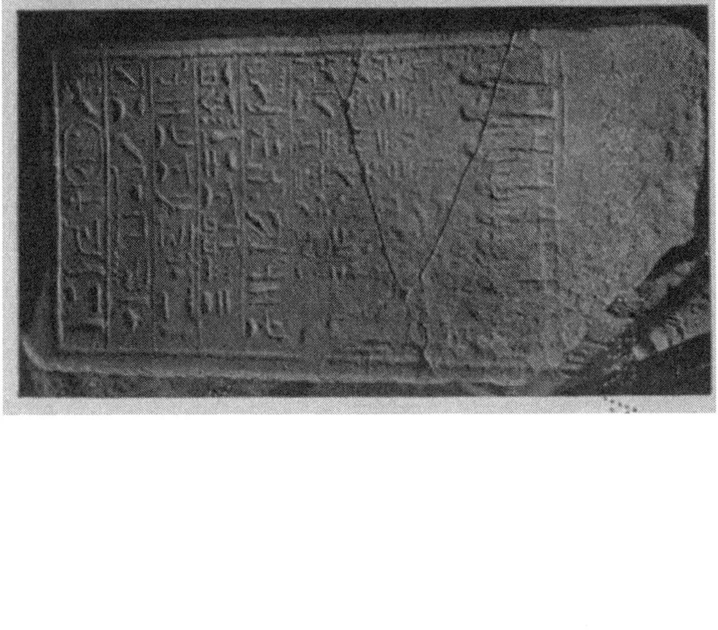

STAFF OF DIRECTION

"chief scribe," *mer sesh*, occurs once in early times; and a "scribe of the treasury," *sesh en perui hez*, in the Middle Kingdom.

Usually lower than the scribe came the "guards of the store-house," or store-keepers, *ari āt*, of whom there were generally four; less often there were one or two, and rarely three or five. In an administration where there was no currency the store-keeper was practically banker as well; such a condition is best called to mind by the old tithe-barn system in England, where any person or corporation having a claim upon land received their dues or rents in kind, and had to take charge of large quantities of produce each season. Thus the store-keeper was a very important factor, though without any responsibility for direction.

The "chief of the boats," *mer adetu*, is named in four expeditions, and the boats or boatmen in four others. The boat service must have always been an essential part of an expedition, as the train of asses could not go to and fro with stores between Suez and Sinai, owing to want of water on the road. The whole provision must have been brought down by boats to Burdéys, and then taken on donkey-back up to Serabít or Magháreh.

The "general," *mer mashau*, was employed occasionally. We find him under Pepy I, and in about a third of the expeditions of the XIIth dynasty. In one case no less than 10 generals are named, probably inferior officers who took a title for the Sinai service.

A wider office, that is found only in the larger expeditions, is that of "controller," *shenty*. Two or three of these were employed together, but we cannot now distinguish their functions.

Once a "chief physician," *ur sunnu*, was taken. This was in a party which seems to have been specially well organized, to judge by the fine record of 90 foremen miners, arranged in parties of ten with separate chiefs.

So far we have been following the most complete

period of records, that of the reign of Amenemhat III in the XIIth dynasty. In the earlier expeditions of the Vth and VIth dynasties to Magháreh, the official system was different. Under Assa the expedition was managed by two "princes," *sar*, without apparently any definite official experience. In the VIth dynasty a "seal-bearer of the god" was in charge, but he had not the other offices of chief in the *diwan*, or chief of the north land, these more specialised offices having been apparently part of the later system of government.

In the Vth dynasty the "sage scribe" and the "deputy scribe" were employed. Next to them was the commander of recruits, *uz neferu*. Two inspectors, *uba*, follow in the list; and three "interpreters for the princes," *sehez saru*, completed the chief staff. This mention of interpreters shows that Egyptian was not understood by the Retennu or Aamu, nor was Semitic known to the upper class of Egyptians.

In the VIth dynasty a further growth is seen. The expedition was directed by a "general" or a "seal-bearer of the god." And next to him in importance came classes of officials only found at this age, bearing the title of "in the eyes," *am merti*. The later phrase, "eyes and ears of the king," is well known, and these eyes doubtless refer to the royal presence, so that this title was equivalent to the Tudor phrase, "standing in the presence." They were legates from the court, who had their place about the king, and took their orders from him. These officials are named in the same order under Pepy I and Pepy II. First are two entitled "the legate, chief of the land" (*mer ta*), which is probably the first form of the title "chief of the north land," held by the leader of the expeditions in the XIIth dynasty. Next are two named "the legate, chief of the store-house," *mer āt*, who was replaced later by the four guardians of the store-house. Thirdly come two named "the legate, chief of the elders," *mer uru*, a title which

117 STELE OF SINEFERT. 118 STELE OF 100 NAMES, UPPER HALF. YEAR 4, AMENEMHAT III.

THE MINING OFFICIALS

shows that these elders were not a consultative body, but were the foremen or managers of the workmen.

In this age there were also interpreters attached to the "commander of recruits," *sehez uz neferu*. All of the above officials also had their normal positions in Egypt, and belonged to the home government.

Returning now to the great expeditions of the XIIth dynasty, we see also that another class of officials were appointed, solely for the work in Sinai. The principal of these were the inspectors, *ubau*. There are three titles which we cannot distinguish in functions : (1) *ubau*, with the bird *ba*; (2) *ubau* with the winged vase, as it may be called ; and (3) *ubau*, or *andu*, with a netting-needle sign. Of these there were usually two or three of no. (2), once there were fifteen of no. (1), once one of no. (1) with no. (2), and once seven of no. (3). How far these differed in their work cannot be traced without other examples.

The elders or foremen, *ury*, are named once, where three of them come between the controllers and the inspectors.

The guards, *heru*, are named under the title of the "overseer of the guards," *her heru*, of whom one was in a large expedition, and two in the best organized party.

An "overseer of the treasury," *her en perui hez*, appears once at Magháreh in the XIIth dynasty.

One of the most usual officials was the "overseer of the house of the superior miners," *her per kaiu*. These regulated the living of the better class of miners, probably managing the commissariat. There were usually two of these officials in an expedition, sometimes but one, and there is one instance of three.

A similar official is once mentioned as having charge of the house of the Aamu, or Syrians, who were employed.

An office that must have been of importance was that of the *sau*, which occurs once. In the same expedition there occurs an interesting title, the "chief of the gang," *mer sa*. This is a new sense of the word *sa*, which means primarily "back" or "backing." In a long list of a hundred foremen of miners, *neter kherti em hat*, every tenth man is called *mer sa*, showing that the nine men after him were his *sa*, or "following." He is thus apparently the same as a "chief miner," *kai*, under whom there were 4 to 45 miners. We thus learn that the organization was in parties composed of ten foremen miners, each party with a chief foreman, and doubtless each foreman miner having three or four labourers under him.

Of the purely technical men several classes are known. The principal was the "deviser of minerals," or prospector, *mes en āati*. That this was an important office is shown by only two being employed in each of the four expeditions where they are named (see fig. 119), and where 300 and 450 men were engaged. It has been thought that this was the title of a mason or stone-cutter, but it is far more important than that, as there is only 1 in 150 to 200 persons of the whole expedition. In the enormous expedition of Ramessu IV to Hammamat, there are 130 *mes en āati* named; but as there were over 8,000 men, that is less than one prospector to 60 men. This would be none too many to search out fit places for work, and devise fresh work as the sources became exhausted. The root of the title is, of course, *mes*, birth; and the derived meanings of *meses*, to draw a figure, and *mesmes*, planning or invention, sufficiently explain the *mes en āati* as the prospector who was to search out fresh sources of minerals.

After the turquoise was found, an official had the duty of gathering it, and keeping the stock together, as as it was very valuable, and might be easily lost or stolen. We find in one expedition the collectors, *uha*, a word derived from *uha*, to gather. They come next after the prospectors, and before the controllers, *shentyu*.

A sculptor, *mesenti*, is once mentioned, required no doubt for the work on the temple and the steles. Another

119 STELE OF SEBEK-HER-HEB, YEAR 40, AMENEMHAT III.

120 BASES OF STELES, FACING THE SACRED CAVE.

THE LABOURERS

kind of sculptor is the *kheti*, derived from *khet*, to carve; three of these came in one expedition. In another expedition three copper-smelters, *khemti*, were named. They may have been employed in the reduction of the ore at the Wady Nasb, or in making and repairing the tools of the workmen who were engaged on the temple.

The cook or baker, *pesy*, is named in one party. It is curious that there were not more men employed in the preparation of food, as it takes one man's time to bake and cook for twenty or thirty men, so that a dozen or twenty cooks would have been required for an ancient expedition.

There are also two obscure titles which can only be discussed at greater length than we can do here.

We now turn to the labourers. Of the superior miners, *kai en neter kherti*, two or four are named, the four looking after 45 common miners. Elsewhere five superiors, *kai*, are named, as well as three *kai uaz*. The bulk of the miners, *neter kherti*, were divided into a superior class of foremen miners, *neter kherti em hat*, of whom ninety are named at once, and the common labourers, *neter kherti*, of whom there are recorded in different expeditions 45, 200, 200, and 255, with 37 royal miners. In the beginning of the reign of Amenemhat III we find at Magháreh 734 soldiers named, and the mention of so large a number suggests that the troops were used for mining before more specialised parties were sent.

For the temple building there were, in one year, 75 "people of monuments," *sa en mennu*. At another time there were 50 "people of the temple of Amen," *sa en per Amen*. Many times peasants, *sekhti*, were sent, as many as 30, 30, and 43 being recorded. The only work in Sinai for which a common peasant was required would be driving the transport donkeys. In the instance of 43 peasants a train of 500 asses is named; this would imply a dozen asses to each man, which would be quite as many as he could manage.

The sea transport was a most important part of the organization, as the food supply was essential, and a failure in that might starve the whole service. Unfortunately, it is not often recorded; twice over, twenty boatmen, *sa en bet*, are named, and twice a single boatman, while four times the "chief of the boats," *mer depet*, appears. Twenty boatmen imply that five or six boats were employed. In another expedition 30 *ahau* boatmen are named.

The employment of foreigners by the Egyptians shows that much the same relations existed between Egypt and the desert as we find at present. Three expeditions of Amenemhat III were accompanied by the "brother of the prince of the Retennu, Khebdet," or "Khebtata" (*sen heq en Retennu*). On two steles he is shown riding on a donkey, led by a man in front, and with a driver carrying his water-flask behind. He was doubtless employed to manage the Bedawyn and to serve as a hostage for their good conduct. In just the same way, on a lesser scale, the brother of the sheykh was usually with our party, to ensure good terms with the neighbourhood. In one expedition, six Retennu are named. It is evident, then, that the Retennu were inhabiting Southern Palestine and Sinai at that time, and were the Tennu of the Tale of Sanehat. The Aamu Syrians also appear, ten in one year, twenty in another; and an overseer of the house of the Aamu is likewise named.

We can now form some general picture of the arrangement of one of these great mining expeditions, having the practical conditions of work and life in this region before us, as a background to the details recorded on the monuments. So soon as the inundation was over in November and December, stores would be accumulated at the head of the Heroöpolite Gulf, the officials would arrive, and the organization would be settled.

The stores, as they were received, would be in charge

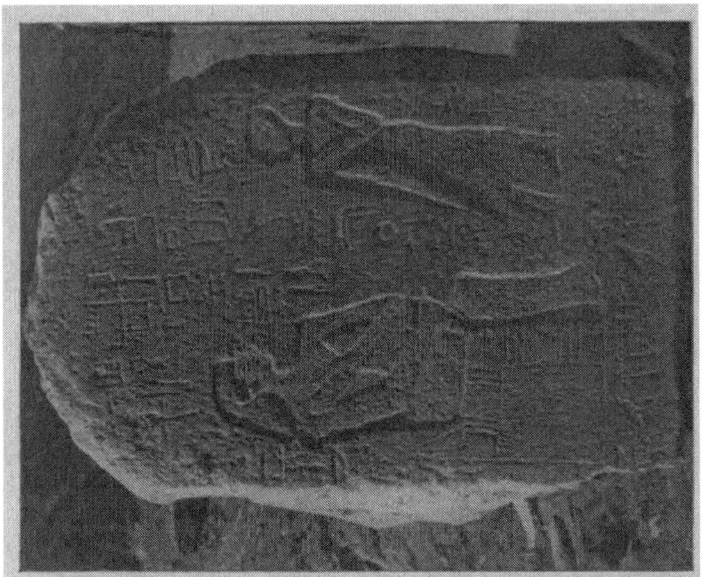

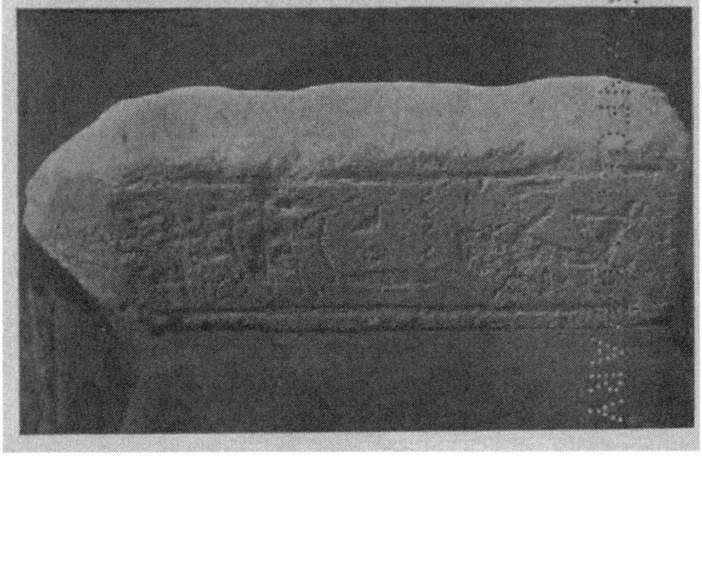

123. STELE OF YEAR 27, TAHUTMES III.   124. STELE OF YEAR 11, QUEEN HATSHEPSUT.

of the guards of the store-house. The scribes of the expedition, and the commissary or seal-bearer, who gave all the receipts and tallied the stores, would be in attendance. When these preliminaries were finished, the head of the party would come and take command of his staff. He was a chief of the *diwan* of the palace, with full official training; he could act in the king's name with his seal, and he was experienced in dealing with foreigners, since he was chief of the north land. The gangs of workmen would arrive at the starting point; but not a day too soon, as they and the asses consumed about five tons of provisions daily.

To get across the desert the full train of 500 asses would be needed, each carrying its own food and water and supplies for one man for three days, down to Gharándel, and enough food for two days more to the spring of the Wady Nasb, where the main halt would be. Then 300 asses would be sent down the Wady Bába to the coast at Burdéys, to bring up the boat supplies.

The maintenance of the camp would be kept up much on these lines. Each man requiring 3 lb. of supplies and each ass (say) 15 lb. daily, this for 500 men and 500 asses would be nearly 5 tons a day of food. Such would form 50 ass-loads; and as the round journey from the coast to Serabít and back would take five days (allowing for loading and delays), this would mean that 250 asses would keep up the whole food supply from the coast. Water might be put at 4 gallons per head per day; we actually lived on 1½ gallons each, but a larger allowance is more likely. Thus an ass would carry enough for three men; and so, if a single round to water was made each day, then 200 asses would be required to keep up the water-supply. This leaves 50 out of 500 as a margin for sickness and delays.

The stores were brought down by boats; and as there were 20 or 30 boatmen, probably about 6 boats were employed. If the round trip up the gulf and back, loading and unloading, took 12 days, this would mean a boat-load every two days. And two days' supply was about ten tons, which would be a very likely load for such boats, as they needed to draw close inshore with very little water. Thus, all the quantities of men, asses, and boats seem to have been well proportioned and reasonable, allowing for delays and waste, without causing any embarrassment.

At the work of a large expedition (fig. 118) there were 100 "foremen miners"; and as there were 400 or 500 men in such a party, each foreman had three or four labourers under him for crushing the rock where quarried. The foremen miners were made up in gangs of ten, one of the ten being "chief of the gang." Eight such chiefs formed the upper rank of the workmen.

These workmen were looked after at work by two or three inspectors; and the camp was organized by overseers, who managed the houses of the superior miners. The safety of the whole camp from petty thefts was secured by one or two chief guards of the camp, while for external security from Bedawy raids, an officer and soldiers were in some cases provided. The earliest expedition of Amenemhat III consisted entirely of soldiers.

The technical work was provided for by sending usually two prospectors to discover the minerals, and determine where work should be undertaken; and sometimes two collectors were also appointed, to secure the turquoise when extracted. A copper-smith was sent to repair and make the tools required. And when building at the temple was in view, then masons and sculptors were also despatched. The driving of the string of baggage-asses was not the work for miners, and peasants were sent, each having about a dozen asses to drive to and from water, or for the coast supplies.

Foreigners were also employed, sometimes Retennu, sometimes Aamu, and the brother of the chief of the Retennu came as manager of the natives, and perhaps as a hostage.

125. STELES OF XII DYNASTY, PARTLY RE-WORKED BY RAMESSU III.

THE RECORDS

The preparation of the record of the expedition, on a great stele of the local sandstone, was a special care. It must have been begun early in the time, as it entailed some weeks of work. The chief of the party was the main person commemorated; but all the staff are usually named, and after it was finished and erected, probably after the high officials had left, the lower workmen used to scratch in their names on the blank ends and margins. By the time the hot weather came on, all this body of men were on their way back to Egypt, accompanying the bags full of the precious gifts of the "Mistress of Turquoise."

CHAPTER IX

THE LESSER AND FOREIGN MONUMENTS

BESIDE the multitude of large historical steles, which were inscribed with records of the expeditions, there were also many lesser monuments of kings and of private persons, which give us further light in many ways. These were mostly found in the Sanctuary and the Portico, and nearly all of them were broken. Seldom could we recover all the pieces of any one thing; the destruction of the whole of the offerings and dedicated objects was deliberate and vindictive. We shall notice in describing the glazed offerings how the greater part of the fragments of them have weathered away and disappeared.

The oldest offering here which can be dated was inscribed by Sneferu, the last king of the IIIrd dynasty. He was represented here by the royal hawk, fig. 126; this bird was of life size, carved in fine grey marbly-limestone, and very smoothly finished. There is hardly enough to show the artistic quality of the figure; only the wing edges remain on either side of the breast, and an end of the pattern down the neck. The block has been violently broken, and was used to pound other stones; but happily, this was done by so unintelligent a destroyer that he never touched the name upon it. The engraving of the cartouche is perfect in the firmness and evenness of the lines; it is from the hand of a workman of great precision and good taste, who has fully given the fine character of the early hieroglyphs. No later work here is at all like the quality of this, which can only be compared with the

126. GREY MARBLE HAWK OF SNEFERU, III DYNASTY.

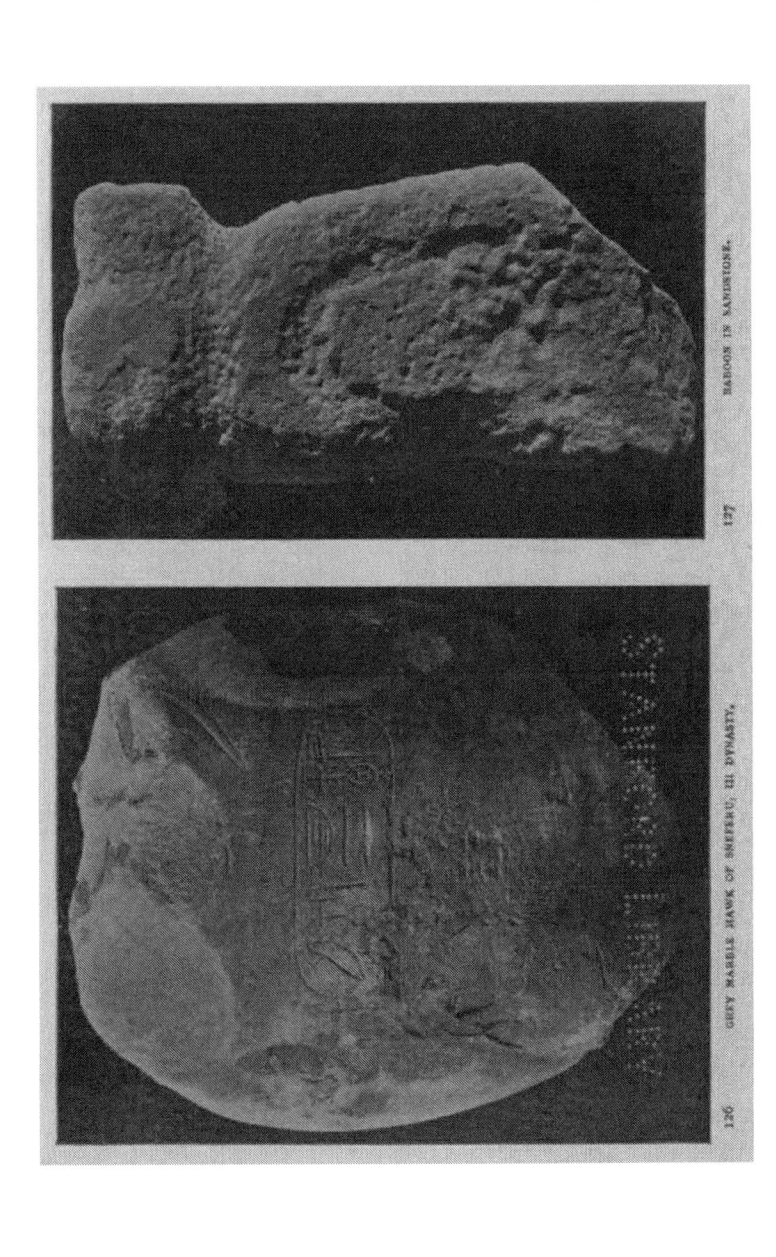

127. BABOON IN SANDSTONE.

style of the early pyramid period. That Sneferu specially favoured hawk figures is seen by those in his temple at Medum. There I found five hawks, one of blue glaze, one of grey limestone (in colour not unlike this from Serabít), and three of common white limestone (PETRIE, *Medum*, pl. xxix, pp. 9, 34). The many references to this king on later monuments here, which we have noticed in Chapter VII, show how well he was known as the founder of the shrine of Serabít; thus the evidence of the hawk, which is a contemporary monument, is confirmed. This figure is now in the British Museum.

Another piece of early work which we should not have expected here is the rude figure of a baboon in sandstone, fig. 127. This is of the same family as the rude limestone figures of baboons which were found in the early levels of the temple of Osiris at Abydos (see PETRIE, *Abydos*, ii, pl. ix). There seems no reason for the baboon being venerated here; nor, indeed, is any reason known for its veneration at Abydos, though the baboon was found there more commonly than any other figure. As it is not connected with the official worship of either place, may it not be that it was worshipped by some special tribe, perhaps the people of Middle Egypt, from the region of Hermopolis, where the baboon was sacred? Where such people were employed they might readily offer their own tribal offerings. This baboon is now in the Ashmolean Museum, Oxford.

A sculpture found in the portico shows a remarkable group of kings, seated at one long table, on which their hands are laid, fig. 128. The latest named is Senusert I, on the right-hand side; so probably the carving was done in his reign. Next to him is his father, Amenemhat I; beyond him is Mentuhotep III, Neb·hapu·ra, of the XIth dynasty; and at the left hand is a king whose name is quite lost, but who is doubtless the earliest king who was adored here, Sneferu, of the IIIrd dynasty.

The veneration of Sneferu by Senusert I is specially

shown by a seated figure made in his honour (see fig. 129). It is inscribed, " Monument made by the son of the Sun, Senusert, for the Horus Neb-maat Sneferu, his father." The work is thick and clumsy, a fault increased by the difficulty of the material; fine lines or delicate forms are scarcely possible in soft sandstone. Another figure of the same character, fig. 129, has traces of a better-cut inscription on the side, but this is unfortunately too much weathered to be read. The thickness of the work, and lumpy limbs, are even more evident here.

We also found the body of a hawk of sandstone; it was so worn that for some time no one saw what it was. At last I noticed that it had been a hawk, and long after that, a favourable light showed the cartouche Kheper-ka-ra, of Senusert I, upon the breast. This remains by the north door of the temple.

Of the reign of the next king, Amenemhat II, there is part of a seated figure of the goddess Hat-hor, fig. 130; this was dedicated by the chief captain of the ships, named Sneferu, born of Maketu. It is interesting that we have in the British Museum the tablet naming the same man, who was father of the chief chamberlain Sneferu. The mother, Maket, is likewise mentioned on the tablet (LIEBLEIN, *Dict.*, 123). At Serabít was also a fine tablet representing a chief official (divine sealer and chief of the north land) named Ankh-ab, offering loaves to Amen. From his titles he was probably the head of an expedition. A figure of King Senusert III, a mere block with a head to it, and curiously lumpy, was found in the lesser *hanafiyeh*. It was dedicated by five officials—a chief chamberlain, Merru, two inspectors, a scribe of the cattle, and an Aamu or Syrian named Lua, or Luy, the Semitic Levi; it is interesting to find this name here before 3000 B.C. Several other seated figures were found; some are of Hat-hor, including one dated in the 24th year of Amenemhat III, by Merru, the chief of the expedition.

128 GROUP OF SENUSERT I, AMENEMHAT I, MENTUHOTEP III, AND SNEFERU.
129 BASE OF FIGURE OF SNEFERU MADE BY SENUSERT I, AND ANOTHER EARLY BASE

130   HAT-HOR, DEDICATED BY SHIPMASTER SNEFERU, AND FIGURE OF UNKNOWN KING.

131   UNKNOWN QUEEN, OF LOCAL WORK.   132   HAT-HOR, LIMESTONE, XII DYNASTY.

THE FIGURE SCULPTURES

Coming down to the XVIIIth dynasty, there is a head of a queen, fig. 131, which is quite different in the feeling of the work from ordinary Egyptian carving. The sculptor has had but little traditional teaching, and has tried after his own fashion to give the expression. It is out of shape and of untrained work, and shows the local ability probably of some mason who had no pretensions to being an artist. The shoulder is very sharp and square, and the head-dress unusually detached. On the same page, fig. 132, is a bust of Hathor from a seated figure in very hard limestone. It is somewhat weathered, but the work is good and lifelike; so much so that it does not seem to have been done by mere rule, but to have been a careful life study from a vigorous model. It is probably of the XIIth dynasty.

Turning over to fig. 140, we see a much later head of Hathor of Ramesside age, from a figure of about half life-size. It has not the natural vivacity of fig. 132, but it stands alone in the peculiar character and expression of it. Travellers unaccustomed to the usual figures of the goddess have often dilated on the mysterious expression of her face in the latest and most debased examples at Denderah, and they have been bewitched by its enigma. But here is a Hathor which, even if one knows well all others, is one of the most baffling of faces. The immense width of it at the ears, the capaciousness of it, and the questioning, sleepy eyes, give it a strange and unfathomed character. The professed source of the type is shown by the double uraeus, which stamps it as being idealised from a living queen. And that queen in the reign of Ramessu II is certainly Nefertari, who also wore the double uraeus on the forehead. Her actual portraits (see PETRIE, *History*, iii, figs. 31, 32) have much less force and character than there is in this idealised head of the "Mistress of Turquoise," but they are obviously the source of the artist's type.

126 THE LESSER AND FOREIGN MONUMENTS

Another queen has left here one of the most striking portraits ever carved by an Egyptian (fig. 133). The well-known queen Thyi, the consort of the magnificent monarch Amenhotep III, has until now only been known to us by some relief sculptures, and not by any named figures in the round. It is strange that this remotest settlement of Egypt has preserved her portrait for us, unmistakably named by her cartouche in the midst of the crown. The material is dark green schistose steatite, and the whole statuette must have been about a foot in height. Unhappily, no other fragment of the figure remained in the temple, and the head alone has been preserved. The haughty dignity of the face is blended with a fascinating directness and personal appeal. The delicacy of the surfaces round the eye and over the cheek shows the greatest care in handling. The curiously drawn-down lips, with their fulness and yet delicacy, their disdain without malice, are evidently modelled in all truth from the life. After seeing this, it seems probable that the supreme fragment of a queen's head in marble from the temple of Tell el Amarna is the portrait of Thyi, and not of Nefertythi (PETRIE, *Tell el Amarna*, pl. i, 15). This is the more likely as a queen's head found this year at Gurob, and bought for Berlin, is unquestionably in accord with the flat portraits of Nefertythi, and does not resemble the marble head. Moreover, Mr. N. Davies has observed that only the statues of Akhenaten and Thyi are depicted as being in the temple where the marble head was found.

Turning to the new portrait, we gather some details about the queen. The ear is represented as being pierced, as is also the case with her son Akhenaten (*Tell el Amarna*, pl. i, 9). The crown which she wore was probably of openwork, in gold. The two winged uraei wave their length in loops around the head, till they meet at the back; while in front they are the supporters of the cartouche with the name. From the two sides of

HEAD OF STATUETTE OF QUEEN TYYI. DARK GREEN STEATITE. XVIII DYNASTY.

134 MENTU-MERTI OFFERING TO SUTEKH.

135 STELE OF RAMESSU 4, NAMING THE ATEN. XIX DYNASTY.

the cartouche depend the two uraei over the forehead, the emblem of the great queen of Upper and Lower Egypt. This piece alone was worth all the rest of our gains of the year; it is now in the Cairo Museum.

A rare figure of a god is seen on a tablet, fig. 134, which was dedicated by the royal courier Mentu-nekht, who is shown offering a bouquet of flowers. The god is a strange figure of truculent aspect, wearing a tall, pointed cap with two horns in front, and a long streamer hanging from the top of it. The name in front is *Sutekh aa pehti*, "Sutekh the great and mighty," the great god of the Hittites, worshipped specially in Syria. Some figures of this god have been published already by Mr. Griffith; they are from places in the east of the Delta—Tanis, Nebesheh, and Zagazig—and from Beyrut, in Syria (*Proc. Soc. Bibl. Archaeol.*, xvi, 87). It is particularly interesting to see repeated here the figure of Sutekh, as on the stele of 400 years, and more clearly showing the two horns. This is entirely different from the figures in Egypt of the god Set, although the Egyptians easily confounded their Set with the Syrian Sutekh, and even used the same hieroglyph for both. The adjectives "great and mighty," however, are distinctive of Sutekh.

A beautiful piece of work remains in the lower part of a limestone tablet of Ramessu I. The portion which is preserved of the figure is carefully wrought, and in the dress resembles the work of Akhenaten; it shows that what we know as the distinctively coarse Ramesside work did not begin till the second Ramessu. The inscription gives for the first time the complete names of the king; the vulture and uraeus name, and the Horus on *nubti* name, were only imperfectly known before. Another curious survival of Akhenaten's time is that the king is said to be "prince of every circuit of the Aten." To find the Aten mentioned thus after the ruthless Amenism of Horemheb is remarkable. Hitherto the latest mention of it was under King Ay (*A. Z.*, xxix, 125). Ramessu is said to restore monuments to glorify the name of his mother Hat-hor, "Mistress of Turquoise." Another tablet in sandstone, representing the king offering to Hat-hor, was also found here. It is rare to meet with any inscriptions of this king, as he only reigned for two years.

Of Ramessu II there was a fine statue here, holding a pillar at the left side; but only the lower part and pedestal of it could be found, fig. 136. The favour to the king of Tahuti, god of Punt, as well as of Hat-hor, is unusual. The best part of this statue, however, is the graceful figure of the princess Bantantha, on the side of it. The upper part of the figure is given here, fig. 137, and is certainly a careful portrait. If we compare this with the beautiful portrait of this princess on the side of the statue of her father at Memphis (PETRIE, *History*, iii, fig. 35), we shall see the exact similarity in the narrow eye, the long, straight nose, the thin, long lips, and the general expression. Slightly as the eyes are indicated, by blocking in the sandstone, yet the effect of the whole is so closely the same that this might well have been a careful copy of the Memphite figure. It shows how closely both followed the original. The name has been rather blundered upon this, Bagesutanth for Bantantha, suggesting that the sculptor did not know hieroglyphs very well, although he was so good an artist. This statue was inserted in a base-block 25 × 17 in., and 10 thick; as this base lay in the cave it seems that the statue was placed there originally, but had been dragged out to the portico to break it up.

Either the upper part of this or of the next figure seems to have been removed of late years. The natives stated that eighteen years ago a traveller took away the upper part of a statue on camel-back to Suez. It is to be hoped that the present owner of this part will communicate with the British Museum, where the lower part just described is now deposited; or else with the Brussels Museum, where the lower part of the following figure is

136. BACK OF STATUE OF RAMESSU II. 137. FIGURE OF BARTANTHA.

kept. Either of these parts can be obtained in exchange, as neither have been registered by the museums, pending the connection with the remainder. The other figure was the lower part of a group of Ramessu and Hat-hor, hand in hand; the upper part of the figure of Hat-hor was also found, but that of the king is still missing. This was likewise in the portico.

An almost life-size bust of a queen was found. The face was bruised and rounded, but on the back is an inscription dated in year 33, probably of the reign of Ramessu II from the style. Several monuments of private persons also adorned the temple. But as they are of no interest except for the inscriptions, they will be dealt with in the atlas of inscriptions, *The Egyptians in Sinai.*

A remarkable group of figures was found in the temple, of a ruder style than the regular Egyptian figures, and some bearing inscriptions in unknown characters. The best of these is shown in fig. 138. The general form is a usual type of Egyptian figure, but the style is very clumsy, and the head rises up in too cylindrical a shape. This exaggeration is more marked in other examples. The inscription on the front is shown larger in fig. 139. This group of five signs is repeated on four diverse monuments, so that it is not a personal name, but some religious phrase. From instances where the signs are in vertical arrangements we learn that the writing here is from left to right. Beside this figure, and parts of others, there is a figure of a sphinx of small size, fig. 141. This has along the upper sides of the base a line of inscription, which contains the same signs as those in fig. 139. On the shoulder is a square containing a dedication to Hat-hor, "Mistress of Turquoise," in ordinary Egyptian hieroglyphs. And between the paws, as on Egyptian sphinxes, is a Horus-name, which is very rough and small, and which seems only to contain the sign of the sickle, *maat*. We can hardly doubt that this is the

Horus-name of Sneferu, as on another late work (fig. 144, no. 4) we have seen how Sneferu was adored by Hatshepsut, both in the Shrine of Kings and in the making of a memorial stele, and it would not be surprising if a sphinx were carved in his honour. But it is clearly of local work, and not done by a trained Egyptian sculptor. The fault of representing the forehead as too receding is the same as in the local bust of a queen, fig. 131.

Other examples of such inscriptions were carved over the mine at L on Map 3. On looking over the broken rocks about that mine, my wife noticed a fragment with some signs upon it, which could not be recognised. I searched farther, and on turning over a fallen block I found more signs. I then brought over some men to the place and turned three or four large pieces which had fallen from a cut front of rock; thus we exposed portions of other inscriptions, which I reconstituted. At last it was clear that we had remains of about eight tablets, roughly cut, with broad grooves round them to isolate them, in the general form of an Egyptian round-headed tablet. But none of the inscriptions were intelligible as Egyptian, of any hieratic or debased type. A figure of the god Ptah was evident, very roughly outlined; but not a word of regular Egyptian could be read. There was a mixture of Egyptian hieroglyphs, but most of the signs are quite apart from such.

How much can be concluded about this writing, while we are yet unable to connect it with signs of known values?

1. It is a definite system, and not merely a scribbling made in ignorant imitation of Egyptian writing by men who knew no better. The repetition of the same five signs in the same order on the figure and on the sphinx from the temple, as well as on three of the tablets over the mines a mile and a half distant, show that mere fancy is not the source of this writing.

138. SANDSTONE FIGURE, FOREIGN WORK AND INSCRIPTION.

139. FOREIGN INSCRIPTION ON ABOVE. XVIII DYNASTY.

THE FOREIGN WRITING

2. It is always associated with work of a style different to all the usual Egyptian work here, a peculiar local style which was not followed by any one trained in Egyptian methods.

3. The direction of writing was from left to right, contrary to later Semitic and most Egyptian writing.

4. It is used about the XVIIIth dynasty. The only indication of date that I could find at the mine, L, was a bit of buff pottery with the red and black stripe which we know to be characteristic of the time of Tahutmes III, and perhaps rather earlier, but not later. The figure, fig. 138, was found at the doorway of the shrine of Sopdu, which was built by Hatshepsut. The sphinx is of a red sandstone which was used by Tahutmes III, and not at other times. The veneration of Sneferu, apparently named on the sphinx, was strong under Tahutmes III, but no trace of it is found later. Each of these facts is not conclusive by itself, but they all agree, and we are bound to accept this writing as being of about 1500 B.C.

I am disposed to see in this one of the many alphabets which were in use in the Mediterranean lands long before the fixed alphabet selected by the Phoenicians. A mass of signs was used continuously from 6,000 or 7,000 B.C., until out of it was crystallized the alphabets of the Mediterranean—the Karians and Celtiberians preserving the greatest number of signs, the Semites and Phoenicians keeping fewer. The outline of this signary will be found in *Royal Tombs of the First Dynasty*, p. 32. The two systems of writing, pictorial and linear, which Dr. Evans has found to have been used in Crete, long before the Phoenician age, show how several systems were in use. Some of the workmen employed by the Egyptians, probably the Aamu or Retennu—Syrians—who are often named, had this system of linear signs which we have found; they naturally mixed many hieroglyphs with it, borrowed from their masters. And here we have the result, at a date some five centuries

132 THE LESSER AND FOREIGN MONUMENTS

before the oldest Phoenician writing that is known. Such seems to be the conclusion that we must reach from the external evidence that we can trace. The ulterior conclusion is very important—namely, that common Syrian workmen, who could not command the skill of an Egyptian sculptor, were familiar with writing at 1500 B.C., and this a writing independent of hieroglyphics and cuneiform. It finally disproves the hypothesis that the Israelites, who came through this region into Egypt and passed back again, could not have used writing. Here we have common Syrian labourers possessing a script which other Semitic peoples of this region must be credited with knowing.

140 QUEEN NEFERTARI AS HAT-HOR. XIX DYNASTY.

91 SPHINX OF FOREIGN WORK AND INSCRIPTION. XVIII DYNASTY.

CHAPTER X

THE ALTARS AND THE OFFERINGS

HAVING already described the sacrifices and ablutions in the worship of the "Mistress of Turquoise," as shown by the remains at Serabít, we now turn to the smaller religious objects, which further explain the system of worship here.

In figs. 142 and 143 are the altars and other small stone objects of the temple. The separation here on two pages has been ruled by the direction of the lighting; for with objects photographed at various times and places a uniform light or scale could hardly be maintained. The scale of the first page is about $\frac{1}{8}$ (from $\frac{1}{7}$ to $\frac{1}{9}$), and that of the second page is about $\frac{1}{5}$ (from $\frac{1}{4}$ to $\frac{1}{6}$), excepting the tank, no. 16, which is $\frac{1}{13}$.

The plainest and roughest of the altars were nos. 14 and 15, which were found in the Portico; no. 15 has been merely rough-chipped, no. 14 has been dressed over. The altar no. 13 is well finished, and on the top the surface was burnt for about a quarter of an inch inwards, black outside and discoloured below. This proves that such altars were used for burning; and from the small size, about 5 to 7 in. across, the only substance burnt on them must have been inflammable, such as incense. This altar is a foot high; it was found in the shrine of Sopdu, and is now in the British Museum. The tallest altar of incense was no. 4, which is 22 in. high; there is a cup-hollow on the top, $3\frac{1}{2}$ in. wide and 1 deep. It was found broken in two, in the court. A larger and more elaborate altar was found in the Sacred Cave, no. 3. It has been much broken about the top, but it had originally a basin hollow about 9 in. wide and 4 in. deep, which might perhaps have been for libations. Around the narrowest part is a thick roll 4½ in. high. The whole altar was 25 in. high. Two small altars, nos. 1 and 2, were also found in the cave or portico; they are more nearly of the type of vase-altars of the XIIth dynasty found in Egypt, of which the only published example seems to be the top of the altar in *Illahun*, vi, 10. A similar but taller altar, no. 12, was found in the shrine of Sopdu; and a rude one of this type, no. 7, was in the Shrine of the Kings, but had been much broken.

Most of these altars seem to be intended for incense, and in one case there is the mark of burning on the top; they thus agree with what we know of the Jewish system, where a small altar was reserved specially for incense. We have here, then, another instance of Semitic worship, differing from that of Egypt, where incense was always offered on a shovel-shaped censer held in the hand.

Another form of altar was found in the Shrine of the Kings. It is a flat block, no. 8, with two shallow saucers on the top of it. In no. 9 we see half of another such block. The saucers are 10 in. wide over all and 7 in. across inside. These were evidently for a purpose different from that of the tall altars. They would hardly be for a drink-offering, as—in Egypt, at least—altars for libations had a spout by which the wine flowed down to the ground. But they might well be for the meal offerings, or cakes of flour and oil, a kind of pastry which was usual, as we see in the regulations of the book of Numbers (xxviii. 5, 9, 12, 13, 20, 28; xxix. 3, 9, 14). The worship in Palestine of the Queen of heaven, which was a regular title of Hat·hor, as it was of Ashtaroth, is mentioned by Jeremiah. The Israelite women who had fled into Egypt said to him, "When we burned incense to the queen of heaven, and poured out drink offerings unto her, did we

ALTARS, AND EARLY HATHOR CAPITAL.

CONICAL STONES (10, 11), ALTARS (12-15), AND TANK (16).

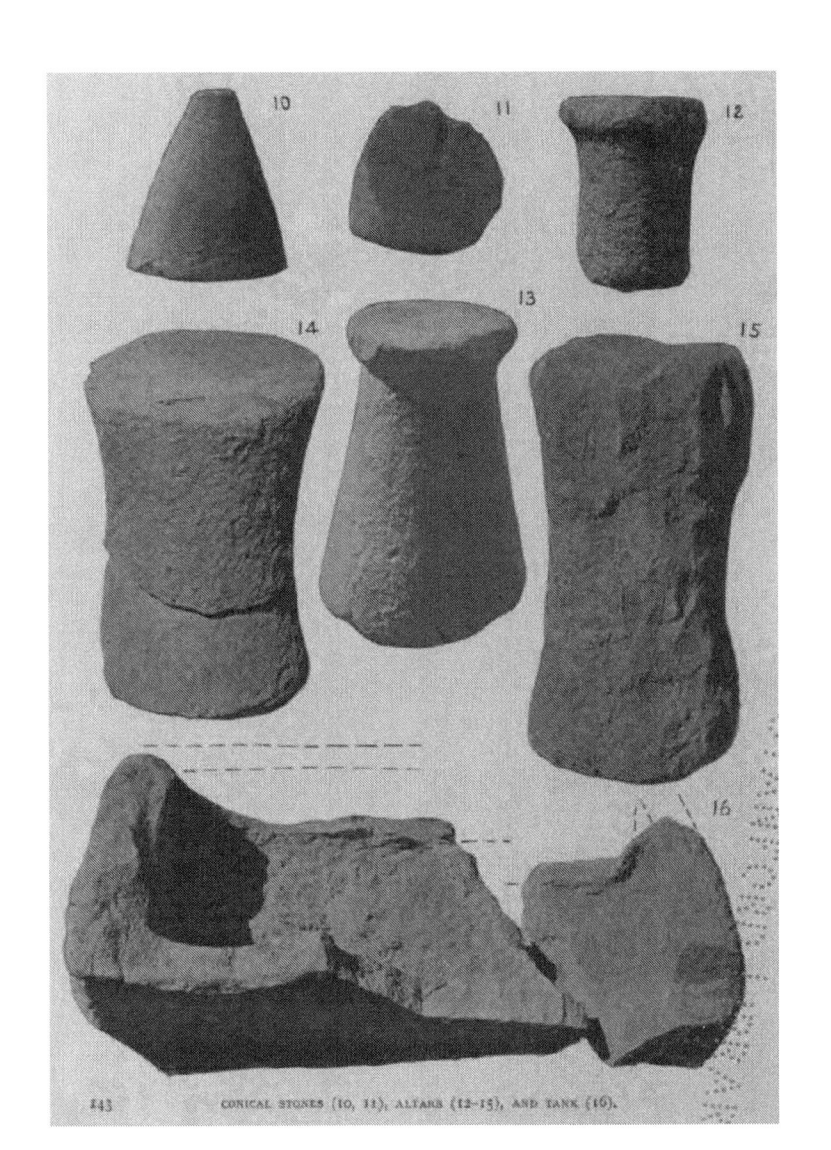

make her cakes to worship her, and pour out drink offerings unto her, without our men?" (xliv. 19).

A portion of a circular tray of sandstone, no. 6, is also from the Shrine of the Kings, but it is difficult to understand. From the width, about 20 in. across, and the thinness of the middle, only 3½ in., it cannot have been a base or cap for a column, where any great weight was in question. It is rough beneath, so cannot have been for setting upon an altar, capping it. It seems rather like part of a stone dish, to lie on the ground for receiving offerings.

Among the fragments in the portico was found a roughly wrought head of Hathor from a column, no. 5. The stem below is octagonal, like the columns in sandstone of the XIth dynasty found at Koptos (PETRIE, *Koptos*, p. 13), and those in limestone of the XIIth dynasty found at Kahun (see *Illahun*, pl. vi, 1). From the workmanship this certainly cannot be placed in either the XIIth or the XVIIIth dynasty. The fluted columns of Amenemhat IV (3250 B.C.) continued to support the portico till the end of its use in the Ramesside age, 1150 B.C.; half of one was still in place, and no trace of any other column was found. This rough capital is not likely to belong to the fine period of Senusert I, and it seems that it is a fragment of an earlier portico, perhaps built at the close of the XIth dynasty by Mentuhotep III.

In the shrine of Sopdu were found two cones of sandstone, alike in shape and size. One of them (fig. 143, no. 10) is now in the British Museum. The other (no. 11) was somewhat worn. Both of these cones have a small groove on the base (see no. 11), which would seem to be only accidental if it were not the same on both. We need but allude to the Syrian worship of the conical stone, as it is so well known in the figures represented in the Syrian temples shown on coins and gems, the El Gabal, or sacred stone, which Elagabalus brought to Rome from his Syrian home, and the many references to it in writers. But it is not so well known that the veneration for conical stones still lives in Palestine. In the village of Bureyr, from which my workmen were drawn for excavating at Tell el Hesy (Lachish), I saw this adoration kept up. A piece of ground between two houses was fenced in front with a stone wall, and all untrodden, tangled with weeds. At one side was a hollow in the wall, with a stone shelf across it, which at once reminded me of the shelves in similar hollows in the prehistoric temple of Hagiar Kîm in Malta. On this shelf was a cone of stone, the lower block of a Roman mill. I inquired why it was there, but no one would tell. We happened afterwards to find another such Roman millstone in the excavations at Lachish, but I left it at the camp when we closed the work. After travelling for some days, my donkey man (who was from Gimzu) turned the conical stone out of his saddlebag, to my great surprise, and said that he could not take it all the way home. I asked him why he had brought it at all, and of what use such a stone could be to make it worth while to load his beast with it for a two or three weeks' journey. The only answer I could get was that it was "a good stone"; and evidently he would have gladly taken it to his house if possible.

At the base of the illustration, fig. 143, is the stone tank, no. 16, which lay outside the north door of the temple, and which has been already described in the account of that building.

In fig. 144 are some examples of stone work from the temple. These are all half the size of the originals, as are most of the following pages of small antiquities. The flint knife, no. 1, was found in the enclosure south of the *hanafiyeh*. It is of the type well known to belong to the XIIth dynasty, and published from Kahun (see *Illahun*, vii, 7; xiii, 6). The straight edges of the handle end were covered by a wrapping of fibre to protect the user's hand, as was found in the one at Kahun.

144. FLINT KNIFE, XII DYNASTY. ALABASTER VASES INSCRIBED, XVIII-XIX DYNASTIES.

STONE VASES

The alabaster vases had been plentiful in the temple, but all were reduced to fragments. Their forms were tall cylinders, cups, and globular vases with a loop handle on each side. There were also many vases in the forms of figures of the god Bes or of the cow of Hat·hor. The earliest vase, no. 2, is the finest in the engraving of it. The titles rather differ from those elsewhere. First comes a declaration of relationship only, "Royal wife, royal daughter and sister"; then follow special titles, "Great royal wife, daughter of a great royal wife, royal mother, Aahmes Nefertari, living for ever." This queen was the wife of Aahmes, the founder of the XVIIIth dynasty. From her being named "royal mother," this vase belongs to the time of her son Tahutmes I, and so may be about 1560 B.C.

There was also another vase, less finely engraved, of Tahutmes I (no. 3). The fragment of a flat slab, no. 4, was probably of the XVIIIth dynasty by the work, but it bears the Horus-name *Neb·maat*, which is that of Sneferu. It is another example of the veneration of Sneferu in later times. As there is here the stem of an *uas* sign at the side, this was part of a larger group of hieroglyphs giving the other name of the king and some titles. It was not part of a scene, as the Horus-name would not in that case be so low down.

Parts of alabaster cups were also found, with inscriptions around the swell of the body. The scribe Pa·nehesi, "the negro," who is named on no. 5, was of the time of Amenhotep III; his stele was placed in front of Amenhotep's building, in what was afterwards enclosed as chamber E. Probably nos. 6 and 7 are parts of similar cups.

Some large figures of the cow of Hat·hor were dedicated here by Merenptah, the son of Ramessu II. His coarse rough engraving is seen on the flank of one of these kine in no. 8. These figures are hollowed out as if to serve for vases. Such figure-vases of clumsy

138 THE ALTARS AND THE OFFERINGS

work are favourite objects in the XIXth dynasty, the fashion having been copied from the vases in the forms of girls, calves, dogs, hedgehogs, etc., made by Greeks at that time. No. 9 is part of an alabaster base of a statue. No. 10 is part of a vase of Merenptah (1220 B.C.), with both of his cartouches. The head of Bes, no. 11, was part of a cylindrical vase with his figure on it, and cartouches on the breast; this was probably of Merenptah, by the workmanship.

Two exquisite alabaster cups of lotus form were dedicated here by Amenhotep III. The fragments that remain of one of these (fig. 145, no. 1) show the petals of the lotus flower surcharged with the inscription of the king. Some pieces of a kneeling figure of alabaster, nos. 3, 4, 5, hollowed out as a vase, seem to be probably of the XVIIIth dynasty. But a piece of a solid figure, no. 2, has the drapery in an entirely un-Egyptian fashion, copied from a loose garment, which was twisted round the body, with a corner thrown over the shoulder, much as modern Arabs do now. This was probably part of a figure of one of the Aamu; or, if it were as early as the XIIth dynasty, it might be from a figure of Khebtata, the brother of the Retennu prince (see p. 118). The two small heads, nos. 6 and 7, are from tubular vases of alabaster, probably of the XIXth dynasty.

The greater part of the offerings were of glazed ware—vases, bowls, and cups; beside lesser quantities of plaques, *menats*, bracelets, wands, sistra, animals, etc. These objects had all been broken up, so that not a single whole thing was found. The fragments formed a layer, two or three inches thick, over all the sanctuary and portico, and extending outside of the sanctuary on the north for a distance of some feet. It is clear that the Bedawyn revenged themselves on the Egyptians by overthrowing and smashing all the offerings that had been accumulated here during many centuries. We hoped that, as the site had been very little dug over before our clearance, we

145. PIECES OF LOTUS CUP, AMENHOTEP III. PIECES OF ALABASTER STATUETTES.

DESTRUCTION OF OFFERINGS

might be able to reconstruct many of these broken offerings. The way to test such a question is to select the classes of objects which are most distinctive, and find from them what proportion can be joined together. We accordingly searched all the *menats*, bracelets, wands, sistra, and plaques exhaustively. Every fragment was collected, sorted over, and every possible joining was tried. The result was that very few pieces could be fitted together; for instance, not a single one of a dozen sistrum-heads fitted any handle that was found. The general conclusion was forced on me that we have not more than about a third of all the glazed ware that had been broken up. What, then, has become of the rest? We found many hundredweights of fragments, but half a ton or more of pieces must have entirely disappeared. They could not be hidden around the temple, for the whole space is bare rock, and we turned over all the sand and earth in the neighbourhood. The only conclusion seems to be that the greater part of the pieces were scattered upon the rock around; that there they gradually disintegrated under the sun and dew and frosts, and every loose grain was blown away by the high winds which sweep over the plateau. Thus the pieces have in three thousand years entirely disappeared in dust, and only those have been preserved which were hedged round by walls and stones sufficiently to keep a layer of sand and earth over them.

These fragments of vases in fig. 146 are, then, only the best of the inscriptions which were to be found among some hundredweights of fragments and chips. The oldest is no. 1, a pear-shaped vase of Tahutmes I (1530 B.C.), with a dedication to "Amen, lord of the thrones"; it was, therefore, made for Thebes rather than for Sinai. The piece no. 2 is from a similar vase, with the names of Tahutmes III and Hatshepsut (1490 B.C.). By this time vases were specially made for offerings to the "Mistress of Turquoise," as we see on the piece no. 3.

140 THE ALTARS AND THE OFFERINGS

The titles are unusual here, as Hatshepsut is called *Suten net*, and not *Suten baty*, the crown of Lower Egypt being substituted for the bee. These vases were all thick and soft in the body, with poor glaze, which easily decomposes. A far finer ware was made under Amenhotep III (1400 B.C.); in the piece of a flat dish, no. 4, the material is hard and clean, with the signs inlaid in violet upon a green ground. Another vase of this king, no. 5, also has the inlaying.

In the XIXth dynasty, Sety I (1320 B.C.) dedicated some tubular vases, nos. 6, 7, and 8, of various designs. His son, Ramessu II (1270 B.C.), made more vases than any other king; many are large tubular jars, such as the piece no. 9, which honours the goddess Tefnut. Cups were also usual, as in no. 10, which names Hat·hor. Cups are also found of Merenptah (1220 B.C.), such as no. 11; of Sety II (1210 B.C.), naming Hat·hor, no. 12; of Queen Ta·usert (1205 B.C.), who has left a good many offerings here (see no. 13); and lastly of Ramessu III, no. 14.

The forms are pear-shaped vases with necks from Tahutmes I to Amenhotep III, tubular vases of Sety I and Ramessu II, and cups from Merenptah to Ramessu III. The forms of cups with and without stems were made at the same time. In all, parts of 73 vases were found with inscriptions. The best set of these is now in the Museum of Fine Arts at Boston, Mass.

In fig. 147 are shown the pieces of inscribed bowls and of pottery with foreign patterns. The use of inscribed bowls extended through the whole period of the glazed vases. There is one of Queen Aahmes Nefertari; a piece with the name of Tahutmes, probably the IIIrd, no. 1; many of Ramessu II, as in no. 2, with both cartouches. Those of Merenptah are the commonest, sometimes with only one cartouche, as in nos. 3 and 4, but also often bearing both cartouches. Sety II has left

146   PIECES OF GLAZED VASES
OF TAHUTMES I (1), TAHUTMES III (2, 3), AMENHOTEP III (4, 5), SETY I (6, 7, 8),
RAMESSU II (9, 10), MERENPTAH (11), SETY II (12), TA USERT (13), AND RAMESSU III (14).

147 PIECES OF GLAZED BOWLS
OF TAHUTMES (1), RAMESSU (2), MERENPTAH (3, 4), SETY II (5), RAMESSU III (6, 7),
AND WITH FOREIGN DESIGNS.

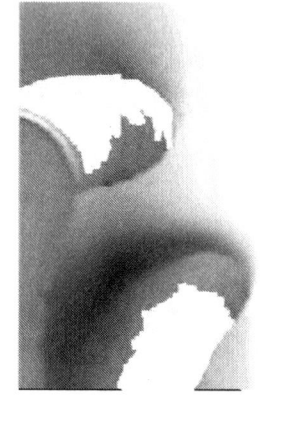

GLAZED VASES

a few bowls, usually with the notched palm-sticks at each side of the cartouches, as in no. 5. These notched sticks represent the primitive tally of time, and so came to express a very long duration. Placed around the king's name they are the equivalent of the expression, "ever living." Ramessu III (nos. 6 and 7) also left three bowls here, of clear, coarse work, like most of his products.

Many pieces of glazed pottery show a good deal of foreign influence in their designs. Bowls of thin ware are found with the spiral wave pattern and wavy lines (see nos. 8, 9); both of these belong to foreign sources. In no. 10 the spiral wave is joined with the basket-work pattern, which is also foreign in origin and usually Libyan. No. 11 is a pretty piece of a cup, which is purely Egyptian. The spiral wave was boldly worked on large vases, as in nos. 12 to 15, recalling the glazed pottery from Greece. A plant pattern occurs in no. 16. The pattern of diagonal squares (no. 17), with dots in them, is quite foreign in the source of it; as also is the square diagonally divided, in no. 19, with spots in it. The rosettes of violet inlay in green glaze (no. 18) are of the style of Amenhotep III, and probably are of foreign motive. Lastly, the basket-pattern band round no. 20 is also familiar on Greek vases of this age. Probably most of these patterns are due to the importation of Greek vases, and the copying of their designs by the Egyptian workers in glazed pottery.

The *menat* was a flap of metal, wood, or glazed pottery, which was placed at the back of a necklace, with the intention of counter-balancing the weight of the beadwork in front, and preventing it dragging on the neck. It may well be seen, with the collar complete, in the hand of Hathor, on one of the pillar sculptures from the tomb of Sety I in Florence; also in some of the scenes of Sety I at Abydos, as in CAULFEILD, *Temple of the Kings*, xvi, 8. *Menats* are not known in the earliest times, and are very rare, if known at all, in the XIIth dynasty. But in the XVIIIth dynasty they are common, and continued to be made with royal names down to the end of the XXXth dynasty. They bear the names of the Persian kings, unlike the scarabs, which ignore the foreign dynasties. These *menats*, shown in fig. 148, begin here with the great queen Aahmes, the foundress of the XVIIIth dynasty; no. 3 bears her name, and probably no. 2 is of her also, by the titles, "royal daughter, royal sister." A daughter of King Aahmes also appears in no. 4, which has the name of Amen·meryt. Amenhotep I appears on no. 1, and his wife Aahmes on no. 5. Some fragments of thick, coarse work are put together under no. 7, as being probably of the same age; the top piece is of a king, the lower pieces of Queen Neferu·ra, wife of Tahutmes III. Hatshepsut and Tahutmes III left the greatest number of *menats* here, and examples are given in nos. 9 and 10; several of theirs are noticeable for the very thin, delicate lines of the drawing. There are a few of Amenhotep II, such as no. 8. The great change in this class was made in the time of Amenhotep III, by his new style of glazing in two colours inlaid, an art which had been practised by Mena in the Ist dynasty, but had fallen into oblivion. Parts of two *menats* of Amenhotep have the beautiful violet inlay in a light blue ground, as in no. 11. He also made the usual style of *menat*, as in no. 12, but of more regular and finished work than in earlier reigns. A new form of pottery *menat* came forward in the XIXth dynasty, with a head of Hat·hor on the top, as in no. 13, of Ramessu II. Figure *menats* are known in the XVIIIth dynasty, made of copper, such as one from Kahun (*Kahun*, x, 77), with the figure of Sekhet. The *menat* no. 14 is very rudely inscribed, and cannot be read with certainty; the cartouche is probably intended for that of Queen Ta·usert—compare that on the vase, fig. 146, no. 13. Sety II appears on one example,

148 GLAZED MENATS
OF AMENHOTEP I (1), NEFERTARI (3), MERYTAMEN (4), QUEEN AAHMES (5), TAHUTMES I (6), RANEFRU (7),
TAHUTMES IV (8), HATSHEPSUT (9), TAHUTMES III (10), AMENHOTEP III (11, 12), RAMESSU (13),
TA·USERT (14), SETY II (15), RAMESSU IV (16).

149   GLAZED BRACELETS
OF SETY I (1), RAMESSU II (2, 3, 4, 5, 14), MERENPTAH (6), SETY II (7), TA-USERT (8, 9, 15, 16, 17), RAMESSU III (10, 18, 19), RAMESSU IV (11), RAMESSU V (12, 20), RAMESSU VI (13).

MENATS AND BANGLES

no. 15, and Ramessu IV on one other, no. 16; but none are known of Ramessu III, who offered so many objects of other classes.

From having as many as fifty *menats* to compare, we can draw some conclusions as to their history. They all have plain backs until Hatshepsut, and plain backs continue in some cases till Amenhotep III; after that they are all painted on both sides. The two with heads are of Ramessu II. On the disc at the lower end the lotus flowers are square, with the stem and the buds diagonal, till Amenhotep II (see no. 8); the buds are square, with the stem and the flowers diagonal, under Amenhotep III (see no. 11); then there are eight buds under Ramessu II, and four buds only under Ta·usert, no. 13. These differences will serve to date uninscribed examples and fragments. The best set of these *menats* is now in the British Museum.

A class of offering which only came into use in the XIXth dynasty is that of bracelets and bangles; they are, however, the commonest of all, nearly half the cartouches found being of this class. Examples are given in fig. 149. A few are known of Sety I, as no. 1, but the greater part are of Ramessu II: some thick and convex on the outer face, as no. 2; some larger in the band, as no. 3; some flat on the face, as nos. 4 and 5. Where there are inscriptions beyond the name and titles, they are always in honour of Hat·hor. Very wide bracelets appear under Merenptah, no. 6. This form continues of slightly less breadth under Sety II, no. 7, and his daughter, Queen Ta·usert, nos. 8 and 9. Ramessu III reverted to the rounded face, as in no. 10, which continued under Ramessu IV, no. 11, Ramessu V, no. 12, and Ramessu VI, no. 13.

A different class of armlet is the narrow bangle, of which the thickness is only a little more or less than the breadth. These are either rounded or triangular in section. The rounded ones are of Ramessu II, no. 14,

Ramessu III, as no. 19, or Ramessu V, no. 20. The triangular bangles are inscribed on one face only; they are of Ramessu II, Sety II, Ta·usert, as nos. 15, 16, and 17, and Ramessu III, no. 18. Beside these inscribed bracelets and bangles there are many with patterns,—the wavy line, no. 22; wavy line and spots, nos. 23, 25, 26, and 27; with spots between lines, nos. 24 and 28; and with cross-lines, no. 29. There were also many plain ones, but it was difficult to say how far such were only the plain parts of bracelets which were inscribed. The fitting together of these was exhaustively tried, by sorting all the bracelets and then trying every piece to every other which could belong to it. But very few could be put together. The best set of these armlets is now at Chicago.

The oldest class of all this glazed ware is that of the wands, fig. 150. Ivory wands have been found at Hierakonpolis, probably of the IInd dynasty; these have a curiously bent form (*Hierakonpolis*, i, xiii, 1, 2), which is explained by the wands with gazelle-heads used by the dancers of the Vth dynasty, in the tomb of Anta (PETRIE, *Deshasheh*, xii). From this bent shape has descended the form seen in nos. 1 and 2, and it influenced the form even to the end, in no. 9. The use of the wand in ceremonial singing, doubtless accompanied with dancing, is mentioned in the Tale of Sanehat, where the king's daughters bring their collars, their wands, and their sistra, and display them during their song (*Egyptian Tales*, i, p. 122). The earliest of the glazed wands from Serabît is of Tahutmes I, no. 1. That the ends belong to this example is not certain; they are only placed with it as being similar in style and work. Of Amenhotep III we have a nearly complete wand, no. 2, though broken in five pieces. This shows the length of the straight part—these earlier wands, when complete, were about 16 in. long; they had a lotus-flower pattern at the end, then a straight stem with bands around it; at the bend

150   GLAZED WANDS (1-13) AND RING-STANDS (14-16)
OF TAHUTMES I (1), AMENHOTEP III (2), SETY I (3), RAMESSU II (4, 5, 6), MERENPTAH (7),
RAMESSU III (8), RAMESSU IV (9).

WANDS AND RING-STANDS

was the cartouche, with a sacred *uza* eye on each side of it, and then a short tapering part led to the end, with another lotus pattern. In the XIXth dynasty they have only one sacred eye, and are much thinner and flatter, as in those of Sety I, no. 3; they are not quite so thin under Ramessu II, nos. 4 and 5. No. 6 is of a Ramessu, with the cartouche parallel to the wand. Under Merenptah the wands are rougher, as no. 7; there are none of the rest of this dynasty. Those of Ramessu III are of poor glaze and soft. All have the cartouches parallel to the wand; four have both cartouches, as no. 8, and two have only a single name. Of Ramessu IV (no. 9), one has an eye, another has only the name; the wands are small, pale blue-green, and of hard material. Some varied types of ends of wands are given in nos. 10-13. The best set of the wands is now at Brussels.

A large number of pieces of ring-stands for supporting vases were found, and a few rough ones were complete. Such ring-stands are unknown in prehistoric times, but red pottery rings begin with the earliest dynasties. There is good reason for their use, as in a country which is rainless, and therefore very dusty, it is impossible to place a damp, porous jar on the ground without its picking up dust and becoming dirty. It was necessary to stand it on a dry support, which would not hold the dust; and the ring-stand with a pointed vase resting in it is the most satisfactory arrangement, and lasted in use for over four thousand years. Many of these glazed ring-stands are plain; others have a few bands, with spots, upon them, as no. 14; the commonest pattern is with a fringe of lotus-petals, as no. 15; and one has a group of the head of Hathor, with two cats guardant at the sides, no. 16. Some of these ring-stands are inscribed, see fig. 151. Here no. 1 is of Ramessu II, "beloved of Hathor, Princess of Turquoise." Merenptah has both cartouches on no. 2, and Ta·usert both upon no. 3. At first sight, no doubt, these objects of Queen Ta·usert might be attributed to Ramessu II, as she carefully imitated the appearance of his names as far as possible. The objects from her temple at Thebes (PETRIE, *Six Temples*, xvi, xvii) first showed what forms she took in imitation of her ancestor; and the coarseness of work of her glazed objects here at once calls attention to this class, and makes us notice the details which distinguish her name. There are some other rings, which may be stands or large armlets; they were made by Sety II, and have the group of the head of Hat·hor and cats, as on no. 16, just described. The best of the ring-stands are now at Chicago.

The sistrum was the special emblem of Hat·hor. A large golden sistrum was the most sacred treasure of her temple at Denderah, and the name of the capital of the next nome—Diospolis—was the "temple of the sistrum." This sacred instrument was so much used that it gave the name to a class of priestesses, as bearers of the instrument. It essentially consisted of a rattle made of metal discs sliding on a bar, which was placed through the sides of a frame. This frame was attached to a handle, which had a head of Hat·hor at the junction. We should have expected to find a larger proportion of sistra at a shrine of Hat·hor, but they are not common. The principal examples of the heads are shown in fig. 151, nos. 4-11. These have all been broken from handles, but none will join any of the handles found here, nos. 16-20. Some were complete with only the head on the handle, as nos. 4, 5, 9, and 11; others had the frame above, which carried the cross-bars, as nos. 6, 7, 8, and 10. Part of the top of the frame of 10 remains, showing the architectural cornice with which it was finished. Indeed the frame of the rattle was modified by the Egyptians in architectural usage to form the house hieroglyph of the name *Hat*·hor, "house of Horus." These sistrum-heads are all double, with a face on each

151 GLAZED RING-STANDS (1-3) AND KHATRA (4-20)
OF RAMESSU II (1), MERENPTAH (2), TA-USERT (3), AMENHOTEP I (16), RAMESSU II (18),
SETY II (19), RAMESSU III (20).

152 GLAZED PLAQUES OF HATHOR.

SISTRA AND HAT·HOR TABLETS

side; fragments of three or four large ones were found, like no. 5, which were of glazed pottery. One here, no. 11, is of schistose steatite. The handles are of Amenhotep I, no. 16; Queen Aahmes Nefertari, by the titles, no. 17; Ramessu II, no. 18; Sety II, no. 19; and Ramessu III, no. 20. Thus they extend over almost the whole period of the offerings here. The best set is now at Boston, Mass. Some small glazed heads of Hat·hor were also offered, which are single faced, and without a long handle, as nos. 12, 13, and 15. Also there were here some of the little standing female figures, like no. 14, which are commonly found dedicated to Hat·hor, as at the temple of Deir el Bahri.

Beside the sistra there were also votive tablets of glazed ware with the head of Hat·hor, of which examples are shown in fig. 152. These vary in the details. Some have the more architectural treatment of the wig of hair descending in two rolls to the base, as no. 1. Others show a pole supporting the head and wig, as in no. 2, where the pole is on a flat stand, and in no. 8, between two trees. Others have a wig of straight hair, as nos. 3, 4, and 7. Some fragments have the name of Hatshepsut, as no. 5; and some, with the name of Tahutmes III, show part of the pole, and therefore have belonged to such heads of Hat·hor, see nos. 10 and 11. The form of the top of the head-dress varies, but it is generally a rough copy of the cornice of uraeus serpents, which was the regular architectural finish of the shrine or house of Horus on the head. The prominence of a definite pole here suggests that these are copies of some great mask of Hat·hor upon a pole, which was set up at the festivals. The number with the pole was about 27, with the plain wig 18, and with the striped wig 5—a total of 50. Of these, 1 is of Amenhotep I, 2 are of Hatshepsut, and 5 of Tahutmes III.

Another type of tablet had the Hat·hor head cut in outline, the flat surfaces being painted, as in fig. 153.

148 THE ALTARS AND THE OFFERINGS

Such heads had stems, copied from the pole which is shown on the square tablets; it is not certain that the stem below no. 1 belongs to the same specimen. The head-dress is much like that on the square tablets, in 2, 4, and 5. But no. 3 is elaborated with the shrine on the head, bearing two cats rampant, looking backwards. This shrine-type is most familiar in the great capitals of the columns at Denderah; but that temple is of late Ptolemaic time, and debased in its style. There were about 40 of these heads among the offerings.

The cat seems to have been specially related to the worship of Hat-hor at Serabît, though this connection is not known elsewhere. The cat supporters of the head of Hat-hor on fig. 150, no. 16, and other ring-stands, and on the capital, fig. 153, no. 4, show that it belonged to this goddess. We find not only figures in the round, of cats and other *felidae*, as in fig. 153, nos. 6-11, but also flat tablets with figures of cats, in fig. 154. So far as these are dated, the cartouches are all of Hatshepsut and Tahutmes III, see nos. 2, 3, and 6. The cat is sometimes on a pedestal, as in nos. 9 and 13, and in some others not shown here. Hence it seems as if it were treated as a sacred animal. In one case the cat is between two papyrus plants, no. 11. Among these tablets, one has the name of Hatshepsut, and two have the name of Tahutmes III. Dr. Hoyle, who has made a special study of ancient representations of animals, has examined all these animal figures, as many have been given to the museum of Owens' College, Manchester, under his charge. He reports that fig. 153, no. 6, is a cheetah, and possibly no. 8 also; no. 10 is a serval; and no. 7 is unlike any species known, as it is barred transversely. In fig. 154 nearly all the animals are servals, the best being nos. 9, 10, 12, and 14. No. 7 is, however, very doubtful; and no. 4 is probably a different species, but is not identified.

Having now described the offerings which bear the

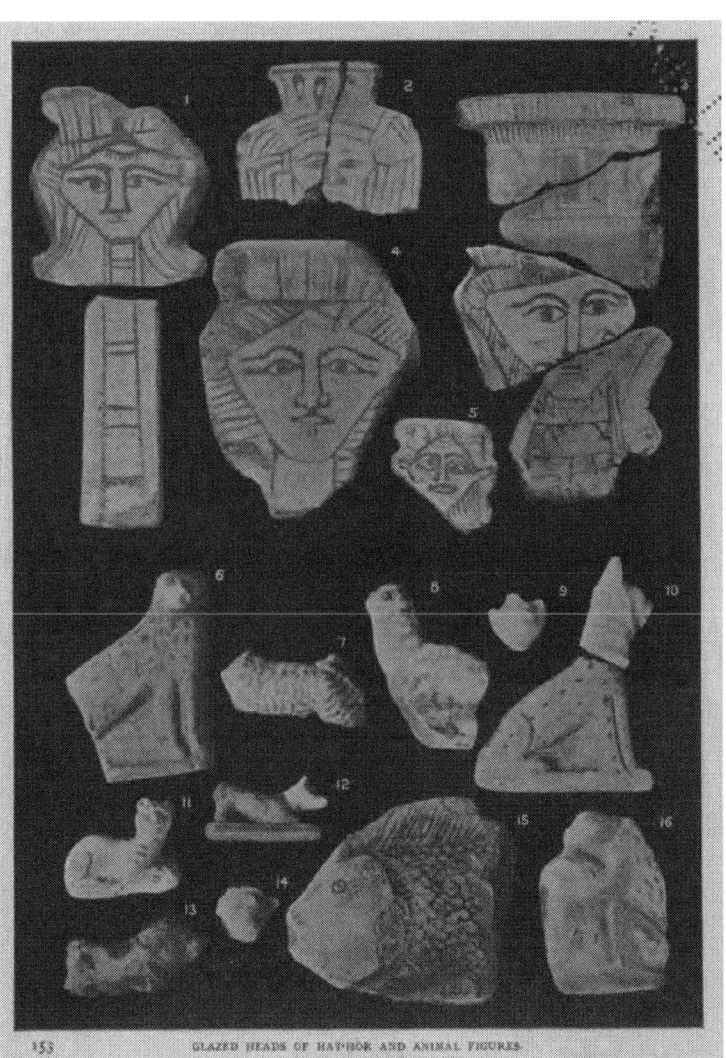

153 GLAZED HEADS OF HAT-HOR AND ANIMAL FIGURES.

154 GLAZED PLAQUES OF SERVAL CATS.

HISTORY OF OFFERINGS

names of kings, it is desirable to give a list of the numbers of such objects, so as to compare the relative amounts of offerings in different reigns. For this purpose we may also add those already known, and published by Captain Weill; these are 14 in all, and are here sorted in with 433 cartouches which I obtained:

	Vases and cups.	Bowls.	*Menats.*	Bracelets.	Wands.	Ring-stands.	Sistra.	Hat-hors.	Cats.	Totals.	*Per annum.*
Aahmes Nefertari	—	—	3	—	—	—	1	—	—	⎫	
Merytamen	—	—	1	—	—	—	—	—	—	⎬ 9	·4
Amenhotep I	—	—	1	—	—	—	1	1	—	⎬	
Queen Aahmes	—	—	1	—	—	—	—	—	—	⎭	
Tahutmes I	3	—	1	—	1	—	—	—	—	5	·2
Hatshepsut	2	—	11	—	—	—	—	2	1	16	·7
Tahutmes III	3	1	16	—	—	—	—	5	2	27	·8
Amenhotep II	1	—	3	—	—	—	—	—	—	4	·2
Amenhotep III	4	—	7	—	7	—	—	—	—	18	·6
Sety I	6	—	—	3	8	—	—	—	—	17	·6
Ramessu II	28	10	3	93	25	6	3	—	—	168	2·5
Merenptah	10	21	—	16	7	7	—	—	—	61	3·0
Sety II	2	5	1	17	—	—	3	—	—	28	5·6
Ta-usert	4	—	1	22	—	3	—	—	—	30	6·0
Ramessu III	15	3	—	19	6	—	2	—	—	45	1·4
Ramessu IV	—	—	1	7	3	—	—	—	—	11	1·8
Ramessu V	—	—	—	6	—	—	—	—	—	6	1·5
Ramessu VI	1	—	—	1	—	—	—	—	—	2	·4
	79	40	50	184	57	16	10	8	3	447	

From this table we see how each class of object rose into importance and then diminished. From the total cartouches of each reign, divided by the number of years in the reign, we get the number of named offerings *per annum*. Probably we must multiply this by three, to allow for those which have perished. We see that there was a tolerably constant average all through the XVIIIth dynasty and Sety I, originally about two named offerings *per annum*. Then this rose greatly in the XIXth dynasty to perhaps ten or twenty *per annum*, and then decreased in the XXth dynasty. It is not to be supposed that these offerings were made every year in regular amounts; but the numbers show the relative quantity of offerings in different reigns, and the general amount of attention given to the place.

Many small objects of interest were also found apart from the large classes, and such are shown in fig. 155. The upper half of this plate down to no. 14 is nearly of full size; from 15 onward the photographs are half the natural size, like all the previous plates. No. 1 is a woman's head, with the hair dressed in the manner usual when engaged in active work, such as that of the bread-makers (NEWBERRY, *Beni Hasan*, i, xii and xxix), and performers (xxix) in the XIIth dynasty. Nos. 2 and 3 are pendant figures of the youthful Ramessu II; 4 and 5 are delicate pottery cartouches of Sety I; 6 is a pendant of a lotus-leaf on a tank of water; 7 is a quarter of a scarab of the new type of cattle-hunt of Amenhotep III, first published by Mr. FRAZER in his *Catalogue of Scarabs*, frontispiece; 8 is a pretty trefoil in blue glaze, which belongs to the early XVIIIth dynasty. No. 9 is a spiral bead of dark violet glaze: it is remarkably like the gold bead found in Neit-hotep's tomb at Naqada, and the lazuli beads found in Zer's tomb at Abydos; we may suppose that it is of the early dynasties, and has survived perhaps from Sneferu's offerings. Nos. 10-13 are very unusual little figures, which have been attached to objects, 13 having part of the edge of a bowl held in front of the figure; the heads have strange tufts of hair upon them, one behind and two in front on 11, one in front and two behind on 12. No. 14 is a crystal bead of flattened form to wear in a necklace; 15 is a votive ear of glazed pottery; 16 is a face from a limestone statuette; 17 is a blue-glaze clustered papyrus column, of the regular type of the XIIth dynasty—four pieces of this were found; 18 is a glazed pottery head of the god Bes; 19 is a piece of a plaque of very fine glazed ware, probably of

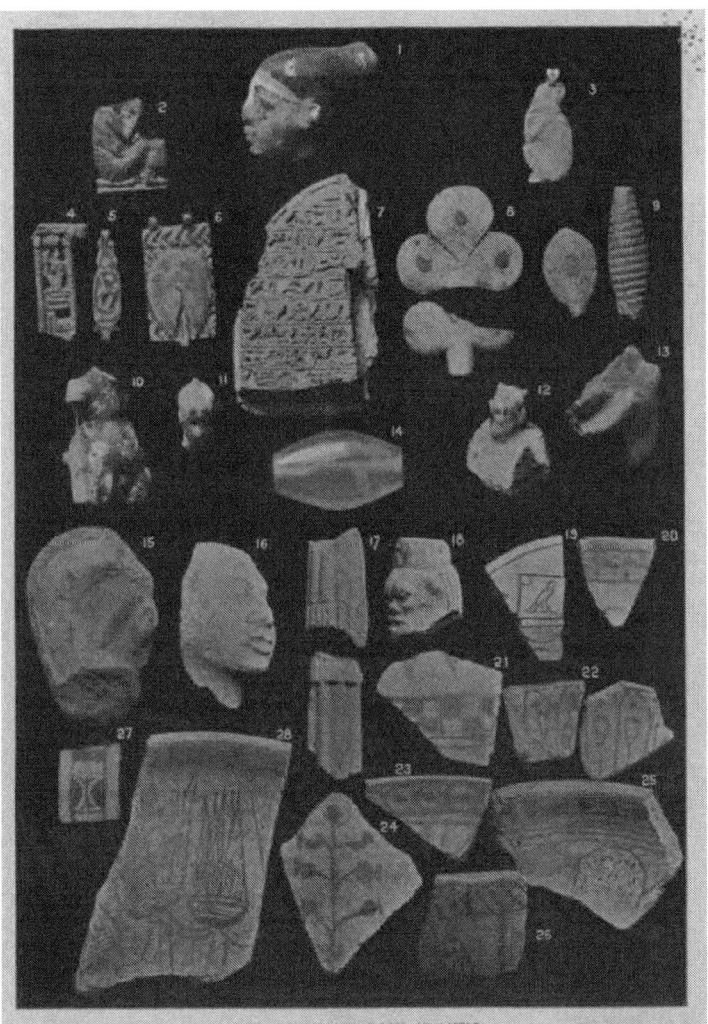

155. GLAZED FIGURES AND PIECES OF BOWLS.

156   PIECES OF GLAZED VASES WITH ANIMALS AND PLANTS

152 THE ALTARS AND THE OFFERINGS

tablets with figures of foreign subjects of Ramessu III found at Tell el Yehudiyeh. The art of these has a relationship to that of the finely modelled and coloured reliefs of stucco found at Knossos.

There had also been large cylindrical glazed vases with painted scenes and patterns. In fig. 158 the upper vase has the scene of a girl presenting flowers to a king, with long trails of convolvulus hanging down behind her. The pattern of garlands and feather-work is of violet on white. Another flower pattern on a similar vase is by its side. Below are parts of a vase painted in brown on a bright yellow ground, with a kneeling figure holding two notched palm-sticks, the emblem of eternity; and a lotus flower is on the opposite side. These large jars, about a foot high, of the brightest-coloured glaze, must have been very effective in decoration.

Large quantities of beads were found amid the broken offerings, about half a hundredweight. These had formed collars and necklaces, dedicated to Hat·hor, to which the *menats* had been attached. The various shapes of the beads are shown in fig. 159. Those in the top line are of green and black glaze, and seem as if made to imitate plaiting with coloured straws. The rosettes are of the usual work of Amenhotep III and IV, as also the pendants with palm-leaves, next below. The coarser pendants in the fourth row are of the late XVIIIth dynasty, or perhaps of Ramessu II. The imitation scarabs of blue pottery come next; and below are the long pointed pendants of the XVIIth dynasty. In the lower part the rosette beads and notched beads are of the XVIIIth dynasty, as also the long dark beads sprinkled with white chips; these were glazed over with blue, and thus made to imitate dark turquoise-rock with specks of turquoise in it. The rough ball-beads were probably made up with the long beads below into necklaces for the *menats*, and the disc beads of the bottom string were not originally strung, but were stitched on to a pectoral of cloth. The

157. PIECES OF TWO JARS WITH RELIEFS, RAMESSU III

158. PIECES OF TALL JARS WITH COLOURED GLAZES, RAMESSU III.

collar and *menat* are represented in the hands of Hat-hor, on the slab from the tomb of Sety I now at Florence.

We have now given some idea of the great mass of offerings which were presented at this shrine of the "Mistress of Turquoise" by the kings who sought her favour in their mining. Doubtless there were other offerings of metal, and valuable materials, which were seized on by the plunderers when the Egyptians abandoned the place, and the wild Bedawy tribes wrecked everything that they could destroy. For over four thousand years the Egyptians had more or less dominated Sinai; but the degradation of their kingdom, under the later Ramessides and the Ethiopian occupation, let this side of their territory slip finally from their power.

CHAPTER XI

THE MINES OF SERABÍT EL KHÁDEM

IN Chapter IV we have described the mines of Maghareh and the mode of mining there. At Serabít the methods were the same as at Maghareh, but there were variations in some features. There is not the same amount of dating by tablets cut in the rock at the mines, and the history of the mining is not, therefore, defined. On the other hand, there are so few monuments in the temple before the XIIth dynasty that we may presume the mining to be nearly all of the XIIth and XVIIIth to XXth dynasties.

The main group of mines is along the west side of the valley 3, about F on Map 3; see also the view with the heaps on the left, fig. 68. These are caverns cut in from a little over the level of the floor of the valley; for this upper end of the valley is here only about fifty feet below the plateau, before it plunges down about three hundred feet in the great falls east of F. The most southern has been reworked in modern times, and much broken up. To the north is a cave, about thirty feet long and nearly as wide, from which a stratum has been worked out about six feet high; the roof of the further part of it has fallen in. Beyond are surface-quarries of the turquoise stratum, and large banks of chips have been thrown down into the valley, which deepens here about F. A party of our men turned over these heaps for some days in search of tools. Some perfect stone crushers were found here, shown in fig. 56, together with many pieces of rejected turquoise.

159 GLAZED BEADS OF XVIII–XIX DYNASTIES.

To the south of the temple, near the fall of the valley, a small cave has been cut, about three or four yards square, the roof of which has partly fallen. The chip-banks having retained the rainfall in the cutting, a little earth has accumulated, and the natives now plant a few rows of corn, with the chance of its reaching maturity. In the same way the quarry rubbish thrown down the valley on the north of the temple, from the quarries which are close under the temple level, has held up the rains, and made a bed of soil in two patches of perhaps half an acre altogether. These are duly ploughed and sown, and had wheat about six inches high in March ; though whether there was rain enough for it to mature this year seemed doubtful.

On the opposite side of the valley 3, at H, there are two mines which run in some way below the top of the hill, as that rises up thirty or forty feet above the ferruginous stratum on this side of the valley. These mines are about five to six feet high, and go twenty or thirty feet into the hill. At the inner end the upper part only is cut away, showing that the top was worked first, just high enough for a man to crouch or lie at the work, and then the lower part was removed by cutting down. The sides of these and the other mines here are fairly upright, and are not rounded out like the mine of the IIIrd dynasty at Magháreh. Inside the cave, on a wall facing the entrance, is a tablet cut in the rock ; unfortunately it has been carved in a soft red stratum, which has powdered away so much that nothing is now legible.

Between this and the hill to the east is a sharp ravine, which must be passed at the head to reach the mine G. This was a wide excavation, about 35 ft. square, running only a few feet under the surface, and without any pillar or support. A large part of the roof has fallen in, where it is thinnest, on the south side. No trace of inscriptions remains here.

The group of inscribed mines is at A to E. This is a narrow neck of hill between the valleys 2 and 3. It was first attacked from the head of valley 3 at A; the stratum of turquoise sandstone was worked back here until there was some ten feet of unproductive rock over it, and large banks of chips had accumulated. On the face of the upper rock two inscriptions of Amenemhat II were cut; the arrangement of these is rude and irregular, and they were evidently done by a man who could read ordinary documents, but who had no training or practice in setting out or carving inscriptions. Failing to continue this as an open mine, a small tunnel, 2 or 3 ft. wide, was run into the turquoise stratum. This was also attacked from the south side of the neck at D, and a tablet was cut on the rock showing that the expedition of Sinefert under Amenemhat III had worked here. Another tablet was also carved at C by Ptah·ur, who led the expedition in the 45th year of Amenemhat III. The workings inside the hill were irregular and complex, so a pit was sunk from the top to give air and light, and it bears a fine inscription of Sebek·her·heb, who was working here in the 44th year of Amenemhat, as we know by his Bethel stele. This pit has been miscalled a reservoir, as we noticed in Chapter V. My workmen turned over the chips inside this mine for a day or two, without finding anything more than a few pieces of wood. This region was also worked in the XVIIIth dynasty, further tunnels being run irregularly at E; there is a scene of Tahutmes IV, dated in his 4th year. The tunnels are nearly choked with chips, and could not be examined without clearing them out. The plateau to the east of this is deeply cut up by valleys, yet the turquoise level is not denuded from the hills left between them. No mines, however, could be found in these hills, though I looked carefully over the ground as far as the map extends. My wife also looked over the hills between the Wady Umm Agráf and the

Ras Suwíq without finding the mine and tablet of the 7th year of Tahutmes IV, which is said to be two miles south or south-east of the temple. The so-called reservoir inscription is described as being a mile south of Serabít, and it is really half a mile south-south-west; so the tablet described as two miles south or south-east might be looked for at one mile south, which would be on the south side of Wady Umm Agráf. But I went over that side, and looked along the course of the valley, without finding any trace of workings. So there is still this mine of Tahutmes IV to be rediscovered; also the tombs said to be found by Gardner Wilkinson, three-quarters of an hour south-east of the temple, which might be on the plateau in the map if three-quarters of an hour's walk around the valley-head is intended; also the miners' huts said to be found by Major Macdonald at a distance of two hours,—all of these needed more time to find than we could spare from the copying and mapping of Serabít.

On the west of the temple there are no inscriptions by the miners, excepting those in unknown signs. At J the knoll of hill has been largely quarried away in an open mine, and parts which were undercut as caves have been broken down in the modern search for turquoise. Another mine at K has been cut into the side of the hill looking down the valley; the work does not extend far in, and seems to have been abandoned as unprofitable. The largest mine of the Wady Dhába is at N. The wide openings of it, and great banks of chips, catch the eye from the ridge of the Bethels near the temple. There have been several mines here run together, with one opening to the north of the headland, and the main cutting to the south. The opening has been squarely cut 80 in. wide and about 12 ft. high. The working was done by a chisel or pick half an inch wide, and another pointed chisel. The surfaces of the working were large sweeping curves of about four feet diameter, thus producing a series of hollows which merge together. In this the mine resembles that of the IIIrd dynasty, and is, therefore, perhaps the oldest mine here. The vertical cracks of rock were followed in the working, but were very little used for the permanent sides of the holes. The ceiling is all closely chiselled over, and is fairly flat. The first cutting was in galleries about 70 in. wide, with supports of about 20 to 30 in. between them. These supports have been later cut away, so throwing the whole into one irregular cavern about 50 ft. wide. The height of each working was originally five or six feet, but the different strata of turquoise rock led the miners to open various levels, until the whole broke together into a cave about 13 ft. high; this leads back to an upper and lower level, with a shelf of rock between, which is broken through in parts. The three paying strata, of 20 in., 55 in., and 10 in. of red sandstone, were separated by blanks of 25 and 20 in. of yellow sandstone.

Further to the north is a mine at L, which is in a neck of the plateau, and opens out into the valleys 7 and 8 on both sides, like the mines at A—E. The photograph of the working is given in fig. 72. On the east side a trench has been opened, about ten feet wide and high, running almost across to the west side. The north side of this trench is shown in the photograph. It has been cut at several levels, but the lower level is the only one which extends far in. The tablets with unknown signs are on the face of the trench at the shallower end to the east, on the right hand beyond the part photographed. One of the lower galleries leads through the hill, and opens into a large cavern which looks down into valley 8. This cavern runs to about forty or fifty feet in, and is about twenty-five feet wide and twelve or fifteen feet high. In order to get more air and access three square shafts have been sunk from the top of the hill down into these workings. The galleries are

POSITIONS OF MINES

about 70 in. high, and 30 to 40 in. wide, just large enough to work in easily; they were cut with a chisel four-tenths of an inch wide, and the sides are fairly even and straight, not like the working of mine N. The roof has only sparse chisel-cuts on it, showing that the rock was got out by undercutting and breaking away lumps of it. Altogether the working is like that of the mine of Tahutmes III at Magháreh; and I found a scrap of pottery here of buff body, with red and black lines, which belongs to that age. So this mine may be fairly put to the earlier half of the XVIIIth dynasty.

Rather below the level of this, at a little to the north, is a series of other mines, marked M. These have only been cut in from the east, and do not open out on the west, as the hill is so much thicker. There are some wide galleries, and the largest work opens out a large cavern perhaps fifty or sixty feet across, see fig. 73; from this, galleries turn off on the north, and it widens out to the south at the inner side, and so connects with the other galleries. The character of the galleries and working is shown in fig. 73. The cavern was a good deal higher originally, as the floor is now deeply covered with banks of chips. Outside in the valley are large banks thrown down from these workings; and the best way of seeking for the ancient mines is to search for the spoil-banks along the upper levels of the hills, looking from the opposite side of a valley.

In the chip heaps both at Serabít and at Magháreh were found the large crushers equal at each end (fig. 56, nos. 1, 2, 3), the picks with a groove round the head to bind them to a handle (fig. 57, no. 1), and the heavy pointed mauls, which must have been grasped with both hands (fig. 56, no. 4; fig. 57, no. 2). Those figured here are, however, from Serabít, as at Magháreh we only found broken specimens. But in the mines the tool-marks do not agree with the broad pounding blows that would be given with such clumsy instruments; and copper chisels seem to be certainly indicated by the clean cuts of uniform breadth whereby the stone was removed. It appears, then, that these stone tools were rather those used by the labourers for breaking up and crushing the masses of rock which were dislodged by the miners. The tool in fig. 57, no. 3, is a borer for drilling stone vases with sand. It points to an actual making of vases here, which we should not have expected, as any suitable stone would have to be brought here in the block.

Besides the large stone tools, there were many thousands of flints found near the mines. These have been collected also by previous travellers, and a wild notion has been formed that they were set in wooden handles, and used as chisels, struck with a mallet. To make any cuts in the sandstone, such as the chisel-marks, would soon snap a flint; yet there were very few broken ones, compared with the large number found. The real use of these flints is shown by the wearing and smoothing of the ends, due to grubbing against sandstone. In fig. 60 are the various types which we found. In the top line the first six are all entirely rounded at the point by wear in the sandstone; this was probably done when scoring round the nodules of turquoise to get them out of blocks of rock. Next are five examples of the pointed flints, which are seldom worn much, and seem as if intended for some work not in sandstone. Lastly are two of the long fine flakes, which were rather common. There seems to be some relation between the pointed forms and the worn flints. They were found at Magháreh principally in three places: A (Map 2), a heap of chips at 60 ft. above the valley, and 270 ft. down the valley from Sahura's tablet; B, a heap of chips at the same level, and 160 ft. down the valley from Sahura; R, scattered flints on the hill-side below Ra·n·user's tablet. In these places we found at—

A, flints largely worn, 1 in 8 pointed;
B, flints less worn, 1 in 20 pointed;
R, flints little worn, 1 in 30 pointed.

These numbers depend partly on the selection made at Magháreh; but as this was done all at once, it is not likely to be very different for other places. It seems that the proportion of pointed flints increases where they were most used for working in the sandstone.

The large flints in the second line were apparently used for working the rock, as many of them are worn. In the lower part there are portions of well-flaked tools, which belong probably to early times, as they were found on the surface and have no connection with the mining. The last three flints are heavily worn by working in sandstone.

Now, these worn flints were found mainly in the heaps A and B at Magháreh, and no black stone crushers or large tools were with them. On the contrary, scarcely any flints occurred where the crushers and picks were found, below the mines of Sa-nekht and Tahutmes III at Magháreh, and below the mines of Amenemhat II and the well-worked mines at Serabít. Also, there is no trace of working with flints in the rock surfaces of the mining of the Egyptians. The conclusion, then, seems to be that the large stone crushers and picks were used by Egyptian workers, and the flints were used by Bedawy grubbers of all periods to scrape the turquoises out of the rock without regular mining.

Turning to the tools of the Egyptians, it seems that they used metal in all ages for their heavy work. The chisel-marks in the mines are too uniform to have been made by such clumsy tools as the large stone picks, and the regular breadth of the cut shows a metal chisel to have been used. The stone picks and crushers must have been for breaking up the masses of rock, and crushing it to search for the nodules. We actually found two copper chisels in the temple at Serabít. They lay with ashes, stone dust, and rubbers of sandstone for facing surfaces of stone, in the northern half of chamber E, which had been used as a workshop. The forms are shown in fig. 160; the lengths are 6½ and 7½ in. They were probably used by the masons for cutting stones in building the chambers C to A of the temple, and are, therefore, of the late XVIIIth or XIXth dynasty. One has a wide flat cutting edge, fairly sharp, and therefore for facing the stone; such dressing may be seen on the Sutekh stele, fig. 134, and the altars in fig. 142, nos. 8, 9. The other chisel is of a rarer type, as it narrows to the end and is blunt; this was evidently for the rough-hewing, as on the altars in fig. 142, no. 3, and fig. 143, no. 15. Such a chisel must have been used for the mining, as the breadth of the cut agrees, and the thickness in the middle was needed to bear the force of the blows without bending.

A crucible was found at Serabít which was almost complete (fig. 161). The form of the crucible shown in hieroglyphs has been a puzzle hitherto, as it rose up so high above the spout. Here we see that in order to get a sufficiently refractory material the Egyptians had to use a very weak paste for the body, which easily crumbles away. It was, therefore, not practicable to lift the crucible with a heavy charge of melted metal in it. The only way to empty it was to roll the crucible forward on its round bottom. Thus the form required was a hemisphere, prolonged upward to allow for accidental tilting in the fire and to give a better hold in moving it, yet with a spout for the ready delivery of the metal. Thus they arrived at the form which we here see in reality, and which is used as the emblem of copper in the hieroglyphs.

163. COPPER CHISELS FROM TEMPLE, XIX DYNASTY.

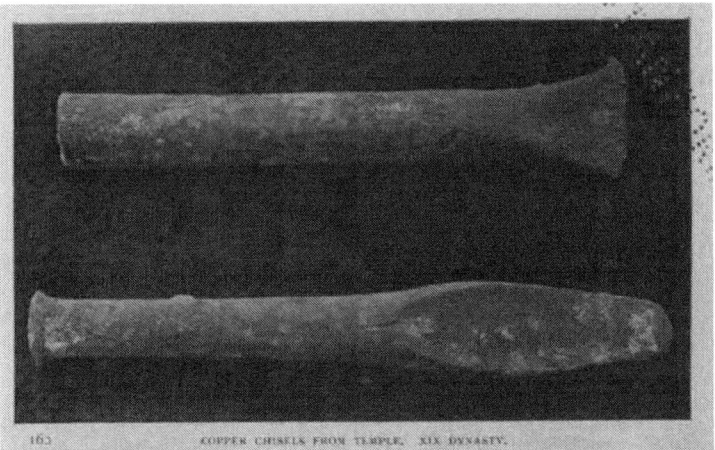

161. CRUCIBLE FOR MELTING COPPER, FROM TEMPLE.

CHAPTER XII

THE REVISION OF CHRONOLOGY

THE work at Sinai has brought to light one monument of chronological importance, and has called attention to another such record; and as no account of the present knowledge of Egyptian chronology is generally available, it seems well to give here an outline of the materials before us, the mode of applying them to the question, and the main results for the history of Egypt. As this is a subject which involves some things not commonly known, it is but natural that many people—even of those acquainted with Egyptian matters—should set it aside as being too intricate or too uncertain to be profitably considered. Yet every one has some interest in the whole question of whether Menes founded the kingdom of all Egypt five thousand years before Herodotos, or at only half that distance of time; and any one who has to deal at all with history requires some workable series of dates for reference. Though some details are intricate, and have never yet been properly worked out by astronomers, yet the main facts of the scale of the whole time are very simple, and easily followed by any reader of this volume. It is desirable to put an end to the blind negation with which almost every one treats the subject, as at present authors and curators of museums throw themselves entirely upon some of the most uncritical and obsolete guides. Where I here give facts or conclusions without reservation, they are matters generally accepted and undisputed; where there is a difference of opinion worth any notice it is stated, with the reasons on both sides. To save needless complication I shall here describe all celestial movements as they appear to us, and appeared to the Egyptians; the purely astronomical reality is a theoretical view which we need not touch here.

We are all familiar with leap year, when we put an extra day in the calendar to keep the account true. The whole checking of the chronology rests on the unquestioned fact that the Egyptians ignored leap year, and counted only 365 days. There have been defects in every calendar, simply because the motions of the earth have no exact relation to each other, or to those of the moon. The Muhammadan calendar falls short eleven days each year, by taking twelve lunar months as the year, which only amount to $354\frac{1}{2}$ days. Thus the whole Arab months shift round the seasons in about thirty years. Another instance is the imperfect Old Style calendar of Russia at present, which has shifted thirteen days, so that (if continued) the months would shift round all the seasons in about 50,000 years. Now the Egyptian slipped his months backward a quarter of a day each year, by not keeping up the enumeration as we do with a 29th of February. As the months thus slipped backward, or the seasons appeared to slip forward in the calendar, in 1,460 years the months shifted round all the seasons. Strictly the year does not contain exactly an odd quarter of a day, but ·242; so that the rotation of the months would take place in 1,500 years. But as the earth's rotation is slackening, the fraction was exactly a quarter of a day within historic times; and we may then call it so, as the Egyptians did. The authority for this is Censorinus, writing in 239 A.D. that " the Egyptian civil year has only 365 days, without any intercalary day, whence the quadrennium so adjusts itself that in the 1,461st year the revolution is completed."

In order to observe the seasons exactly, the mere

THE SOTHIS PERIOD

changes of heat or of growth are too vague; and the Egyptians saw that some connection between the sun and the stars should be noted. As they had no exact timekeeper they could not compare the sun by day and the stars by night; so they adopted the first appearance of a star in the glow of sunrise. But this was necessarily rather vague, and they might even err two or three days in observing it. The shift of the stars in relation to the sun is about two diameters of the sun each day. For their star of observation they took Sirius, the brightest of all the stars, otherwise called Sothis, Canicula, or the Dog Star. As Censorinus says: "The beginnings of these years are always reckoned from the first day of that month which is called by the Egyptians Thoth, which happened this year [239 A.D.] upon the 7th of the kalends of July [June 25th]; for a hundred years ago from the present year [*i.e.* 139 A.D.] the same fell upon the 12th of the kalends of August [July 21st], on which day Canicula [Sirius] regularly rises in Egypt.'

Thus the new year's day of the months—the 1st of Thoth—coincided in 139 A.D. with the fixed astronomical feature of the rising of Sirius in the dawn just before the sun, which was on July 21st. This, of course, differed by a day or two in different parts of Egypt. From this it follows that the months of the shifting calendar, and of our fixed calendar, agreed as follows:

	5702 B.C. 4242 2782 1322 139 A.D.	5222 B.C. 3762 2302 842 619 A.D.	4742 B.C. 3282 1822 362 1099 A.D.
Aakhet season.			
1 Thoth	21 July	23 March	23 Nov.
1 Paophi	20 Aug.	22 April	23 Dec.
1 Hat-hor	19 Sept.	22 May	22 Jan.
1 Khoiak	19 Oct.	21 June	21 Feb.
Pert season.			
1 Tybi	18 Nov.	21 July	23 March
1 Mekhir	18 Dec.	20 Aug.	22 April
1 Phamenoth	17 Jan.	19 Sept.	22 May
1 Pharmuthi	16 Feb.	19 Oct.	21 June
Shemu season.			
1 Pakhons	18 March	18 Nov.	21 July
1 Pauni	17 April	18 Dec.	20 Aug.
1 Epiphi	17 May	17 Jan.	19 Sept.
1 Mesore	16 June	16 Feb.	19 Oct.
5 intercalary	16 July	18 March	18 Nov.

The shift at intervals of four months is given here, from which it is easy to reckon for intermediate times in proportion.

Now in going backward the first great datum that we meet is that on the back of the medical Ebers papyrus, where it is stated that Sirius rose on the 9th of Epiphi in the 9th year of Amenhotep I. As the 9th of Epiphi is 56 days before the 1st of Thoth, Sirius rose on that day at 4 × 56 years (224) before the dates at the head of the first column. As only 1322 B.C. can be the epoch here, so 1322 + 224 = 1546 B.C. for the 9th year of Amenhotep I, or 1554 B.C. for his accession. And as Aahmes I reigned 25 years, we reach 1579 B.C. for the accession of Aahmes and the beginning of the XVIIIth dynasty. This is not defined within a few years (1) owing to four years being the equivalent of only one day's shift; (2) owing to the rising being perhaps observed in a different part of Egypt at different times; (3) owing to various minor astronomical details. But this gives us 1580 B.C. as the approximate date for the great epoch of the rise of the XVIIIth dynasty.

Before that we next find another Sirius rising and two seasonal dates in the XIIth dynasty, and an indication of a season in the VIth dynasty.

The most exact of these early dates is a rising of Sirius on the 17th of Pharmuthi in the 7th year of Senusert III, on a papyrus from Kahun. This is now in Berlin, and was published by BORCHARDT in *Zeits. Aeg. Spr.*, xxxvii, 99-101. This shows that the 17th of Pharmuthi then fell on July 21st, which gives the 7th year of Senusert III at 1874 or 3334 B.C. As he reigned probably to his 38th year, he died 1843 or 3303 B.C. Amenemhat III reigned 44 years by his monuments, Amenemhat IV 9 years, and Sebekneferu 4 years by the Turin papyrus; these reigns bring the close of the XIIth dynasty to 1786 or 3246 B.C. We have, then, to decide by the internal evidence of the monuments of the kings which of these dates is probable, by seeing whether the interval of the XIIIth to XVIIth dynasties was 1,786 − 1,580 = 206 years, or else 1,666 years. This question has been merely ignored hitherto, and it has been assumed by all the Berlin school that the later date is the only one possible, and that the interval was only 206 years.

Setting aside altogether for the present the details of the list of Manetho, let us look only to the monuments, and the Turin papyrus of kings, which was written with full materials concerning this age, with a long list of kings, and only two or three centuries later than the period in question. On the monuments we have the names of 17 kings of the XIIIth dynasty. In the Turin papyrus there are the lengths of reigns of 9 kings, amounting to 67 years, or 7 years each on an average. If we apply this average length of reign to only the 17 kings whose reigns are proved by monuments, we must allow them 120 years; leaving out of account entirely about 40 kings in the Turin papyrus, as being not yet known on monuments. Of the Hyksos kings we know of the monuments of three certainly; and without here adopting the long reigns stated by Manetho, we must yet allow at least 30 years for these kings. And in the XVIIth dynasty there are at least the reigns of Kames and Sekhent-neb-ra, which cover probably 10 years. Hence for those kings whose actual contemporary monuments are known there is required:

XIIIth dynasty	. .	120	years
Hyksos	at least	30	"
XVIIth dynasty	. .	10	"
		160	"

This leaves us but 46 years, out of the 206 years, to contain 120 kings named by the Turin papyrus, and all the Hyksos conquest and domination, excepting 30 years named above.

This is apparently an impossible state of affairs; and those who advocate this shorter interval are even compelled to throw over the Turin papyrus altogether, and to say that within two or three centuries of the events an entirely false account of the period was adopted as the state history of the Egyptians.

This difficulty has been so great that many scholars in Germany, and every one in the rest of Europe, have declined to accept this view. If, however, the Sirius datum is to be respected, we should be obliged to allow either 206 or else 1,666 years between the XIIth and XVIIIth dynasties. As neither of these seemed probable courses, it has been thought that the Sirius datum itself was possibly in error, and here the matter has rested awaiting fresh evidence.

At this point two Sinai monuments come in with decisive proofs that the Sirius datum is quite correct.

Some of the mining records on the steles have months named on them, and a few have the day named. Let us look first at those of the XVIIIth and XIXth dynasties, of which the dates are known within a few years. These are:—(1) Of Amenhotep III, 36th year, Mekhir 19th; this was in 1379 B.C., when Mekhir 9th fell on January 19th. (2) Of Ramessu II, 3rd year, Phamenoth, day not stated; this was in 1298 B.C., when Phamenoth was from January 12th to February 11th—say January 26th for a middle date. (3) Of Ramessu IV, 5th year, Pauni 1st; this was in 1166 B.C., when Pauni 1st was March 9th. (4) Of Ramessu IV (?), 4th year, Pauni, day not stated; this was 1167 B.C., when Pauni was from March 9th to April 8th—say March 24th for a middle date. (5) Probably of Tahutmes III, judging by the style and work of the stele, 9th year, Phamenoth 6th; this was in 1494 B.C., when Phamenoth 26th was on March 26th. (6) Of Ramessu II (?), 3rd year, Epiphi, the day not stated; this was in 1298 B.C., when Epiphi was from May 12th to June 11th—say May 27th for a middle date. Putting all these together, we find the dates to be:

(1) Amenhotep III . . January 19th.
(2) Ramessu II . . January 26th ± 15 days.
(3) Ramessu IV . . March 9th.
(4) Ramessu IV (?) . March 24th ± 15 days.
(5) Tahutmes III (?) . March 26th.
(6) Ramessu II (?) . May 27th ± 15 days.

The season for carving records was, then, from the middle of January to the middle of May, but generally not later than March. This just accords with our experience of the climate. In January the weather is cold, but good for active work; by April the heat begins; in May it is almost unbearable in the valleys. The autumn is not so suitable, as the scanty plants would be dried up or dead; whereas in March the natives live largely on the milk of their sheep and goats, which manage to find some green food after the winter rains.

Having thus found that the mining season was just that time which is known now to be most suitable for work, we are able to make use of two critical records. On a fragment of a stele of Amenemhat III which we found, is a date much weathered. This occurs in the middle of an account of the work, and is not the head-date of the stele. It gives the season, *Aakhet*, and has two strokes under the moon sign, but one of these is in the middle, showing there have been three. This gives then Hat·hor, the 3rd month of *Aakhet*. There is the number 12 before it, possibly the 12th year, but from its small size probably the 12th day. That is so near the middle of the month that we may as well adopt it as the day, with the reservation that the date might be about a fortnight either way. The season of mining with which this should agree, is from the middle of January to the end of March; and the 12th of Hat·hor fell at these times between 1746 and 2090 B.C., or between 3206 and

3550 B.C. This agrees with the Sirius rising, which gives about 1840 or 3300 for this reign.

The other monument is less precise, but more unquestionable in its meaning. In a record of the reign of Amenemhat III, the chief of the expedition, Hor·ur·ra, relates how he came to Serabît in hot weather, when work seemed almost impossible; yet by the favour of Hat·hor he obtained a great quantity of turquoise. He fortunately states that he arrived in Phamenoth, and left in Pakhons. Now this hot weather must have been late in the spring. At the close of summer a little delay would have given good conditions; but a delayed expedition in the spring, caught by an early summer, would be the probable conditions. The heat, according to our feelings, begins late in April; to an Egyptian it probably would begin in May. It seems, then, that Phamenoth fell in May, and Pakhons in July, within an uncertainty of a month either way, as we do not know whether the season were early or late, or in what part of Phamenoth or of Pakhons they travelled. Now this correspondence was in 1754 and in 3194 B.C., with an uncertainty of 120 years either way, or 1870 to 1630 and 3310 to 3070 B.C. This, again, agrees to the Sirius date within the uncertainties, as by that Amenemhat III reigned 1843 to 1799 B.C., or 3303 to 3259 B.C.

These two new data in the subject make it certain, therefore, that the Sirius dating in the XIIth dynasty is correct, and not liable to some misinterpretation.

We now have to face this large question, which of these two cycles of the 1,460-year period—the earlier or the later—is to be accepted? We have shown that there seems to be no possibility of the later period being true, as that leaves only 46 years free for all the large number of unknown kings of the XIIIth to the XVIIth dynasties. Yet, on the other hand, we may shrink from the idea that there was as much as 1,500 years in this interval.

There is one professed clue to settle the matter—the

History of Manetho. This work was in its original form an authority of the highest order. Compiled under the active patron of learning—Ptolemy Philadelphos—and very possibly for the great library which he created, and written by an Egyptian priest who knew how to use all the documents that had come down to his day, it has the strongest external claims to belief. We know how thorough and systematic the Egyptian records were from even the fragments left to our own times: the chronicle of all the years and reigns of the first five dynasties is unmatched in any country, and the fragment of it at Palermo shows how early a systematic record existed; while the later Turin papyrus of the XVIIIth dynasty, or before, giving the length of reign of every king, with summations at intervals, shows how the same taste for precise reckoning was kept up in later times. It was, then, to complete copies of such works that Manetho could refer when constructing his history for the Greek world.

The internal evidence is also strong for the care given to his work and its precision. That Manetho and the Turin papyrus of the XVIIIth dynasty drew from the same sources may be traced even in their fragments which we know. The Turin papyrus gives 1,755 years for the Ist to VIth dynasties, and Manetho gives 544 years for the VIIth to XIth dynasties, making 2,299 years in all; while Manetho states 2,300 years as the total to the end of the XIth dynasty. Hence he had exactly the same total for the Ist to VIth dynasties as we find given more than a thousand years before in the Turin papyrus.

Manetho has been often accused of double reckoning, by stating two contemporary dynasties or kings separately. Every instance in which this has been supposed has broken down when examined in detail. Not a single case of overlapping periods can be proved against him. On the contrary, there are two excellent proofs of his care to avoid such errors. The XIth dynasty we know by the monuments to have covered at least one century, and probably two. Yet Manetho only gives 43 years, evidently because he reckoned the Xth dynasty as legitimate, and until that ended he did not count the XIth dynasty, which was partly contemporary. Again, in the case of a single reign, we find the same treatment. It is well known that Taharqa was reigning about 29 years before the accession of Psametek I. Manetho places three ancestors of Psametek before him, reigning 21 years in all. Here, it has been said, is a clear case of double reckoning of overlapping reigns. But just here is Manetho's care shown, for he cuts down the well-known reign of Taharqa to 8 or 18 years, according to different readings; and this 8 years, with the 21 of the three other kings, makes the 29 years of Taharqa. In fact, he has only counted Taharqa until he takes up what he regards as the legitimate line, and thus he ignores the 21 years of the reign which overlapped those of the other kings.

Of course, there have been many corruptions and false readings in details, and we only have the scanty outlines given by Julius Africanus (221 A.D.), Eusebius (326 A.D.), and George Syncellus (792 A.D.). But the minor errors do not at all justify an entire rejection of what was obviously the general sum and extent of the history. There may also be varying statements about many dates in general history, but that does not justify us in rejecting them all, and taking something entirely different to any of the statements that we have.

Starting from the well-fixed point of 1580 B.C. for the beginning of the XVIIIth dynasty, let us take Manetho, as best represented by his earliest synoptist, Julius Africanus. His statements give:

Dyn.	Years	B.C.
XIII	453	3170
XIV	184	2717
XV	284	2533
XVI	518	2249
XVII	151	1731
XVIII		1580

EARLIER DATE OF XIIth DYNASTY

There is a check on this total in another way. Manetho states that the total from the XIIIth to the XIXth dynasties, inclusive, was 2,121 years. His statement that the XVIIIth dynasty lasted 263 years is very nearly true, but in his XIXth dynasty an error arose by duplicating the long reign of Ramessu II, and stating the whole as 209 years, while it is truly 120 years. These deducted from 2,121 years give his period from XIIIth—XVIIth dynasties as 1,649 or 1,738 years. For this interval, then, from the end of the XIIth to the beginning of the XVIIIth dynasties, we have by—

Sirius' risings	206 or 1,666 years;
Manetho's separate dynasties . .	1,590 years;
Manetho's total	{ 1,649 years, or 1,738 years.

The agreement of Manetho here with the longer interval and the earlier Sirius dating is as close as these errors of transmission allow us to expect. Its evidence for the early date is conclusive. On the one hand, if we accept the shorter period, both Manetho and the Turin papyrus have to be rejected—that is to say, nearly all the consecutive historical documents that we possess. If, on the other hand, we accept the longer period, there is nothing whatever against it but a prejudice, and it accords closely with Manetho and agrees with all that remains of the Turin papyrus.

When we also look outside of Egypt, some evidence of weight is found in Crete. Dr. Arthur Evans has strongly stated that the shorter interval is impossible in view of the long periods indicated in Cretan civilisation between the XIIth and XVIIIth dynasties.

From this point let us go back a stage earlier. We have reached the end of the XIIth dynasty at 3246 B.C. It lasted for 213 years, according to the Turin papyrus, and therefore began in 3459 B.C. From that to the close of the VIth dynasty is 544 years in Manetho, and

174 THE REVISION OF CHRONOLOGY

545 years by the difference between 1,755 years which the Turin papyrus gives for the close of the VIth, and the 2,300 years which Manetho gives for the close of the XIth dynasty. Hence the close of the VIth dynasty is 4003 B.C.; and therefore, the reign of Merenra will be at 4111 to 4115 B.C. Now it is in this reign that we have the statement that Una built a boat in 17 days of the month of Epiphi, to bring down alabaster from the quarry of Hat-nub; but he did not succeed in getting the block down in time before the Nile fell too low, and the sand banks appeared (PETRIE, *Hist. Eg.*, i, 95). The month of this lowness of the Nile may be taken as the end of Epiphi or early in Mesore, say Mesore 5th as a likely average. Now in 4111 B.C. that fell on May 19th. This agrees with the well-known difficulty of getting heavy boats down at the beginning of May or later; I have often had to hire two small boats in April, rather than one big one, in order to get a cargo down the Nile safely at that time. I had supposed that this datum referred to the fall of the Nile at the close of the inundation; but such is impossible in view of our more recent information, and we see that this really referred to the final close of heavy navigation for the year.

Earlier than this we have only one record to check the dead reckoning by consecutive dynasties. The great tablet of Pepy I at Magháreh (now destroyed) was dated in his 37th year, Mesore 6th. The actual date is the year after the 18th biennial cattle census, which must be the 36th or 37th year. As this year is 4131 B.C. according to what we have seen above, this date corresponds to May 24th. This is late in the season, but there is a yet later stele of May 27th at Serabít. So far as the rather vague indications of these last two seasonal events guide us, the Merenra low Nile shows that the season could not be much earlier, and the Pepy tablet shows that it could not be much later. Hence these together well confirm the dating we have reached above.

For the extent of the first six dynasties there is only the authority of the Turin papyrus and of Manetho, without any monumental check on the total amount. As, however, we know of the actual remains of 35 out of the 51 kings recorded, it is only reasonable to accept those lists as substantially accurate. The total of the reigns in Manetho is 1,497 years, the total of the dynastic totals is 1,479 years; but a total at the end of the VIth dynasty in the Turin papyrus is 1,755 years, and with this agrees the total of 2,300 years to the close of the XIth dynasty in Manetho. This discrepancy of 258 or 276 years might perhaps be due to the Turin papyrus having counted a dynasty of kings before Menes. In this uncertainty we shall do best to keep to the numbers of Manetho. The final list for the dynasties, then, will be as follows:

Dynasty	Began B.C.	Dynasty	Began B.C.
I	5510	XIII	3246
II	5247	XIV	2793
III	4945	XV	2533
IV	4731	XVI	2249
V	4454	XVII	1731
VI	4206	XVIII	1580
VII	4003	XIX	1322
VIII	3933	XX	1202
IX	3787	XXI	1102
X	3687	XXII	952
XI	3502	XXIII	755
XII	3459	XXIV	721

The first column of this list may very possibly have errors of a century in it, but it is not likely to vary more than this, judging by the two seasonal dates in the VIth dynasty. The second column must be correct to within a few years, as correct as we can fix the rising of Sirius. The general astronomical question of the place of Sirius, in regard to the precessional movement of the pole, does not appear to have been yet properly calculated.

It may introduce two or three centuries of difference possibly in the earlier dates, but it would in no way affect the reasoning of the question here. If any one wishes to abandon these dates, they must also abandon the greater part of the information that we have, cast Manetho and the Turin papyrus aside, ignore the evidence of Cretan archaeology, and treat history as a mere matter of arbitrary will, regardless of all records. As against this general position of dates there is nothing to be set in favour of any very different schemes, nothing —except the weightiest thing of all—prepossessions.

There are but three courses possible: (1) to abandon all the systematic documents that have come down to us; or (2) to invent an arbitrary change in the calendar sequence, of which there is no evidence; or (3) to accept the results here stated.

In connection with the question of the risings of Sirius in their chronological relation, we must also take notice of the great festival of the *sed*, or ending, which was a royal observance of the first importance. Every one agrees that the *sed* festival came after a period of 30 years, as it is stated expressly on the Rosetta stone; but whether this refers to a period of the king, or to an absolute fixed period, is a question. There have been three theories about this festival: (1) that it came after 30 years of reign, as it certainly did under Ramessu II; (2) that it came after 30 years of princedom, counting from the time when the king had been appointed crown prince; (3) that it came at fixed intervals of 30 years, or approximately so. If it can be shown to have a connection with fixed intervals, it becomes of some importance in the history and chronology. The entirely exceptional use of this festival at intervals of three years by Ramessu II was only an egotistical freak.

That this festival did not refer to 30 years of the king's reign is clear from the regnal years that are recorded for it; these are 37, 2, 16, 33, 12, and 22;

also it occurs in a reign which only lasted 26 years. That it referred to years of princedom seems unlikely, by those years in which it was celebrated. Mentuhotep's feast was in his 2nd year. Hatshepsut (whose festival came about the 40th year of her age) is not likely to have been associated with her father as heir when she was only ten years old, and when he had also a younger son. Akhenaten is not likely to have been associated on the throne as soon as he was born, yet his festival fell about the 30th year of his age. Tut-ankh-amen, who has the reference to "millions of festivals" in his reign, was only 9 years on the throne, and his predecessor only 12 years, so he never saw the 30th year of his princedom. And Ramessu II is known to have been associated with Sety as prince for some years; yet he celebrates his *sed* in his 30th year.

Is there, then, any reason for associating these festivals with a fixed period? We have seen how important was the observation of Sirius for regulating the year, and how the whole cycle of months shifted round the season, and was connected with the rising of Sirius. If, then, the months were thus linked to a cycle of 1,460 years, what is more likely than that the shifting of each month would be noticed? This was a period of 120 years, in which each month took the place of the previous one. And a festival of 120 years is recognised as having taken place; it was named the *henti*, and was determined with the hieroglyphs of a road and two suns, suggesting that it belonged to the passage of time. It is impossible to suppose that this could refer to the length of a reign or a princedom. We may reasonably see in this the feast when each first day of a month fell on the heliacal rising of Sirius, at intervals of 120 years.

Can we, then, dissociate a feast of 30 years from that of 120 years? The 120 years is the interval of one month's shift; the 30 years is the interval of one week's shift. Having a shifting calendar, it would be

178 THE REVISION OF CHRONOLOGY

strange if no notice was taken of the periods of recurrence in it, and a feast of 120 years and another of 30 years are the natural accompaniments of such a system. In the great festival of the renewal of a Sothic period in 139 A.D., the signs of the months are prominent on the coins of Alexandria.

But if this were true we ought to find that the festivals fall at regular intervals of time. There might be small variations, as the four weeks are 28 days and not 30; so there might be times when by keeping to a week-reckoning of intervals of 28 years they mounted up to 112 years instead of 120 for a month. But this would only lead to anticipating the feast by 8 years before it was set right again at a whole month. We will therefore state all the *sed* festivals that are known, although we have not a sufficiently certain chronology in the earlier period to test their dates.

			B.C.	Cycle.	
Narmer	on mace-head				(*Hierakonpolis*, i, xxvi, B).
Zer	seals				(*Royal Tombs*, ii, xv, 108, 109).
Den	ivory tablet, ebony tablet				(*R.T.*, i, xiv, 12; xv, 16).
"	seal				(*R.T.*, ii, xix, 154).
Semerkhet	crystal and alabaster vases				(*R.T.*, i, vii, 5-8).
?	Palermo stone, 3rd line, 3rd space				—
Qa	two bowls				(*R.T.*, i, viii, 6, 7).
"	Sab-ef, overseer of the *sed heb*				(*R.T.*, i, xxx).
Ra-n-user	temple at Abusir				(*A. Z.*, xxxvii, taf. 1).
Pepy I	Magháreh, 37th year	4131?	4121		(L., *D.*, ii, 116, *a*).
"	Hammamat, 37th year	"	"		(L., *D.*, ii, 115, *a, c, e, g*).
Mentuhotep II	Hammamat, 2nd year	?	3522?		(L., *D.*, ii, 149).
Senusert I	obelisk	3439-3397	3402		(L., *D.*, ii, 118, *h*).
Senusert III	Semneh	3339-13	3342		(L., *D.*, iii, 51).
Amenhotep I	Karnak	1562-41	1552		—
Tahutmes I	Karnak	1541-16	1522		(L., *D.*, iii, 6).
Hatshepsut	Karnak	1500	1492		(L., *D.*, iii, 22).
Tahutmes III	Bersheh	1470	1462		(S., *I.*, ii, 37).
Amenhotep II	Karnak?	1449-23	1431		(Pr., *A.*).
Amenhotep III	Soleb	1414-1379	1401		(L., *D.*, iii, 83-8).
Akhenaten	Amarna	1372	1372		(L., *D.*, iii, 100).
Tut-ankh-amen	Qurneh	1353-44	1342		(L., *D.*, iii, 115-8).
Sety I	Abydos	1326-1300	1292		(Mar., *Ab.*, i, 31).
Ramessu II	various	1270	1262		(B., *T.*, 1128).

LIST OF SED FESTIVALS

Ramessu III	. El Kab	.	.	. 1202-1171 1202	(B., *T.*, 1129).
Ramessu IV	. Karnak	.	.	. 1171-1165 1172	(L., *D.*, iii, 220).
Uasarkon II	. Bubastis	.	.	. 857 —	(N., *F.H.*).
	Feast of 12 years, therefore also			869 872	—
Taharqa	. Karnak	.	.	. 701-667 692	(Pr., *M.*, 33).
Nekhthorheb	. Bubastis	.	.	. 378-361 362	(N., *B.*, 57).
Ptolemy I	. Koptos	.	.	. 304-285 302	(P., *Kop.*, 19).

(The references above are those used in my *Student's History of Egypt.*)

Now there is no difficulty in identifying the positions of these cycle dates with the *sed* festivals, remembering that there cannot be exactitude nearer than three or four years, as that is only a single day's shift of Sirius' rising; and eight years' anticipation, as in Hatshepsut, Tahutmes III, Sety I, and Ramessu II may exactly result from reckoning on by weeks of 28 years' shift, instead of 30. But by these all agreeing together it is more likely that the observations were made farther south, say at Thebes instead of Memphis; the different positions of observation in Egypt would make a day's difference in the visibility of Sirius. When there are long reigns, and no dates of the festival, there is of course no proof in the case. But where there are exact dates, as in the four cases named, we see that they agree with the festivals, with the small anticipation which I have noticed. Under Akhenaten there was no anticipation, and it is just then that Thebes was abandoned, and the observations might have been made farther north. The festival of Uasarkon II seems at first sight contradictory, as that fell in 857 and the cycle of weeks fell in 872 and 842 B.C. But it is called a festival of 12 years at Bubastis; also, I have a base of a statuette of Uasarkon, which names festivals of 12 years. And 12 years before 857 is 869, agreeing with the cycle in 872 B.C.

Now it is very unlikely that these five exact datings should agree so closely to a fixed cycle by mere accident, and that the other cycles should all fall within the required reigns. The probability is that the *sed* feasts belong to these cycles, as we have seen is suggested by the length of the cycle of 30 years and that of 120 years.

180 THE REVISION OF CHRONOLOGY

Looking more closely at the designation of the feast, we see that it is often called *sep tep sed heb*, "occasion, first or chief, of end festival." This has always been supposed to mean the first occasion in the reign; but we see that in the 37th year of Pepy I (which must be his second occurrence of a 30 years' period) he has a *sep tep sed heb*; and Amenhotep II, who only reigned 26 years, has a *sep tep uahem sed heb*, "repetition of the chief *sed* festival," as *uahem* is used in other cases for the repetition of a *sed* festival. These examples show that the adjective *tep* refers to the quality of the occasion, "the chief occasion of a *sed* festival." The chief occasion of a *sed* feast was the 120 years' feast on the shift of a whole month. Let us see how this agrees with these *sep tep* feasts:

	B.C.	Cycle.	Sirius rose.
Pepy I	4131?	4121	Paophi 1.
Mentuhotep II	?	?	?
Senusert I	3439-3397	3402	Pharmuthi 1.
Hatshepsut	1500	1492	Epiphi 22.
Amenhotep II	1449-23	1432	—
Repetition of the *sep tep*, so the *sep tep* was in		1462	Mesore 1.
Ramessu III	1202-1171	1202	Paophi 1.
Uasarkon II	857	—	Khoiak 28.

Thus, by the chronology which we have before reached, five out of six certain dates of chief occasions of the festival were on the first of a month, or just at the close of a month. That of Hatshepsut is the only exception; the lengths of reigns of the XIth dynasty being too uncertain for us to here include Mentuhotep II. If such agreement were mere chance, not more than one in four of such feasts should fall on the beginning of the month; it is thus fair evidence in favour of this meaning of the "chief occasion," when five out of six agree to it. The cause of the exception in the case of Hatshepsut is unknown to us.

By the agreement (within likely variations) of the exactly dated *sed* festivals with the epochs of a weekly shift of the rising of Sirius, 30 years apart, and by the chief festivals falling usually on the epochs of the monthly shift, we have a strong confirmation of the connection of these festivals with the epochs of the calendar.

Thus we conclude that when the beginning of a month shifted so as to coincide with the observed rising of Sirius before the sun, a chief *sed* festival was held; and when each week, or quarter month, agreed to the rising, there was an ordinary *sed* festival.

The name of this festival is, however, "the end festival," literally "the tail festival"; it commemorated, therefore, the close of some period, rather than a beginning. Let us look more closely at the nature of this great feast, a study of which may be seen in MURRAY, *Osireion*. The principal event in it was the king sitting in a shrine like a god, and holding in his hands the crook and the flail of Osiris. He is shown as wrapped in tight bandages, like the mummified Osiris figures, and there is nothing but his name to prove that this was not Osiris himself. Otherwise, he is seated on a throne borne on the shoulders of twelve priests, exactly like the figures of the gods. In short, it is the apotheosis of the king during his lifetime. Now, when we see that the king was identified with Osiris, the god of the dead, the god with whom every dead person was assimilated, we must regard such a ceremony as being the ritual equivalent of the king's death. We have the near parallel in the Ethiopian kingdom, where, as Strabo says, the priests sometimes sent orders to the king by a messenger, to put an end to his life, when they appointed another king in his place (*Hist.*, xvii, 2, 3). And Diodoros states that this custom was forcibly abolished as late as the time of Ergamenes, in the 3rd century B.C. Dr. Frazer has brought together other examples of this African custom. In Unyoro the king, when ill, is slain by his wives. In Kibanga the same is done by the sorcerers. Among the Zulus the king was slain at the first signs of age coming on.

182 THE REVISION OF CHRONOLOGY

In Sofala the kings, though they were gods, were always put to death when blemishes or weakness overtook them. The same custom appeared in early Europe. In Prussia the ruler was "God's mouth," but when ill he was bound to agree to self-immolation with the holy fire.

Another mode of averting the misfortune of having an imperfect divine king was to renew the king, not only on occasion of his visible defects, but at stated regular intervals. In Southern India this period (fixed by the revolution of the planet Jupiter) was 12 years, the same as we find quoted for the *sed* festival under Uasarkon II. At Calicut the custom was that a jubilee was proclaimed every 12 years; a tent was pitched for the ruler, and a great feast celebrated for many days, and then any four of the guests that would, fought their way through the guards, and whichever killed the ruler succeeded him. If none could reach the ruler, then the reign was apparently renewed for 12 years. In Babylonia the custom was to slay a series of annual kings. In later times a condemned criminal was substituted, who lived in enjoyment of all the royal rights for five days before his execution. In Egypt this substitution was familiar in modern times at the Coptic new year, when a mock ruler, with tall, pointed cap, false beard, a peculiar garment, and sceptre in hand, held his court and ruled for three days at his will. This dress was then burnt on the man who personated the king.

All of these instances given by Dr. Frazer (*Golden Bough*, i, 218-31) are summed up by him thus: "We must not forget that the king is slain in his character of a god, his death and resurrection, as the only means of perpetuating the divine life unimpaired, being deemed necessary for the salvation of his people and the world."

We see thus how various peoples have slain their divine kings after fixed periods; or have in later times substituted mock ones, who should be slain at appointed times in place of the real king. Such a ceremony was the occasion of a great festival, fixed astronomically, setting aside all the usual affairs of life.

Now let us learn what we can of the Egyptian festival of the *sed heb*, in view of the festivals which we have been noticing. The essential point was the identification of the king with Osiris, the god of the dead; he was enthroned, holding the crook and the flail, as Osiris, and carried in the shrine on the shoulders of twelve priests, exactly like the figure of a god. The oldest representation of this festival on the mace of Narmer, about 5500 B.C., shows that the Osirified king was seated in a shrine on high, at the top of nine steps. Fan-bearers stood at the side of the shrine. Before the shrine is a figure in a palanquin, which is named in the feast of Ra·n·user as the "royal child." An enclosure of curtains hung on poles surrounds the dancing ground, where three men are shown performing the sacred dance. At one side of this is the procession of the standards, the first of which is the jackal Up-uat, the "opener of ways" for the dead. On the other side of the enclosure of the dancing ground are shown 400,000 oxen, and 1,422,000 goats for the great national feast; and behind the enclosure are 120,000 captives (*Hierakonpolis*, i, xxvi, B).

The next detail that we find is on the seal of King Zer (5300 B.C.), where the king is shown seated in the Osirian form, with the standard of the jackal-god before him. This jackal is Up-uat, who is described as "He who opens the way when thou advancest towards the under-world." Before him is the ostrich-feather, emblem of lightness or space; this was called "the *shed-shed* which is in front," and on it the dead king was supposed to ascend into heaven (see SETHE in GARSTANG, *Mahasna*, p. 19). Here, then, the king, identified with Osiris, king of the dead, has before him the jackal-god, who leads the dead, and the ostrich-feather, which symbolizes his reception into the sky.

The next festival that we have represented is that of King Den, in the middle of the Ist dynasty (5330 B.C.). This shows an important part of the ceremony, when, after the king was enthroned as Osiris, and thus ceremonially dead, another king performs the sacred dance in the enclosure before him. This new king turns his back to the Osirian shrine, and is acting without any special veneration of the deified king (*Royal Tombs*, i, xv, 16). We do not learn any further details from the published fragments of the Abusir sculptures of the festival of Ra·n·user.

There are no more scenes of this festival till we come down to the time of Amenhotep III, who has left a series of scenes at Soleb. There we see that the festival is associated with a period of years, as the king and the great priests approach the shrines of the gods, bearing notched palm-sticks, the emblem of a tally of years (L., D., iii, 84). The ostrich-feather is placed upon a separate standard, and borne before the standard of Up-uat (85). The royal daughters also appear here in the ceremonies (86), as in some other instances.

In the festival of Uasarkon the details are much fuller (NAVILLE, *Festival Hall*). We there learn that the king as a god was joined in his procession by Amen, both gods being similarly carried by twelve priests. We also see that the festival, though it took place at Bubastis, was specially connected with Heliopolis, the old seat of learning and science, and probably an ancient capital.

On a late coffin with scenes of this festival (*A. Z.*, xxxix, taf. v, vi), we see the king (or his substitute?) dancing before the seated Osiride figures of himself; the three curtains of the dancing ground are still shown behind him. There are also offerings being made to the Osiride king, as to a god. The erection of obelisks is performed by a man, who makes offerings to the sacred bull, entitled, "Great God, Lord of Anu,

APOTHEOSIS OF THE KING

Khenti-amenti." The royal sons are shown by three figures, who are seated on the ground before "Upuatiu, the king, Commander of earth and heaven."

The details of these festivals thus agree closely with what we should expect in the apotheosis of the king.

The conclusion may be drawn thus. In the savage age of prehistoric times, the Egyptians, like many other African and Indian peoples, killed their priest-king at stated intervals, in order that the ruler should, with unimpaired life and health, be enabled to maintain the kingdom in its highest condition. The royal daughters were present in order that they might be married to his successor. The jackal-god went before him, to open the way to the unseen world; and the ostrich-feather received and bore away the king's soul in the breeze that blew it out of sight. This was the celebration of the "end," the *sed* feast. The king thus became the dead king, patron of all those who had died in his reign, who were his subjects here and hereafter. He was thus one with Osiris, the king of the dead. This fierce custom became changed, as in other lands, by appointing a deputy-king to die in his stead; which idea survived in the Coptic Abu Nerūs, with his tall crown of Upper Egypt, false beard, and sceptre. After the death of the deputy, the real king renewed his life and reign. Henceforward this became the greatest of the royal festivals, the apotheosis of the king during his life, after which he became Osiris upon earth and the patron of the dead in the underworld.

Such a festival naturally became attached to the recurring one of the weekly shift of the calendar, the close of one period, the beginning of a new age. It was thus regarded not as the death of the king, but as the renewing of his life with powers in this world and the next, an occasion of the greatest rejoicing, and a festival which stamped all the monuments of the year with the memory of its glory.

CHAPTER XIII

THE WORSHIP AT SERABÍT EL KHÁDEM

IN the previous chapters we have noticed the evidences of the nature of the worship in the temple, but it will be desirable to place these together, and compare them with similar customs elsewhere.

The earliest form of ritual that we find here is the burnt sacrifice. I have already described the great bed of ashes far and wide before the sacred cave, amounting to about fifty tons even now, and far more before denudation. As there are but a very few bushes, and those of small size, to be found at the level of the temple, it seems that the fuel must have been brought up from the plain or valleys below, a climb of a thousand feet. To bring up such quantities of fuel, and to burn it away from the habitations and the places of work, shows that some important meaning was attached to these fires, and that they were not merely intended to serve a utilitarian purpose. As the ashes are on the hill in front of the sacred cave, we are bound to conclude that the motive of those who thus came here was religious.

The nature of this fire sacrifice we may gather from the remains. The fires were not large, as the ash is all white, and no charcoal of smothered fires remains. No whole burnt sacrifice was offered, as no calcined bones were found; and some kind of feeding at the place is suggested by the finding of a few pieces of pottery jars and of thin drinking cups. These belonged to the age of the XIIth dynasty.

SEMITIC SACRIFICES

The principles of sacrifices have been carefully studied by Robertson Smith in *The Religion of the Semites*, and we must compare his conclusions with what we find. He states that, "Originally, all sacrifices were eaten up by the worshippers. By-and-by certain portions of ordinary sacrifices, and the whole flesh of extraordinary sacrifices, ceased to be eaten. What was not eaten was burned" (*R. S.*, 370). He also writes of "the *zebahīm* or *shelamīm* —that is, all the ordinary festal sacrifices, vows, and free-will offerings, of which the share of the deity was the blood and the fat of the intestines, the rest of the carcase (subject to the payment of certain dues to the officiating priest) being left to the worshipper to form a social feast. . . . The holocaust, again, although ancient, is not in ancient times a common form of sacrifice, and unless on very exceptional occasions occurs only in great public feasts, and in association with *zebahīm*. . . . When each local community had its own high place, it was the rule that every animal slain for food should be presented at the altar, and every meal at which flesh was served had the character of a sacrificial feast" (*R. S.*, 219-20). It is evident that the nature of the offerings here to the "Mistress of Turquoise" would be festal sacrifices, vows, and free-will offerings, as they were for the purpose of honouring the goddess, with prayers and offerings before the work, and the payment of vows after it. And this is exactly what we find; the fat and blood were burnt and perished, and the ashes remain with the pottery from the social feast of the worshipper.

There might also have been larger sacrifices here. In the celebrated account by Nilus of the Sinaitic sacrifice of the 4th century A.D., the camel was slain and eaten in haste between the rising of the morning star and the sun, "the entire camel, body and bones, skin, blood, and entrails, is wholly devoured" (*R. S.*, 320). "Nilus's Saracens at least broke up the bones and ate the marrow, but the solid osseous tissue must from the first have defied most teeth, unless it was pounded, and so it was particularly likely to be kept and used as a charm" (*R. S.*, 362). Thus we need not expect that any remains of the actual sacrifice, even of large animals, would be found here. If any bones were left about they would be quickly consumed by the hyaenas and dogs, as were all the bones of the animals which were killed for food by our workmen. These offerings were made on the top of the hill in front of the sacred cave, which occupied the highest knoll of rock. This was the essential place of offering in Palestine. The pre-Jewish inhabitants always offered upon high places or hills, and the Jews followed the same custom, which was only enfeebled during the monarchy and not abolished until after the Captivity, as we have noticed in the reference to it by Jeremiah (p. 101). This worship on hills was rarely known in Arabia. "That the high places or hill sanctuaries of the Semites were primarily places of burnt sacrifice cannot be proved by direct evidence, but may, I think, be made probable. . . . In Arabia we read of only one sanctuary that had a 'place of burning,' and this is the hill of Cozah at Mozdalifa. Among the Hebrews the sacrifice of Isaac takes place on a mountain, and so does the burnt sacrifice of Gideon. . . . It is to offer burnt sacrifice that Solomon visits the high place at Gibeon, and in general, 'to burn sacrificial flesh' is the usual word applied to the service of the high places" (*R.S.*, 471). The instances are thus almost entirely Palestinian; but we must remember that the position of the bed of turquoise on the hill-top would fix the shrine of the "Mistress of Turquoise," and this would naturally cause the offerings to be made here, so that this position scarcely indicates a link with Palestine rather than with Arabia.

It need hardly be said that hill temples are unknown in Egypt. Not only so, but burnt sacrifices on high places are utterly unknown there. The only instances of burnt sacrifice are (1) the burnt sacrifice of an ox by Ramessu III (*Hist. Eg.*, iii, 153) at a time when Syrian influence was very strong; (2) the revolution in Egyptian worship by Khufu, when "he forbade them to offer sacrifice," and substituted burnt offerings of clay models (PETRIE, *Abydos*, ii, 9); and (3) the representation of an altar with flames, in the reign of Akhenaten. The burnt sacrifices when found in Egypt are thus essentially foreign, and the system is Syrian and not Egyptian. A paper by DR. KYLE (*Bibliotheca Sacra*, April, 1905) points out how the Egyptian sacrifices were presented on altars, but were never burned in the normal ritual.

The many small altars found inside the shrine were used for burning, as one was deeply burnt on the top; this burnt altar is also quite flat, so that no liquid or semi-fluid could have been placed on it. Such a form must have been for incense, as the small size of it would preclude the offering of anything non-inflammable which required a fire beneath it. This agrees with the Jewish custom of having a separate small altar expressly for the offering of incense. The tall pillar altar in fig. 142 is also a Semitic form (*R. S.*, 186, 469). In Egypt such an altar was unknown; and, though incense was offered very frequently, it was always burnt in a metal shovel held in the hand before the god.

Another specially Semitic feature at Serabît was the dedication of cones of sandstone (fig. 143, nos. 10, 11), of which two were found in the Sacred Cave or the Portico. The sacred cone was the central object of worship and impersonation of the deity in Syrian temples. It is shown on the coins of Paphos in the midst of the temple. At Emesa was the sacred conical stone, the high priest of which, when he became Emperor of Rome, signalised his devotion by taking the name of Elagabalus, and brought his stone and his ritual with him to the capital; and other less obtrusive instances are known. No such sacred stone occurs in Egyptian worship.

The specially prominent system of ablutions, the basins for which occupied the principal courts outside the shrines, we have already dealt with in describing the temple (pp. 105-7). The similarity to the ritual importance of ablutions in the Jewish and Muhammadan systems is obvious. One objection has been raised, that the modern Muslim does not wash in the *hanafiyeh* court, but in side lavatories attached to the courts. We see, however, that the Jew was familiar with the idea of the washing being at the water-tank, as it is written, " Thou shalt bring Aaron and his sons unto the door of the tabernacle of the congregation [that is, inside the court, and nearer than the altar], and wash them with water. And thous halt put upon Aaron the holy garments . . . and thou shalt bring his sons, and clothe them with coats. . . . And he set the laver between the tent of the congregation and the altar, and put water there, to wash withal. And Moses and Aaron and his sons washed their hands and their feet thereat ; when they went into the tent of the congregation " (Exod. xl. 12-4, 30-2). With such explicit statements as a parallel, we must suppose that the *hanafiyeh* tank in the middle of the great court of a mosque was originally the actual place of washing ; while the retiring to private recesses was a later modification. In old days before Muhammad the circuit of the Kaaba might have been performed naked by the Bedawyn, much as they go naked into battle at the present time ; whereas Muhammad ruled that from the navel to the knee the body must be clothed, and the separation of the private washing from the public tank follows naturally on this change of ideas.

The system of visiting sacred places for the purpose of obtaining oracular dreams we have already noticed (pp. 67-70) in connection with the shelters for such visitants ; these were at the side of the road leading to

ABLUTIONS, BETHELS, AND SHELTERS

the temple, as a substitute for which the cubicles were built in front of the temple at a later age. The placing of memorial stones or steles in these shelters was also closely parallel to the erection of a stone by Jacob after his dream. There are no such shelters in Egypt, and no such steles placed at a distance before a temple in Egypt, so far as is known. Nor are these steles like those which the Egyptians placed inside temples or tombs. Those are hardly ever inscribed on more than one face; these are inscribed on all sides. Those were descended from the false door of a tomb; these are descended from stones visible on all sides as memorials. The only perfect inscription on one of these (fig. 80) is an oblation to Hat-hor by the *ka*, or soul, of the chief of the expedition. This is not of the usual Egyptian type of steles, as they always desire offerings for the benefit of a deceased person's *ka*; this is simply an adoration of the goddess by the living *ka*.

The chambers or cubicles prefixed to the temple were certainly holy places, and not mere lodging for officials. The walls were all carved with scenes of offerings and adoration of the gods, of which traces remain, and the position of the chambers joined in one with the temple, and leading up to it along its main access, stamp them as sacred buildings. These would not have been provided for the mere secular use of shelter, and those who slept there evidently did so with religious intent.

The shrine was that of Hat-hor, the "Mistress of Turquoise," as she is always called here (figs. 103, 104, 140, 151-3). To suppose that this was an Egyptian imported worship would be a crude misunderstanding. All the ritual that we can trace is Semitic and not Egyptian; and the Egyptians used the name of Hat-hor for strange goddesses, as readily as the Italian worships his old goddesses as Madonnas of various places and qualities. She was worshipped under 24 different names in Egypt at various places; and there is a list

192 THE WORSHIP AT SERABÍT EL KHÁDEM

of different Hat·hors for each of the 42 nomes of Egypt. That a goddess should be the deity of turquoise accords with the primitive importance of women in the Semitic system, as we have noted on p. 33. "Goddesses play a great part in Semitic religion, and that not merely in the subordinate *rôle* of wives of gods" (*R. S.*, 52). The greatest Semitic goddess was Ashtaroth or Ishtar, and it is easy to see how she might come to be called Hat·hor. She was the horned goddess, as Hat·hor wears the cow's horns; she was the "goddess of flocks and herds, whose symbol and sacred animal is the cow" (*R. S.*, 336), and Hat·hor is shown in the form of a cow. Indeed, some have supposed that the name Hat·hor originated in Ishtar. If, then, the "Mistress of Turquoise" was Ishtar, the Egyptian would naturally term her Hat·hor.

After two or three thousand years of worship at the primitive shrine, the Egyptians introduced side by side with it the worship of the god of the East, Sopdu. He was closely associated with Hat·hor, or rather, probably his symbol, the zodiacal light, was identified with the goddess, as she is called Sopdu at Elephantine and Abydos (LANZONE, *Diz. Mit.*, 863). A smaller shrine and cave for him was carved at the side of the older shrine; and on the later steles he appears worshipped as well as Hat·hor.

We have here before us, then, a Semitic cave-shrine, older than the Mosaic system or any other worship known to us in Syria or Arabia. We see in it a great goddess, probably Ishtar, worshipped alone, and later on associated with a god. Her ritual was that of burnt sacrifices and incense offerings; many ablutions were required of the worshipper; sacred conical stones were dedicated in her temple; and oracular dreams were sought, and memorial stones were erected where the devotees slept. The essential features of Semitic worship are here shown in use earlier than in any other instance.

And we see how much of Mosaism was a carrying on of older ritual, how that movement was a monotheistic reformation of existing rites, and how the paganism of the Jews was but the popular retention of more than was granted in the state religion.

CHAPTER XIV

THE CONDITIONS OF THE EXODUS

SOME considerations which bear on our understanding of the narrative of the Exodus have come before us in the course of the work in Sinai, and it would be neglecting some useful clues if we did not notice them. At the same time, it is with regret that I feel obliged to enter on a ground so full of thorny misunderstandings and controversies. The work of pure historical research cannot, however, bear fruit if the conclusions of it are not pointed out; especially as those conclusions, and the very frame of mind which leads to them, may be equally unacceptable to different parties. Yet, in dealing with the borders of subjects which are so very differently viewed by various schools of thought, it is necessary to occupy some definite position in order to avoid accepting incongruous views. My position here is not that of accepting either extreme, or of attempting to assume or enforce any general frame of views. And though I simply endeavour to ascertain a few historical facts which may serve to delimit the ground of controversies, yet it is needful first to clear my position by showing why I do not accept the assurances of the "certain results" of one school or another as binding axioms in advance of my researches. If it be possible to contract the borders of the wide range of historical probabilities or possibilities within narrower limits, there will follow a clearer view of what may and may not be; and we shall be able to grasp better the nature of the crucial questions that yet need to be solved.

There is nothing more perilous in research than building solely on one class of evidence or one method. Every scientific worker knows how results which are most perfect to all appearance, and which seem of flawless certainty, may yet have considerable unnoticed errors vitiating the very method of research. Such errors can only be detected by following an entirely different mode of approach; and even a far less perfect method has its great value in showing that no systematic errors vitiate the refined accuracy that has been attempted. To the historian this should be all the more obvious, as he has not the questioning of uniform nature to rely upon, which can be repeated indefinitely; but all his conclusions, even in archaeology, are based on such poor fragments of human work as we may possess, without the possibility of cross-questioning his sources; and in historical (or still more religious) documents he is at the mercy of the frauds, mistakes, and confusions caused by the many minds who have handed on his materials. In no subject is the converging of different lines of research more essential if we are to avoid creating mere fantasies. How perilous unchecked literary criticism may be is seen by the dominance of Jerahmeel in a large part of the modern critical literature; by the invention of a "double" to Egypt, a *Musri* which is really only Sinai, a part of the Egyptian kingdom (see *Student's Hist. Egypt*, iii, 282); and by the repudiation of a conquest of Judea by Shishak, and the invention of a reading of "Cushi," in the face of Shishak's own sculpture of his conquest (*Student's Hist. Egypt*, iii, 235). After such recent spectacles of the inability of unchecked literary criticism to deal with historical questions safely, we must receive the conclusions of such a method, or of such critics, as suggestions which may—or may not—be confirmed by other lines of investigation.

It is generally agreed that we have to deal with documents in the Pentateuch which are of various sources.

But the more composite a work is, the less can the credit or age of one part reflect on that of another; no single verse can be accredited or discredited by what goes before or after it; there may be single late interpolations, or whole narratives constructed to embody one earlier fact. The question of the origin of every statement must stand entirely on its own basis: if it can be shown to be reasonable, it must be accepted until disproved; if it can be shown to be in accord with other evidence, it must carry weight, no matter with what it may be linked. Hence no archaeological evidence which agrees with any point of the documents can be discredited because it may not accord with other parts of the document. The archaeological fact becomes the touchstone for discriminating the composition of the document.

Much confusion of ideas has arisen in criticism, as well as in every other subject, by proving irrefragably one position, and then, in the satisfaction of that proof, gliding over very uncertain ground to a conclusion which is only one out of many possibilities. To take a fundamental instance, the first proposition of literary criticism is the composite origin of the Pentateuch; but on the strength of this it is too often tacitly assumed that large differences of age, of beliefs, and of character are thereby to be expected. To test this conclusion, let us look at a parallel case, where we can verify our results. Take a modern composite document—say a hymn-book—and see the effect of its composite origin. Just as in the Pentateuch we have Jehovistic, Elohistic, Deuteronomic, Priestly, and other sources, so in the hymn-book we have hymns which are addressed solely to one divine name or solely to another, without using any second name. To all appearances one hymn-writer has never heard of, or wilfully ignores, the names used by others. On counting over the usage in one collection we find that half the hymns are monoymous, and in this half no less than six divine names are used alone, and without any

VARIABILITY OF PHRASEOLOGY

other, in addressing one of two Persons of the Trinity. Of course, the formal doxologies, which are often later additions, are not included, as they have generally no bearing on the hymn itself. After such a view of the variety to be found in writings of one nation, under one government, in one religious community, and composed within two or three centuries, we can only come to this conclusion :—that a composite body of religious documents, which belongs to a people of mixed origin with diverse ancestral tendencies, may show exclusive use of many different divine names in different compositions, at one period, in one communion, and even by one person. And was not the Jewish race one of the most mixed in its origin and influences?—Bedawyn, at first under Mesopotamian influence, then living among Syrians, then drilled by Egyptians, and lastly picking up various kindred peoples in the desert and in Palestine. As Defoe writes of the "true-born Englishman," so Ezekiel wrote of the Jew, "Your mother was an Hittite, and your father an Amorite, and thine elder sister is Samaria . . . and thy younger sister Sodom" (Ezek. xvi. 45). Among a people of such mixed culture we must expect to find at least as much contemporaneous diversity as we find among ourselves; and the study of the names in modern religious writings shows that not a particle of historical value can be attached to the usage of the various names in the Pentateuch. Other evidence for historical diversity there may be in language, in ideas, and in institutions ; but names alone are of no historical value for discrimination of race, place, or period.

And a view of the hymn-book may also teach us somewhat of the varied views and ideas which actually find place in the standard expressions of one body. Many different ancestral beliefs not only tint the writings, but even antagonistic views find place side by side. While half the hymns are trinitarian, there are yet many of rigid monotheism, with scarcely a trace of dogma. Yet we should be entirely wrong if we credited the writers with intentional antagonism, and certainly the compilers of these contemporary products accept them all as equally suitable. In looking at this variety we have no need to touch on the widely different views of Calvinism and Arminianism, and the many exaggerations that are to be found within the corners of Protestant usages; we may find all the diversity above described within the best-accepted hymn-book of the most organized communion.

That such diversity is no peculiarity of recent times we may see by the varied parties of the early Church, and the opposite statements about faith and works. That such diversities are by no means restricted to Christianity is seen in the deadly dissensions of the four great sects of Islam. And that modern ages have not introduced such contradictions we see in the Egyptian pneumatology, where there are four entirely separate and contradictory theories of the future state; all of these are mutually destructive, and yet all were combined in popular belief, so that religious manuals and customs of a single age unite for the use of one person two or three irreconcilable dogmas.

It is often assumed that peoples were less mixed in ancient than in modern times, and that purer stocks existed in earlier history. But this assumption is baseless, and all the evidence we have is rather in favour of greater mixture. Certainly five different races can be seen living contemporaneously before 5000 B.C. in Egypt itself.

Now from these practical studies of the religious literature of mixed peoples, we see that inconsistencies of usage in doctrine and in language are to be expected in a body of contemporaneous writings of such a people; and therefore, such diversities cannot in any given case be taken as a canon of criticism of relative age. The cumulative force of a long document differing widely in style from another long document, and one being a repetition of the other in substance, gives a reasonable basis for historic discrimination. But the attribution of different ages to passages in a document on grounds of differences in tendencies, usages, or language is a very risky proceeding, in view of the known diversity of the Jewish race and culture, which *a priori* is likely to produce contemporary variation, such as we have seen among ourselves.

Let us look at another line of literary hypothesis. The conclusion drawn from literary criticism is that the first attempt at written history in Jewish hands was in the 9th century B.C. Compare this with what we know of surrounding peoples. It is agreed now by those Egyptologists who have most recently worked on the subject—Spiegelberg and Steindorff—that the Israelites sojourned in Egypt, and that an Exodus from there to Palestine took place. Now any people under the control of the Egyptians must have been acquainted with the elements of Egyptian administration. Of that administration as far east as the border of Egypt, beyond Goshen, we have fortunately two views in the reign of Merenptah, probably a few years before the Exodus. One report of a frontier official states each day the number of people and official despatches passing to and from Syria; the other report gives details of some Bedawyn (Shasu) coming to pasture in the WadyTumilat. Thus the smallest details were being reported in true Egyptian fashion, in accord with that system of minute registration which characterized all their administration. The upper class of the Israelites were incorporated in this administration, according to Exod. v. 14-9, where the taskmasters are Egyptians, who drive on the officers of the children of Israel, and these officers address Pharaoh, "Wherefore dealest thou thus with thy servants? . . . and thy servants are beaten; but the fault is in thine own people." The appointment of the persons responsible for the work from among the race who worked, is in accord with the Egyptian system. And can it be supposed that these officers who were responsible for the amount of work were left without any of the training in writing and registering which was essential to every responsible Egyptian? The probability clearly is that the principal Israelites were educated for their office.

Again, the figure of the leader, Moses, is accepted as historical by Steindorff; and his name is taken as obviously the Egyptian Mesu, "the child," of which a different etymology was constructed in Hebrew. If any value is to be given to the account of his education in Egypt, he must have been well accustomed to writing.

When we look to Syria we have the examples of writing for all kinds of common messages in the tablets of Tell el Amarna and Lachish. Moreover, in the age of the Judges we have in the papyrus of Unuamen (*Student's History of Egypt*, iii, 197) a picture of a petty Syrian chief having annals of his ancestors, recording many transactions, which were brought up at once as evidence in a dispute. To go to lower stages, we see by the frontier report, in the age of the Exodus, there were seven despatches sent into Palestine within ten days (*Hist. Eg.*, iii, 107), so constant was the Syrian correspondence. To descend lower in society, we find most valuable evidence in our work at Serabit. There the Syrian or Arabian miners, who were employed by the Egyptians, put up their own statuettes and tablets on the rocks, engraved with a writing of their own; this system of writing was thus in common use among Semitic workmen at about three centuries before the Exodus. That these were not solely the works of the upper class is seen by their rudeness and irregularity, which shows that the makers could not command the abilities of an ordinary Egyptian craftsman.

In the face of such facts as these the presumption is that Hebrew officials, who had been ordered to render an account of work to their Egyptian masters, would certainly have the familiarity with writing which those masters required in every trivial transaction. That they would prepare no registers of their own people is quite unlikely. No doubt such papyri might be damaged; many might be lost in the confusion of the barbaric age of the Judges: but it is at least probable that some such documents would have been copied and handed down, and would serve as the material for the general editing of their history under the early monarchy. That there was an editing of material then is likely enough; but all the external probability shows that it was an editing of actual documents, and not merely of oral tradition. There is, indeed, also strong internal evidence that written documents were used; for if only oral material was available, could we expect any editor of such to refrain from unifying the usage of names and the varieties of style? Could we expect such an editor to insert so frequently two versions of the same statements only slightly varied? The very duplications and variations of the text in Genesis and Exodus are the strongest proof that written documents were before the editors, and that they were so ancient and revered that no unification was to be tolerated.

But having said this much regarding the assumption made in literary criticism, we should note also the assumptions too often made in the conservative view. Great confusion of thought has resulted from the use of two words, *miracle* and *supernatural*; and the meanings of these words have been so twisted that false standards of thought have arisen. We must remember that a miracle is a thing wondered at, without any reference necessarily to non-natural action; everything we ad*mire* is literally a *miracle*. In the good old words, anything unusual was taken to be "a sign and a wonder," a thing which was viewed as a token of interposition in human affairs, and therefore a matter of astonishment.

202 THE CONDITIONS OF THE EXODUS

But the notion of such a phrase implying non-natural action has only grown up with the modern view of natural law. To most ages of mankind there was no dividing line between natural and non-natural; so much is inexplicable to the untrained mind that no trouble was taken to define whether an event would happen in the natural course or not. And events which were well known to be purely in the natural course were viewed as occurring at a special time in order to influence human affairs. As a Rumanian Jew said to me, "I come from a land where miracles happen every day; there is no difficulty about miracles." His countrymen have still the antique mind, which views events as wonders fitted to their daily life. To transfer the statements and views of people in that frame of mind into the precise phraseology of the present age—when the infinitesimal variations of natural laws are the passion of men's lives—is completely hopeless and absurd. To take a parallel case, unless we renounce volition and proclaim ourselves helpless automata, we must recognise the forces of our wills which control nature. Yet these are beyond the grasp of modern phraseology, and we can no more translate all our mental processes into automatic formulae than we can translate the records of the Old Testament into purely modern views.

The other word which has done so much harm is *supernatural*, because it is used for two ideas which we have learned in modern times to carefully keep apart. When the extent of natural law was but little understood, the difference between *co-natural* action and *non-natural* action was dimly seen and little regarded. To those who have learned to see in so much of nature the systems of definite cause and effect, this difference is vital; and to continue to use one word with two entirely different meanings is an incessant obstacle to thought. The larger question of non-natural action is outside the scope of these inquiries; all of the events in the records which we touch on here are expressly referred by their writers to co-natural action. A strong east wind drives the Red Sea back; another wind blows up a flock of quails; cutting a rock brings a water supply to view; and the writers of these accounts record such matters as wondrous benefits of the timely action of natural causes. If we trace here some of the details of these natural causes, we shall only be following the statements of the records with which we deal.

We have now shown why we cannot accept all the conclusions drawn from the diversities of documents on one hand, or the introduction of non-natural causes on the other hand, as setting *a priori* bounds to archaeological argument. And we may now note some matters which may help us to understand better the documents that we have.

The repeated request to be allowed to go three days' journey into the wilderness in order to sacrifice is apparently unmeaning to one who does not know Sinai (Exod. iii. 18, viii. 27). But the waterless journey of three days to Wady Gharándel impresses itself on any one who has to arrange for travelling. It is so essential a feature of the road that this may well have been known as the "three days in the wilderness," in contrast to the road to 'Aqabah, which is six or seven days in the wilderness. To desire to go the "three days' journey in the wilderness" was probably really an expression for going down to Sinai.

The whole question of the direction of the journey and the position of Sinai has been much disputed of late years. The first step is to see what the direct narrative shows, and then to examine if any other indications are discordant with that. The position of the Israelites is said to have been in Goshen (Gen. xlvii. 27), identified with the western end of the Wady Tumilat, where it begins to branch from the Delta. Next, they were employed in building forts in the Wady Tumilat at Pithom and Raamses (Exod. i. 11). The latter of these towns was their rallying point for departure (Exod. xii. 37), whence they travelled to Succoth, which is the Egyptian *Thuku*, a district near Pithom, presumably east of that place, which is now known as Tell el Maskhuta. Thence they camped at Etham, on the edge of the wilderness, and this is therefore somewhere near the east end of the Wady Tumilat. It seems that this is the district of Aduma, as the Bedawyn of this land in the time of Merenptah asked to pass the Egyptian frontier at the fort of Thuku to go to the lakes of Pithom for pasture. The attempt to connect this with the Adim of the tale of Sanehat is impossible, as after reaching the Sati Bedawyn Sanehat passed on from tribe to tribe, and at last reached the land of Adim, where the prince of the Retennu Syrians dwelt. This implies that Adim was in Southern Palestine.

The Israelites were ordered next to " turn and encamp before Pi-hahiroth, between Migdol and the sea, over against Baal-zephon: before it shall ye encamp by the sea" (Exod. xiv. 2). Of these names only Pi-hahiroth has been found anciently, in Paqaheret, of which Osiris was god (NAVILLE, *Pithom*, pl. 8). The sea we know to have extended up through the Bitter Lakes to near Ismailiyeh, for as late as Roman time this was known as the gulf of Heroöpolis, which is Pithom. Now the only Serapeum or shrine of Osiris in this region is that about 10 miles south of Ismailiyeh, described as 18 miles from Pithom-Ero in the Antonine itinerary. And thus the "turn" which the Israelites took would be a turn southwards, down the west side of the Heroöpolite Gulf. There must have been a Migdol-tower on the hills behind them, and Baal-zephon on the opposite side of the gulf. Here they were "entangled in the land, the wilderness had shut them in," not having rounded the head of the gulf, as would have been expected. This part of the gulf was probably the shallowest, as it is now dry land between the Bitter Lakes and Lake Timsah. Here, therefore, was the most likely place for the "strong east wind" (Exod. xiv. 21) to blow the waters back and leave a dry crossing. Hence the "wilderness of Shur" was the east side of the gulf between the present Bitter Lakes and Lake Timsah (Exod. xv. 22). The name of Shur occurs in two other passages; it is "Shur which is before Egypt" (Gen. xxv. 18), and Hagar is said to flee to Beer-lahai-roi, between Kadesh and Bered, in the way to Shur (Gen. xvi. 7, 14). These show merely that Shur was a district somewhere on the east border of Egypt.

From here they travelled into the desert until they reached a stage of three days without water. Now there is nothing to prove the limits of the desert of Shur, or that they continued in that region, so we can only look round for a stretch of desert road of three days' journey without water. This is the feature of the road from Suez to Wady Gharándel; moreover, they reached bitter water at Marah, next before Elim, where there was abundance. This exactly agrees with the bitter spring in the Wady Hawára, two hours before reaching Gharándel. Neither the narration of Exodus nor Numbers gives all that is found in the other; and in Num. xxxiii. 10 we have the next stage of removing from Elim and encamping by the Red Sea; from this point there were five stages to Sinai. It seems clear that the writer of these itineraries knew the road to the present Sinai well. The description exactly fits that road, and it will not fit any other. One theory has been proposed, that the journey was eastward to the gulf of 'Aqabah, in order to accord with the fact of Midianites being east of that gulf. But the account of the journey cannot agree with that, while there is nothing to prove that the Midianites may not have occupied both sides of the gulf of 'Aqabah. There is further a presumption that the writer did not regard Midian as being inaccessible to asses, as Moses returned thence with an ass (Exod. iv. 20). This is possible up the Gharándel road, but could scarcely be done on the longer, waterless route of the Derb el Hagg. There is no reason to doubt, then, the general truth of the traditional position of Sinai, though the precise mountain may not be certain. The argument that the Israelites would not have travelled down to the region of the Egyptian mines has no force whatever. The Egyptians never occupied that mining district with a garrison, but only sent expeditions; at the most these were in alternate years, and in the times of Merenptah only once in many years. Hence, unless an expedition were actually there in that year, no reason existed for avoiding the Sinai district. Beyond this road to Gharándel-Elim and the passage from Wady Tayibeh to encamp by the Red Sea, we do not here discuss the further route, as I did not visit that district. We should note that a month was occupied by the Israelites in the journey to the Red Sea at the plain of El Márkha (Exod. xvi. 1). We see, then, that the traditional identification of the region of Sinai is what we must accept.

The next point is whether there has been any noticeable difference in the rainfall and water-supply of the peninsula. The extraordinary preservation of the sandstone sculptures seems to show that there has never been a much greater rainfall since 5000 B.C. In many cases there does not seem to have been a single layer of sand-grains removed from the face of the rock in the historic period. Another evidence is that of the Egyptian well at Magháreh, where the water-supply is two miles distant, in a pit sunk about 8 ft. deep in the granite, at the foot of the mountain. No one since early Egyptian days would have been likely to do such a serious work as cutting this well. Yet the wide Wady Iqneh has much underground water at present, as shown by the quantity of acacia trees (fig. 35); and if there had been much more water there would have been a good supply close to the mines, without going two miles distant to sink a well in the granite. Again, had

CLIMATE UNALTERED

there been much more rainfall they would not have been three days without water on the road, as in that case other springs or streams would have existed in the valleys between Ayūn Mūsa and Gharándel. Furthermore, as Elim is the principal water station on the road, we can hardly refuse to identify it with Wady Gharándel; and the account of Elim states that the water there was in twelve wells. Yet now there is a running stream down the valley of Gharándel, where the road crosses it, and there is no need to make any wells. There does not seem, then, to be any evidence of a perceptible change of climate in Sinai, any more than in Egypt; if there be a change, it is rather that of increase than of decrease in rainfall.

If, then, the climate is unaltered, the maximum population must be unaltered. The present population of the whole peninsula is put by Baedeker at 4,000 to 5,000; inquiries made by Mr. Currelly from the officials, and natives discussing the question, gave estimates of 5,000 to 7,000. If we say that about 5,000 is the present population, we may then expect that the ancient population was about this number. Now we read that in Rephidim there was but scanty water (Exod. xvii. 1; Num. xxxiii. 14), and Amalek fought with the invading Israelites. This battle was doubtless to defend the good water-supply of Wady Feirán, the most fertile oasis of all the peninsula. The general belief of Christian and Arab writers was that Pharan was Rephidim; and this is certainly the position which the natives would choose to repel an invading tribe. The battle is expressly said to have been very nearly equal (Exod. xvii. 11); and this implies that the Israelites were not in greater force than the great rally of the Sinaites to defend their homes.

We see, then, that by the general condition of the small water-supply on the road and at the wells, and by this crucial case of an almost drawn battle against some 5,000 people—we cannot suppose that the Israelites were much more than this number. As bearing on this, observe the size of the region from which they came. The land of Goshen was at the mouth of the Wady Tumilat, a district of about 60 or 80 square miles, as it did not include the great city of Bubastis. This is about a hundredth of the whole Delta; and this, on the basis of the population before the present European organization, would hold about 20,000 people. This estimate is reckoned on an agricultural basis, whereas the Israelites were a pastoral people—" Thy servants are shepherds, both we, and our fathers" (Gen. xlvii. 3)— and, therefore, a much smaller population than 20,000 would be all that the land could support. Thus we may put the case in brief by saying that not more than about 5,000 people could be taken out of Goshen or into Sinai. If the number of the population stated in Exodus and Numbers were correct, the 600,000 men would imply at least 3,000,000 people, which would equal the whole population of the Delta on an agricultural basis; and there is no trace of a depopulation of the Delta at this period.

We should, then, inquire what might have led to so large an overstatement of the numbers of the Israelites. To assert that this is merely a fanciful exaggeration is to cut the knot by an arbitrary hypothesis. To assert that nothing was written down till the 9th century B.C., and so there was no authority for the facts of the 13th century, is directly in the teeth of the Egyptian training of the Israelites, and of the common use of a Semitic writing in Sinai as early as the 16th century, which we have found at Serabît. The utmost that literary criticism can prove is the composite nature of a collection of documents edited in the 9th century B.C., or, as is asserted for this portion, as late as a priestly writer in the post-exilic age.

Criticism cannot disprove the existence of earlier documents, and we are at least free to inquire whether

CENSUS LISTS

any part of the web of documents of the 9th or 6th centuries may not descend directly from earlier writings.

Our question may, then, be put to these documents. Can they show us why such an exaggeration of numbers should have arisen? Is there any emendation of a likely error which could yield a probable form for the original record? The total number stated in Exodus is the result of the census of separate tribes stated in Num. i; and a later census given in Num. xxvi is stated to belong to the close of the wanderings. These two census lists are, then, the real crux. They stand as follows:

	Num. i	Num. xxvi
Reuben	46,500	43,730
Simeon	59,300	22,200
Gad	45,650	40,500
Judah	74,600	76,500
Issachar	54,400	64,300
Zebulun	57,400	60,500
Ephraim	40,500	M. 52,700
Manasseh	32,200	E. 32,500
Benjamin	35,400	45,600
Dan	62,700	64,400
Asher	41,500	53,400
Naphtali	53,400	45,400

The only difference in order is that Manasseh and Ephraim are interchanged, as marked M. and E.; but probably the names only are reversed and not the numbers, as they agree more nearly with the earlier census as they stand. The difference between the two lists is only what might be expected in one or two generations of fighting and intermarrying. Simeon is largely reduced; but if that tribe had much fighting, for every man killed, a woman and her children might be absorbed by remarriage into some other tribe. At least, there is no obvious falsification shown by the comparison of the lists.

But is there any cause for the great exaggeration common to both lists? Look closely, and the hundreds

210 THE CONDITIONS OF THE EXODUS

are seen to be very peculiar in each list. There is not a single round thousand, there is not a single 100, 800 or 900; and the greater part of the numbers fall on 400 or 500. Let us put them in the order of the digits in the hundreds; we then have:

Manasseh	32,200	22,200	Simeon
Simeon .	59,300	64,300	Issachar
Benjamin	35,400	45,400	Naphtali
Naphtali .	53,400	53,400	Asher
Issachar .	54,400	64,400	Dan
Zebulun .	57,400	32,500	Ephraim
Ephraim .	40,500	40,500	Gad
Asher .	41,500	60,500	Zebulun
Reuben .	46,500	76,500	Judah
Judah .	74,600	45,600	Benjamin
Gad .	45,650	52,700	Manasseh
Dan .	62,700	43,730	Reuben

It is evident that the same cause, whatever it may be, equally affects the hundreds in each list; there is almost exactly the same distribution of the digits. Let us take both lists together and arrange the digits to see their distribution more clearly; here is their total:

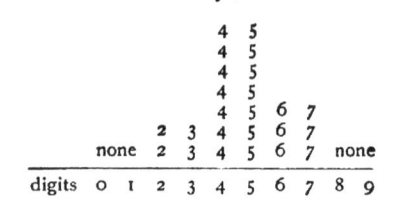

```
                    4   5
                    4   5
                    4   5
                    4   5
                    4   5   6   7
              2  3  4   5   6   7
        none  2  3  4   5   6   7   none
       ─────────────────────────────────
digits  0  1  2  3  4   5   6   7   8   9
```

To any one accustomed to physical questions of numbers, this is overwhelming evidence that the hundreds have here an origin entirely independent of the thousands. The probability of such a distribution occurring by chance has more than a thousand to one against it.

If the hundreds are independent, what then are the

ORIGINAL FORM OF CENSUS

thousands? The word *aláf* has two meanings, "a thousand" and "a group" or "family." Hence the statement in words of 32 *aláf*, 200 people, might be read as 32,200, or as 32 families, 200 people. The statement is ambiguous, and is one which is, therefore, peculiarly liable to corruption of the original meaning in editing an earlier document. We have at least a working hypothesis that the "thousands" are "families" or tents, and the "hundreds" are the total inhabitants of those tents.

Let us test this hypothetical emendation. If it were not true, the thousands then need have no connection with the hundreds, and so the hypothesis would fall through by the absurd results reached for the number of people *per* tent. For instance, if the numbers had no relation in their original meaning, we might find 22 tents for 700 people, or 32 *per* tent; or, on the other hand, there might be 76 tents for 200 people, or 3 *per* tent. What we do find, however, is a much closer relation between them as follows:

	Census 1.			Census 2.		
	Tents.	Nos.	Per tent.	Tents.	Nos.	Per tent.
Reuben.	46	500	9	43	730	17
Simeon.	59	300	5	22	200	9
Gad	45	650	14	40	500	12
Judah.	74	600	8	76	500	7
Issachar	54	400	7	64	300	5
Zebulun	57	400	7	60	500	8
Ephraim	40	500	12	32	500	16
Manasseh	32	200	6	52	700	13
Benjamin	35	400	11	45	600	13
Dan	62	700	11	64	400	6
Asher.	41	500	12	53	400	8
Naphtali	53	400	8	45	400	9
	598	5,550	9·3	596	5,730	9·6

Now the poorest and most short-lived tribe must have averaged five to a tent—two parents, two children to succeed them, and one grandparent, or a child to allow for juvenile mortality. The richest tribes may have had two parents, four or five children, both grandparents, making eight or nine, and herdsmen and servants of the Hebrews and of the mixed multitude who went up with them. Thus the largest numbers here *per* tent are not at all more than might be found in a rich tribe, while the smallest numbers *per* tent are just the minimum possible. The test, then, of the practicability of this view of tents and hundreds is quite satisfactory.

The next test is how far this gives a reasonable view of the changes between the two lists. The diminution of a tribe may be due either to the men being killed in fighting, or to a greater proportion of females being born; in either case, the daughters marrying into other tribes diminished their parental tribe. The only tribes in which there is a difference beyond what is likely to take place by ordinary variation are Simeon, Manasseh, and Dan. Simeon, who was concerned in the plague of Baal Peor (Num. xxv. 14), fell off from 300 to 200, but their tents diminished from 59 to 22. This implies just the consequence of the small families shown by the average of only 5 *per* tent in the first census; in such small families they often had only a single child, and so the number of tents rapidly diminished, even more so than the total number of people. In Manasseh there is a rapid rise from 200 to 700, and in Dan a fall of 700 to 400. An interchange between these would account, then, for the only discordance between the two lists; if there were a large proportion of daughters in Dan married into Manasseh the only serious difference would be explained. But we should remember that this general agreement depends on the hundreds, which have not hitherto been supposed to have any meaning. If the numbers were those of a late census, or were a mere invention, there would be no reason against finding tribes of 100 or 200 having 800 or 900 in the later census, or *vice versa*. The fact that the hundreds of the two lists are so generally in agreement (the average

EVIDENCES FOR CENSUS

variation of a tribe being only 150), shows again that the hundreds have an independent meaning, and are connected.

The third test is to see how far this will agree with the conditions of the country which we have stated. The present population is 5,000 or 6,000, the ancient population was about the same, and the Israelites who fought on equal terms with them must have been also of about the same number. This estimate of 5,000 or 6,000 just agrees with the totals we here reach, 5,550 and 5,730 in the two census lists. The result, then, is exactly in accord with the known historical conditions, both of the number that could leave Goshen and the number that could live in Sinai.

To recapitulate the evidence for this view :—(1) The hundreds group in so improbable a manner that they are proved to be independent of the *aláf*. If, then, the *aláf* are families or tents, and not thousands, (2) the number *per* tent is within reasonable limits, when it might easily have proved absurd. (3) The variations between the census lists are reasonable, when they might have been wholly absurd in the hundreds without being noticeable in the present text. (4) The totals of the hundreds give a population in exact accord with the physical circumstances. Until some other causes can be proposed which shall be likely to produce such grouping of hundreds, and such correlation between hundreds and thousands, as we here see, this reading of *aláf* must stand as the original text, with a probability of a thousand to one in its favour.

The only argument against such a conclusion that I have yet heard is that, if certain high numbers are explained by a likely corruption here, then we are bound to explain all other impossible numbers. This is an entirely illogical requirement. There may be many causes for high numbers appearing, and one cause must not be expected to explain all instances. Moreover, by the very principle of freely proposing interpolations and changes in a composite document, every part of it stands independent as regards its credibility. This corruption of a perfectly rational text may have been the cause of the introduction of other corruptions of numbers in order to agree with it. If a man makes a mistake and writes yards for feet in a survey, he may try to make things agree by other alterations, but it would be quite absurd to require that every error which resulted from this should also be yards for feet. The literary hypothesis of a web of documents woven together in the 9th or 6th century B.C., or any other time that any one chooses, cannot in the least invalidate the internal evidence of any one document being far older than that age. And the internal evidence of perfectly rational and harmonious documents having, by a trivial misunderstanding, resulted in producing the present text, is overwhelmingly probable.

Though we must repudiate any liability when it is demanded that one form of corruption must also be required to explain all other difficulties, yet we may see how far this double meaning of *aláf* will be applicable to rendering families for thousands elsewhere, and how far the original form of the census is in accord with other statements.

The account that at first Moses judged all disputes might be possible with about 5,000 people, but would be very improbable with a much larger number. The appointment of 70 elders is also well in accord with our results. The Egyptian system (in the mining camps) was to name each tenth man as a chief, who looked after the other nine. Now, allowing that 5 tents and under were not represented by a separate elder, there would be 58 elders, each with 10 tents, and the 12 sheykhs of the tribes would make up 70. The account of the rebellion of Korah is insoluble as regards the numbers of the party, and (as we shall see) there is good ground from our present conclusion to regard that as a late account. But the statement about the plague which followed is easily in accord with the original census, the dead being 14 *aláf* and 700. This would mean that 14 families entirely perished out of 598, involving about 130 people, and 570 more died singly in other families (Num. xvi. 49). The next plague that occurred was on the mixture with the Midianites, when 24 *aláf* died (Num. xxv. 9), or 24 tents were swept off. Now Simeon was concerned in this (xxv. 14), and we find that Simeon's tents are stated to have diminished from 59 to 22 between the first and second census. So far we have dealt with all the numbers of the period between the two census lists, and we see that the use of *aláf* for families gives a reasonable explanation of the high numbers in this period. The numbers in later accounts are not in our present view, though some general notice will be taken of them farther on.

Now let us turn back and see some other conclusions which follow from this view. The census of the Levites is not included in that of the twelve tribes. Their numbers of males are given as:

		Num.	30 to 50 yrs.	Num.
Gershonites	7,500	iii. 22	2,630	iv. 40
Kohathites	8,600	28	2,750	36
Merarites	6,200	34	3,200	44
Total stated	22,000	39	8,580	48
First-born of all Israel	22,273	43		

Now it is obvious that these figures of the Levites cannot be treated by supposing the *aláf* to be families. Nor is it possible to take them in accord with the larger numbers of the received census lists; as 22,273 first-born males to 603,500 men would imply that only one man in 13 had any children, even if the eldest being a girl excused counting any boy in the family. On neither the received nor the original form of the census can these figures be accepted as possible. But though this statement is impossible at the time of the wandering, it was certainly possible somewhere between that and the monarchy, when numbers were much larger. To have 22,000 first-born implies that number of families and of men, and so a whole population of about 100,000, or half that if an eldest girl prevented a boy being counted as first-born in a family. The most reasonable view would be that this is a document of the age when there were about this number of Israelites, probably soon after entering Palestine. If so, this would date the establishment of the Levites; and they would be the result of a dedication of first-born, perhaps copied from the sacrifice of the first-born of the Canaanites, among whom the Israelites were then mingling. Whatever date must be assigned to the Levites, it is clear that their census precludes their belonging to the age of the Exodus. There was, then, no tribe of Levi at the time of the census, but it was created as a priestly caste at a later age. This agrees with the narrative of Korah's rebellion being a later passage, as is suggested by its numbers being insoluble. The introduction of it here may have been due to the supposition that it was connected with the plague (Num. xvi. 49), which might well be an original fact of the desert life, as we have noticed.

This will now react further on another question. That the original census was of the Exodus period as stated is the only view possible, as at any time in Palestine the numbers must have been much larger, growing (by accretion more than generation) up to the census of the monarchy, which is none too large for its position. We come, then, to the point that at the Exodus there was no such tribe as Levi; and in the blessing of Jacob (Gen. xlix) each tribe is blessed separately except Simeon and Levi, which are conjoined, pointing to Levi having been only thrust in later by coupling him with his brother Simeon. Moreover, the "blessing" is the worst curse in the whole, and is certainly not that to be allotted to the important priestly tribe. Levi has only been put in here from the recognised association of

THE BLESSING OF JACOB

Simeon and Levi (Gen. xxix. 33-4). This stamps the blessing of Jacob as being not later than the establishment of Levi as a caste, early in the Palestine period. And we can take this blessing back still earlier, as in it Joseph is one tribe, and not yet separated, whereas Ephraim and Manasseh are both present in the Exodus census. This points to the blessings belonging to the Egyptian period. It may be objected that the house of Joseph is mentioned in the conquest of Palestine (Judg. i. 22, 35); but both Manasseh and Ephraim are distinct in the same passage, and the natural reading would be that the whole of their contiguous territory was occasionally regarded as that of Joseph. We have a similar case in England, when we speak of the Saxons in contrast to Angles, Jutes, Mercians, and Northumbrians, all parties of the same invasion; yet when dealing with detail we distinguish Wessex, Sussex, and Essex. So Joseph might be collectively used for Manasseh and Ephraim when acting together, long after the two tribes were recognised as separate.

Now that we have reviewed the earlier statements of the numbers up to the later census, and seen that nearly all of them may be due to the same misunderstanding, we may turn to the great question of how the later high numbers are to be regarded. We are by no means bound to account for them because we can account for the earlier detailed census lists. But the important difficulty faces us, in any case, as to how a body of 5,000 people could conquer their way into Canaan, and how they could become a large people under the monarchy. The royal census lists are by no means in agreement. That of David gives 800,000 for Israel and 500,000 for Judah as the number of fighting men. But under Rehoboam, Judah and Benjamin together were 180,000 men. It seems probable that the former census was really that of the people, and the latter census of the men only. If so, 180,000 men out of 250,000 males implies that a man was in the levy for $\frac{18}{25}$ of his life—that is to say, was enrolled at 14 and struck off at 50, which is quite reasonable. If, then, the whole population of the early monarchy was 1,300,000, this would imply 130 to the square mile, which we may well compare with 200 *per* square mile in Switzerland. The present population is just about half of this amount, but the land is notoriously under-manned in modern times. The census of David, then, as referring to the whole population, would be in accord with that of Rehoboam, and with the conditions of the actual country.

What about the growth in the intermediate times? And how did 5,000 people force their way into Palestine? The Egyptians had been raiding Palestine severely and frequently, and their last clearance of it before this was in 1194 B.C. This accounts for no gold having been found by the Israelites except at Jericho, farthest from Egyptian plundering. Also, it shows that all powers of resistance had been broken down, and Palestine was ready to be a prey to the desert tribes, just as Italy was a prey to the Lombards after Justinian had harassed the Goths to destruction. That 5,000 people, or say 1,800 fighters, should effect a lodgment in a wrecked land like Palestine is not more astonishing than 8,000 desert fighters of 'Amr forcing their way to the heart of Egypt, inhabited by 5,000,000 men and garrisoned by a Roman army. There probably was, however, some joining of desert tribes from the Jethroites and others, which increased the numbers. In Palestine, therefore, within 8 or 10 generations at the most, we have to look for an increase of apparently 1 to 200. Even apart from accretion, they may be supposed to have increased rapidly in a land far more favourable than that which they had been trained to live in. In England the population has been known to grow at the rate of 5 times the number in a century; the shorter generations among the Jews might increase this to 7 or even 10

GROWTH OF THE ISRAELITES

times the number in a century, for an average marriage age of 20 instead of 25 would make this increase. So in two centuries we might find a natural growth from 1 to 50 or even 100, without exceeding conditions actually known. It seems, then, that, roughly speaking, the formation of the population of the early monarchy was one-third or perhaps half due to natural increase, and the rest was caused by accretion and conquest. The absorption of the Gibeonites, the placing of the ark with a Gittite, the presence of a Hittite among the captains of David, who also had a bodyguard of Cherethites, Pelethites, and Gittites, all show how much the numbers of Israel were enlarged by accretion.

The basis for considering the numbers in the accounts between the Exodus and the monarchy is, then, a nucleus of 5,000, rapidly increasing and accreting during two centuries until it became 1,300,000. This growth probably began during the residence in the fertile plains of Moab; in that land all the tribes who were against those whom the Israelites fought would naturally ally themselves with Israel. Thus there is no impossibility in 40,000 entering Palestine as stated (Josh. iv. 13). The 3,000 attacking Ai, of whom 36 were slain, is very probable; so also is 5,000 in the second attack. And 12,000 for the whole population of Ai and Bethel—men and women—is very likely (Josh. viii. 17, 25). Nor, again, is any number less than 10,000 likely to be slain in a crushing defeat of populous Moab, when it was subdued under the hand of Israel (Judg. iii. 29), in a great reversal of their positions. By this time we may well expect that the Israelites numbered a quarter of a million. The mention of 10,000 men with Barak (Judg. iv. 6) can be no exaggeration in so great a battle. One of the largest numbers is the 120,000 slain out of 135,000 (Judg. viii). This was a great panic rout by night, when the enemy was trapped in his flight at the fords of Jordan, and under such conditions in any history of great tribal wars, extermination is to be expected. The attack on the Israelites, who numbered several hundred thousand, would hardly be by fewer than 100,000, and the extermination which follows on defeated tribal movements is well known to us in Caesarian times, and the wars of the Goths, Huns, and Lombards. There is nothing impossible, or even improbable, in the numbers involved, though the account of the fight may leave out of view much of the decisive conditions which were pre-arranged, and pin our attention to the incident of Gideon. The last great fight before the monarchy, the civil war with Benjamin, demands a roll-call of 426,000 of all Israel (Judg. xx. 15, 17), which is rather less than under David and Rehoboam. One in ten of Israel are said to have been levied, or 40,000, to fight 26,000 of Benjamin. The extermination of a defeated tribe under these conditions is not astonishing. The only figures that we need set aside are those of the 22,000 and 18,000 Israelites who were slain. They seem to be due to a confusion between the numbers engaged (40,000) and the number slain. But the totals of men involved, and the catastrophe which befell the tribe, are not surprising.

Now we have seen how much there is in the general cry about the great exaggerations of the numbers of the priestly writer in Judges. So far as what may be called national documents go, there is nothing impossible. The large amounts of all of them fall well into place in the history of a people who rapidly expanded their political growth up to the time of the monarchy, when we find a total stated which accords with the conditions of their position. The question of the setting of the history, of the editing of it, and the introduction of collateral records and traditions, is quite outside of our scope here. But we see that the supposed discredit of it as being radically encumbered with exaggeration is quite untrue, and that there are no large numbers which disagree with the known conditions of the history.

THE EGYPTIAN VIEW

We thus come to the same position as we did in the examination of the census lists. The internal construction of those lists bears witness to an original form which is consonant with the known conditions. And such an original form could not be invented in later ages, nor would the present form, if invented, bear the peculiar relations of numbers from which we can discriminate the original document. That original form must, then, have been transmitted in writing from the age of the Exodus. The accounts of the numbers involved in the later history are also consonant with it, and therefore have probably also been transmitted. We are led thus to the view of a body of historical written documents having descended to the times when they were incorporated with the traditional material. At what time that was done our numerical and archaeological evidence does not at present show; and we may leave critics to suit their own inclinations regarding this, without their conclusions in the least affecting the results which we have here reached.

Finally, let us sketch out what a cultivated Egyptian would have said of the Israelites' history, so far as we can at present understand it. "A Bedawy tribe had wandered down from Mesopotamia to Southern Palestine. There they had connections with various neighbouring peoples, Moabites and Ammonites, whom they looked on as akin to themselves. A dearth in Syria made them emigrate into Egypt, where a part of them stayed on as settlers in the eastern border of the Delta. These were employed by Ramessu II on his public works. The attack on their kindred Israelites in Palestine by Merenptah made them restless, and this was encouraged by other Bedawyn coming into the same district. One of them who had been well educated by us had run away into the desert, and settled in Sinai. Seeing that the land there was sufficient to support his kindred, he came back and tried to get permission for them to go on a pilgrimage to a sacred mountain. This was refused; but many troubles of bad seasons, and a plague at last, so disheartened us that, in the confusion, some thousands of these tribes escaped into the wilderness. They safely crossed the shallows of the gulf, but a detachment of troops following them was caught and swept away. After settling beyond the reach of our government, and living in the desert for many years, they took advantage of the victories of Ramessu III in Palestine. After he had completely crushed the Amorites and other inhabitants, these Israelites (with many of their kindred tribes) pressed in to occupy the bare places of the land, and succeeded in taking many of the towns. In the half-empty land they quickly increased, and took into their alliance many others of the kindred peoples, so that in a couple of hundred years they became as many as half of our own Delta people. So soon as we had recovered from our divisions in Egypt we resumed our place in Palestine, and took a large quantity of gold from the king of these Israelites, as we had done before from all the Syrians; but since those times the Assyrians have hindered our former suzerainty." Such an account may be only one side of the truth, but it is somewhat the way in which the old-established kingdom of Egypt would look on this episode.

We have now seen how far some fresh information from Sinai, and some new examination of our documents, may lead us in understanding the history of Israel. Probably no party will be content with such results; but such seem to be the data for future dealing with this question. Only a few more points have been cleared of the many which are yet in darkness. But if we can at least gain some clearer view of the limits of uncertainty, of the problems yet to be solved, and of the checks from other sources which limit the bounds of speculation, we shall not have made this review of the subject in vain.

In conclusion, it only remains for me to add that the work of this last season in Sinai has served to put in order the Egyptian inscriptions previously known there, and to fix their places and connections which were uncertain before. It has also uncovered many new inscriptions, and the whole of these two or three hundred inscriptions have been drawn full-size in facsimile, and many of them photographed. The publication of these will form the largest body of texts from any year's work. The plan of the Temple of Serabít was but vaguely known before. Many more walls have been found, and also the Shrine of the Kings; and the whole is now fully planned and modelled, and the architectural details restored as far as possible. The district of Serabít has been planned for the first time, and the positions and character of the mines recorded. The considerable mass of offerings found in the Temple includes the finest portrait known of Queen Thyi. The fuller records now obtained have enabled us to reconstruct the old Egyptian organization of the expeditions. And the views that result from these studies regarding the early Semitic ritual, restore what has hitherto been only a matter of conjecture. Never has a working party been more closely occupied with copying, and seldom have the resulting conclusions been of greater interest.

CHAPTER XV

TOR TO MAGHÁREH

BY C. T. CURRELLY

WHILE Professor Petrie and the others of the party entered Sinai from Suez, I went up to Quft, and brought our fellahin and Ababdeh workmen across the Arabian desert to Qoçeyr. It was somewhat difficult to get the fellahin to face the terrors of the desert, especially as one village received a special warning, by the appearance of an *Afrit*, that the expedition would end in disaster. On reaching the Red Sea we experienced some difficulty in securing a boat; but Mr. Snellus, of the Umm Ruz Gold-mining Company, kindly sent us his steamer and took us across to Tor.

The present village of Tor consists of a very few buildings, which are grouped around a monastic house belonging to the Convent of St. Catharine. It has a poor and rather dilapidated appearance. The houses are of mud brick and timber, and are by no means well built.

Although there is hardly anything that could be called a harbour at Tor, it is possible for boats to put in. In the narrow and reef-bound gulf of Suez the north wind frequently blows for several days at a time, so that it may require a month or two for one of the flat, keel-less boats of the Red Sea to beat up against the wind to Suez. It became profitable for the traders to unload the merchandise at Tor and convey it by land. Tor was a station in Phoenician days, and had its period of greatness during the middle ages. But the only things of the past that remain are an arch and some walls, nearly buried by the sand; these belonged to an early monastery, which was abandoned in the fourth century. Our road led straight up the desolate G'aa desert. On the right the mountains rise, ridge upon ridge, a great tumbled mass of ruddy stone that culminates in the majestic Serbál. It would seem as if all the other mountains were placed but as a setting, that the grandeur of this great mountain might stand revealed. On the left a line of low, rocky hills cuts off the G'aa from the sea.

The G'aa is a gravel-strewn waste littered with boulders, and here and there dry beds of little streams. Along these there are many hard-leaved bushes, which have developed the power of using, and parting with, as little water as possible. If rain falls plentifully during the winter, a good deal of vegetation appears, which soon dies down, and the valleys are dotted with dead bushes.

When we camped I was anxious to see how the Bedawyn prepared for the night. As soon as we had uncorded the loads, the camels were fed. Maize and ground beans were mixed up into a very thick paste and put into the nose-bag—a rare treat, for, as a rule, the Bedawy camels get little beyond what the valleys provide. The Bedawyn told me that in winter a camel can go nearly two months without water, but that in hot weather need of water for so long a period would cause it to die. The Ababdeh said their camels would go from 15 to 30 days. When the camels are being worked, the Bedawyn try to give them a drink once every four days. One reason why a camel can do with so little water is that there is very little evaporation from the skin. Behind the ears, however, there is a growth of long hair, and during the excessively hot weather I have seen this very wet; no doubt it was developed to keep the base of the brain cool. A donkey can go for one day without water; but on the second day he sickens, and on the third day he dies. These Bedawy camels are much lighter than the heavy camels of Egypt and of the Arabian desert; and while the Egyptian camel can carry as much as seven or eight hundred pounds' weight, the Bedawy camel can barely carry a weight of three hundred pounds.

The saddles are not removed when the camels are turned loose for the night, perhaps in order to be ready for flight in case of a raid; but as the Ababdeh take off the saddles at night, I am inclined to think that carelessness is at the bottom of the custom of the Bedawy. One thing in the saddle interested me. It is held on with the double "cinch," and the straps that fasten the cinch to the saddle are tied exactly as the Canadian ranchman ties his. The saddles also closely resemble one another, and the connection seems clear: the Canadian learned his way from the Texan, who copied it from the Mexican, who took it from the Spaniard, who had the Moor for a master, and the Moor copied the Arabian, or perhaps the Arabian learned the method from the Libyan country.

The Bedawyn make a little fire with the roots of dead bushes as soon as they encamp, even in the hottest weather, which serves to provide coals for their pipes; for the Bedawyn are always smoking. In Sinai they grow a little tobacco. The pipes are made of pottery, and fitted with a stem about 30 in. long, so that the bowl of the pipe may rest on the ground; this part of the bowl is usually protected by a band of sheet copper. Two little chains are attached to the stem. One supports a long, needle-like cleaner, and the other a pair of forceps about 7 in. long, with which the smoker picks up coals from the little fire. A very great deal of charcoal fumes must be drawn into the lungs, as the smoker invariably inhales the smoke.

On the following morning we started at sunrise—the camels rarely stray more than half a mile away from the camp—and early in the day we reached the first little oasis. This is in a little bay, that opens off from the G'aa into the great hills. Some moisture soaks through the ground and feeds a few palms, and there is a small well with about two cubic feet of water. These palm-trees differ in appearance from those of the Egyptian palm-groves, where every leaf-stalk is worth a farthing, and where the leaf is cut off as soon as it ceases to be of use to the tree.

Some few miles further up there is a pass which leads into a grand amphitheatre of hills, with an oasis of great beauty, around which the rocks rise to a great height—in some places perpendicularly—and give a feeling of extraordinary grandeur to the scene.

On the second day we camped about three o'clock in a little dry stream-bed, the bank of which gave us welcome shelter from the cold wind. Our reason for stopping here was that the sheykh said that there was not another place for miles that was level enough for a man to lie down. About half of the men were immediately set hunting for flints, for many palaeolithic chips lay about, and I soon chanced upon a very good implement, fig. 163 (the largest). We picked up many others, all of which were much the worse for wear. One of the men came upon four flakes about five inches long that fitted together; the edges were unrubbed, and they lay within a few yards of each other. Sir John Evans considers that these could not positively be called palaeolithic, but that no one could say they were not, as the patina was very rich. This seems to me to be a very important find in relation to climatic changes in the country. Here were flakes lying in the bottom of one of the lowest valleys, just as they were chipped from the nodule of flint so many thousands of years ago. Had there been much moisture during any of the time these certainly would have been covered over and rocked about till the edges would have lost their sharpness.

What I saw later confirmed me in the view that there had been practically no climatic change during the period in which neolithic man had been in Sinai.

On the third day we left the G'aa, and turned to the right into the Wady Feirán, from which we passed to the left into the Wady Mukatteb. Here are numerous Sinaitic inscriptions, which have been copied and published ; so we did not stay, but made our way into the Wady Sídreh and the Wady Magháreh, where we met Professor Petrie and the others of the party, who were already at work copying the inscriptions.

CHAPTER XVI

GEBEL MUSA AND THE NAWAMIS

BY C. T. CURRELLY

WHEN the work of clearing the temple at Serabít el Khádem was nearly completed, a Bedawy returned from Suez with less than half of the supplies that he had been ordered to bring, and so we had to start two or three days earlier than we had intended, in order not to be short of food. Some time before, it had been arranged that I should go to the monastery of St. Catharine, on behalf of the Egyptian Research Account, to dig over the rubbish heaps, and Mr. Frost and I therefore started at once. Yusuf, the son of the Ababdeh sheykh, hurried on to Tor, in order that he might meet us at the monastery with more provisions. Professor Petrie kept a third of the men to finish the work at the temple.

We went down the valley at the head of the Wady Umm Agráf, in which we had been encamped, crossed a high pass, and then dropped into the Wady Ramleh. I was surprised at the number of flowers that were growing in this valley. Many small plants in the dry sand of the ancient stream-bed had very little root, and must have drawn their nourishment from the air. In places there were also large plants in bloom.

As we ascended to the water-shed we came to a Bedawy cemetery, in the centre of which was a tomb which, according to the Bedawyn, was erected to a very holy sheykh of the past. The building was roughly constructed of blocks of untrimmed granite, with roof beams of timber, which had evidently been brought from Suez, and which supported the flat granite slabs that formed the roof. The sheykh lay in a rough wooden box covered with white cotton, on which was a quantity of long, grass-like weed. The chief ornament of the tomb was an ordinary Egyptian lantern for carrying candles.

The other graves either had stones placed at the head and at the feet, or a little pile of stones was made over the grave, and a quantity of the votive weed was entangled among these stones.

The Bedawyn told me that the dead are buried without delay if possible, but never at night. A sheep is then sacrificed and eaten, and another is sacrificed ten or thirty days later. It is a frequent custom for the friends to leave a little hand-mill and a wooden mixing bowl by the side of the grave, so that the dead man may not lack suitable implements to prepare his food.

The second day we proceeded up the Wady Labweh. The country was more rolling, and travelling was easier than along the canyon-like wadys. While we were crossing the water-shed into the Wady Berrah it began to snow heavily. The effect on the Egyptian fellahin and the Ababdeh was strange. These men of Upper Egypt knew nothing of snow, and they came running to me, crying, "What is it, master?" An Abādi who was walking near me said, "Why, the Lord is sending us rice from heaven." They caught the flakes on their black cloaks, tasted them, laughed, and were much excited. I wish I knew the story of that fall of snow as it will be told around the Ababdeh fires in a few generations. May not this be the manna which fell from heaven when the children of Israel moved along these valleys?

The explanation that manna dropped from the tamarisk and other bushes does not seem to me to meet the case. There are few bushes, and their dropping fruit would make no impression on the minds of people accustomed to food-bearing trees. I think we must agree that the manna came down from the sky, not from low bushes. The attributes of the manna as given in Exod. xvi. are: that it was a small round thing, ver. 14; like coriander seed, white, ver. 31; and that it melted in the sun, ver. 21; it would pack, ver. 18; it came down from heaven, ver. 4; and it tasted like wafers made with honey, ver. 31. According to the account in Num. xi. 8, it tasted like fresh oil. Evidently both writers made it the most delicious thing they knew of, but they differed in taste. Snow answers to all the attributes described, excepting the one of food, which naturally comes as an addition. That is what the Abādi felt at once. We were short of food, the Lord is merciful, and we were going to the Holy Mount, where the camel of Muhammad placed a foot before his ascent into heaven. If the story of manna does not reflect the startling effect produced upon the Hebrews by the sight of snow, the only other explanation that appeals to me is that the story itself is literally true. No people would speak of food that fell from bushes.

The second evening we camped near the Wady Erthameh, and on the morning we continued in the Wady Berrah for a time, and then turned to the left through some very rough country, and by way of the Wady Soleif dropped into the Wady esh Sheykh. The higher hills were covered with snow, and there were fine effects of the light shining through the mists and the rain. Towards the close of day we reached a grove of tamarisks that promised a fire and warmth. Clouds hung low down on the mountains, and as they floated past pieces were torn from them by the jagged sides of the mountains, and held till another grey mass came along and took this waif of cloudland into its folds. These mountains are very impressive, especially as one approaches Mount St. Catharine and the Gebel Musa. The following day we went through the pass that leads out of the Wady esh Sheykh, the grandeur of which strongly impresses the traveller. The mountain sides come close together, rising to a great height on either hand. Their magnificence is enhanced by the soft red colouring of the stone, and by their absolute barrenness.

In the Wady esh Sheykh there is the tomb of the Neby Saleh, the prophet Saleh. It is a small, ugly stone hut, and, like all the sheykhs' tombs in Sinai, it makes no pretensions to structural beauty. Prayers said at the tomb of a sheykh are specially effective. I have never seen a Bedawy pray in the orthodox Muhammadan manner, although some of them do so; but once, when riding through the Feirán, I saw a young Bedawy suddenly drop on his knees and throw out his arms in the direction of a sheykh's tomb.

During the long talks we had around the fire, I tried to find out if the Bedawyn knew anything of their religion. Only one thing seemed well fixed in their minds—namely, that all of their own faith were going to heaven, and all others were not, a theological position in which they do not stand alone. They seemed to know very little of the Prophet, but accept the position that Muhammadanism was forced on them by war. It is the boast of the Sudánys that they accepted it at the written exhortation of the Prophet.

A few stories were known. I was told how the prophet Harun made a golden gazelle—the local animal—which the people worshipped, and that for his wickedness he was driven into the wilderness, where he died of thirst. One of our Egyptians told a strange mixed story of the prophet Issa (Jesus Christ). Our Lord said that He should not rest in the ground, which caused His family to place His coffin on a camel. This they turned loose, and it is still marching through the air.

I did not succeed in getting any trace of a flood story. All the Bedawyn I questioned said that they had not heard of such a flood. The fellahin, however, have the rainbow story that we have received from the Hebrew Scriptures.

The creation story was told by one of the Egyptians as we were sitting round the fire, and the Bedawyn said they knew it; but I think it was because they were anxious to make me feel that they knew something. Howa sprang from the ground, and then came Adam, who seems to have been both her son and her husband. From these came the human race.

The same fellah then told another story that differs from our account. The prophet Abraham turned Ishmael and his mother from the tents. Together they wandered forth into the desert, till the water-skin was empty. Gradually the boy grew weaker and weaker. At last he could go no further. Twice had his mother left him and rushed eagerly on, to find that the soft blue pool she saw in the distance was but a mirage. Sadly she came back to face the death she now knew to be inevitable, but could not remain near him in the final agonies. That she might not see him die, she went a short distance away; but she turned her eyes, however, to the spot, and saw him raise one foot and bring it down on the earth, when suddenly a spout of water sprang from where his heel had struck. She rushed back and put some to his lips.

During our marches the Bedawyn had three meals each day. Usually they have but two. Very early in the morning they awake and put some more bushes on the fire. The youngest boy who can be expected to do anything grinds some maize with a small hand-mill. The next youngest mixes the crushed meal with a little water in a wooden bowl. A flat stone is made very hot, and the pasty meal having been spread about an inch thick on the stone, this is either propped up against the fire or covered with live coals. Coffee is made by roasting the berries in a small, long-handled ladle, and then grinding them to powder in a heavy pot with the end of a stick. The pot is grasped firmly with the feet, and the stick is worked vigorously with both hands. The coffee-pot is placed on the fire, and the coffee well boiled. This is usually taken in the afternoon. After the breakfast the group around the fire smoke and talk till nearly noon; then those who are still awake roll over and find a comfortable position for their midday sleep. They collect later in the afternoon, and smoke and chat till evening. A few of the younger ones gather enough dry bushes to keep the fire going during the night; then the same meal of maize and salt is taken, and they smoke and chat far into the night. If there be a fair number of them around the fire, talking may be heard all through the night.

Nothing can be more aimless or lazier than the life of the average Sinai Bedawy. Camels, sheep, and goats are driven into a valley. A little girl or a boy stays with the sheep and goats, and some one manages to know where the camels are. The men and women sit by the black goat's-hair tents and do nothing. At rare intervals a tent has to be made. The weaving is done on a loom placed on the ground. I was told that the woof is of wool, and the warp of thick, coarse black goat's-hair. The tent is pitched with a roof almost flat. Bushes piled against its sides give additional shelter. The front is left open.

The men wear a white cotton garment, which reaches to half-way between the knees and the ankles. This is loose, and has a curious sleeve running to a sharp point, which reaches almost to the ground. Sometimes the two points are tied together behind the wearer's neck. A very wide girdle of leather is purchased in Suez. The wide girdle and the long shirt emphasize a boy's athletic figure. Over the cotton garment a woollen cloak, or a blanket, or both, are worn. During cold weather a sheep-skin is usually worn. It is untanned, and not made up in any way. The two hind legs are tied together, then it is slung over the shoulders, and shifted to windward as occasion requires. They all wear sandals of raw dudong-skin, which is very hard and will wear for two or three months. A week's hard walking will, on occasion, cut through a strong pair of our boots.

The Bedawy is fond of weapons. He usually carries a dagger of the Palestinian pattern—a seven-inch blade curved at an angle of about 135 degrees, sharp on both edges and with a thick brass handle. The swords are commonly old cavalry blades. They sling the scabbard around the neck by a cord. Guns of different descriptions are carried, usually flintlocks and matchlocks, and a few old flintlock pistols, and even some revolvers are seen. A bandolier is made of plaited leather, which passes over one shoulder and is joined and fringed off much like a sergeant's sash. To this at intervals cartridge holders are attached, either of brass or wood; and usually there is a pouch on the bandolier, for the flint and steel and the powder-soaked cotton for lighting a fire. The steel often hangs loose from a chain.

Although their country is admirably suited for the wearing of skins as clothing, the natives are so lazy that they will sooner be cold than take the trouble of tanning the hides of their sheep and goats. They know how to tan, however, and make some braided ornamental leather-work for their camel-saddles. They also weave very good saddle-bags of wool, and prepare dyes of many colours from herbs and seeds that grow in the valleys.

The women wear a dark-coloured garment about seven feet long. A girdle around the waist holds it up so that the bottom reaches to the feet, and the part above the girdle falls in a fold. A head-shawl is invariably worn. A veil is usually worn, also. I have come suddenly upon tents and have found the women veiled. I have seen some attempts at embroidery on the dresses, but the work

was very poor. In the little silk-work I saw the mise
able aniline-dyed silks of commerce were used.

A marriage or a death makes a break in this mon
tonous existence. The men marry when they grow
beard, and the girls when they are considered to l
women, about the age of fifteen. Although wives a
purchased, I could not hear that the price for a girl
fixed, as is the custom among the Ababdeh. The mː
who dies is at once buried, as stated above. If l
leaves a family, the boys go to his people, and the gir
are taken by the mother's relatives. A widow is n
as valuable as an unmarried girl.

In the case of murder the idea of the blood-feud st
holds good; but I do not think they would kill t
murderer, as the feud may be compounded for a su
between £50 and £100. Anyway, the feud is n
carried on further than the persons immediately co
cerned. There is also an old custom whereby a murder
may be bought off from punishment inflicted by t
Government, by the payment of a hundred camels. Th
is, of course, a very serious affair, and means that t
whole tribe contributes towards raising the sum require

I found the Bedawyn of Sinai mean, thieving, ar
lying. They would bully when they could, and crinȝ
and whine if disagreeable things happened. I certain
have never met men who seemed to me to possess so fe
qualities with which one could have any sympath
There are certainly exceptions, and one finds some wh
are not bad. I mentioned some whom I considered to l
better than the others to one of the older monks, who hɑ
been forty years at the monastery. He said, "They a
all pretty much the same, if you know them long enougl
the ones you name are a little more clever." Our men
antipathy to them was very marked, although they can
to the country favourably disposed towards the Bedawy

Late in the afternoon we arrived at the valley in whiȼ
the monastery is built. The cold was intense, and tl

water in our tanks froze to the thickness of over an inch during the night.

Mr. Frost and I had an interview with his Eminence the Archbishop, and obtained permission to dig over the rubbish-heaps outside the monastery. As the next day was Sunday, we were able to attend a service in the church. It was very long and tedious, and we both suffered from the bitter cold. Monday was an important Muhammadan festival, and the men asked for a holiday, that they might pray in the mosque on the top of the mountain.

The Gebel Musa is one of the sacred places of Muhammadanism, and I expected to see numbers of Bedawyn assemble for the festival; but not one came. Our men went up and said their prayers with a feeling of the solemnity of the occasion. Rather to my surprise, I found out that their prayers were addressed to the prophet Moses; and one of the men told me his prayer was a request to Moses to take away his craving for the expensive tobacco.

A considerable quantity of rubbish had been thrown over the wall of the monastery, and we were hoping that some information might be obtained by digging over the pile. One day was enough, however, to show that there would be nothing, for the earth was moist right through to the underlying rock, owing to the melting snow, which saturates the soil. Anything like papyrus or parchment must be destroyed. Besides, the rubbish pile was very small, and I found out that everything had for generations been put into the garden.

The monastery building is a large rectangular fort, built of hewn granite (see no. 164). Tales are told of Justinian sentencing the architect to death because the building is commanded from the heights behind. This hardly looks as if Justinian thought that the burning bush was on this identical spot. Formerly the only entrance was over the wall, and people were pulled up in baskets by a windlass. Now there are little footholds, where one may climb some distance up one of th[e] buttresses to ring a bell, on doing which an outer gate i[s] opened. This leads to a court, and a small door give[s] access to the monastery. The centre of the convent i[s] occupied by the church, the appearance of which i[s] marred owing to the fact that it stands below the lev[el] of the pavement. On the side of the courtyard opposite t[o] the entrance to the monastery is a gate that leads to th[e] garden. In it is the crypt (see nos. 165, 166), in whic[h] the bones of the monks of many generations lie, neatl[y] piled together, with the skulls in pyramids, to the le[ft] of the pile of smaller bones that is shown in the phot[o]graph. At the door is the skeleton of an old porte[r] Stephanos, in a silk shirt with a skullcap. A numb[er] of boxes near the door contain the remains of notables [of] the past; while an iron chain still holds together bone[s] of two Indian princes, who dwelt in the mountain[s] chained together in such a way that both of them coul[d] not at the same time lie down to sleep. The photograp[h] of the garden is taken from the door of the crypt.

During our first visit to the monastery it was neces[-]sary for me to remain with the workmen. On my secon[d] visit I was able to ascend to the top of the Gebel Mus[a]. Stones have been arranged in such positions that the[y] form a rough series of steps, from the bottom right to th[e] top of the mountain. A short distance from the bottor[n] there is a little spring of water, where it is said th[e] Virgin appeared to the monks, when they were ascendin[g] the mountain for the last time before they abandoned th[e] monastery, which had become unbearably infested witl[h] lice. The Virgin promised to remove the plague, an[d] on their return the monastery was found to be free fron[n] them. Some distance higher up there are two archway[s]. Years ago pilgrims confessed at the first arch, and gave [a] certificate of absolution to a monk at the second gateway[,] who then allowed them to ascend to the top of the moun[-]tain. Near the summit, on ground that is more o[r]

164 THE MONASTERY OF ST. CATHARINE, FROM GEBEL MUSA.

165 THE MONASTERY GARDEN.

166 THE CHARNEL HOUSE.

167 VIEWS FROM NEAR THE TOP OF GEBEL MUSA.

168 VIEW LOOKING TOWARDS THE TOP. 169 CHAPEL OF ELIJAH.

less level, stands the chapel of Elijah, built on the spot where he is said to have lived during his stay in Horeb (see no. 169). The view from the summit of the mountain is imposing (no. 167). The surrounding mountains rise in peaks very close together, and the altitude enables one to appreciate the form of Mount St. Catharine, to the south.

The gulf of 'Aqabah is seen in the distance, but there is no view of the Red Sea. A chapel, which is badly built, is used for services when pilgrims are at the monastery. It consists of blocks that once formed an earlier and evidently a better chapel. There is also a tiny mosque a few feet from the church, where on very rare occasions a Muhammadan may say his prayers. We were fortunate enough to see the sun sink in its full splendour into a great bank of cloud.

The easiest descent is by a road that Abbas Pasha made, when he hoped to build himself a summer home on the top of the Gebel Musa. This road is partially in ruins, but it is much safer to descend this way than to try to scramble down the rocks in the dark. As we walked slowly, it took us about three hours to descend to our camp, which was pitched by a little spur that runs out into the plain of Er Raha. The monks point out this as the place where Aaron made the golden calf.

As soon as it was evident that nothing was to be gained from the rubbish heap of the convent, we left for the valleys to the north and the east, to see if anything could be found during the few days we still had in the peninsula. We returned by way of the Wady esh Sheykh and by the tomb of the Neby Saleh, turned to the right, and passed just south of the Gebel Umm Luz. The Palestine Exploration Fund map shows old copper-mines near the Wady Ragaita, and we decided to examine these first.

In the Wady Ahmar we came to a little spur that runs out into the valley. This had been made use of for a smelting place. The wind, blowing either up or

down the valley, would give a good draught, and alon[g]
the crest of the hill some smelting had been done b[y]
the aid of pits. These were sunk usually from eightee[n]
to twenty-five inches deep, and stones were built in[to]
a rough low wall around the edge of the holes. T[he]
size of these holes varied, some being a few feet acros[s]
others larger. The form also varied very much. [We]
could see little indication of a definiteness in their for[m.]
The crest of the little spur was covered with a thi[ck]
layer of ashes, but we found only one bit of slag.

We carefully cleaned out and planned the pits. Gre[at]
numbers of flints of good workmanship lay about i[n]
the ashes; and a considerable quantity of quartz an[d]
pieces of stone hammers were found at intervals. T[he]
quartz showed the bulb of percussion, a mark of inten[-]
tional fracture; and some shell fragments, and o[ne]
unfinished shell bead, made one think that bead manu[-]
facture had been done on the site. A short distan[ce]
from the spur, in a little valley at right angles to t[he]
Wady Ahmar, is an open pit from which a quantity [of]
copper ore had been dug.

This ash bed was very hard to understand. [If]
these were pits for making test-smeltings for coppe[r]
it would be intelligible; but in that case, what was t[he]
use of the flints? In the middle of the site there w[as]
a cairn of stones, piled over the body of a man. Tw[o]
beads were found, and proved to be ordinary Egyptia[n]
beads, well known after the XIXth dynasty. One wa[s]
of wound glass, with the two ends of the glass threa[d]
showing plainly, and the other was a double-eye bea[d.]
The illustrations (nos. 170, 171) show the good wor[k]manship of the flints. The drills in particular a[re]
slender and long in the point, and the triangular dril[ls]
are very even along their sides. Some are certain[ly]
arrow-heads, and it is probable that the leaf-shape[d]
implements may have served a similar purpose.

When we were returning to camp in the Wad[y]

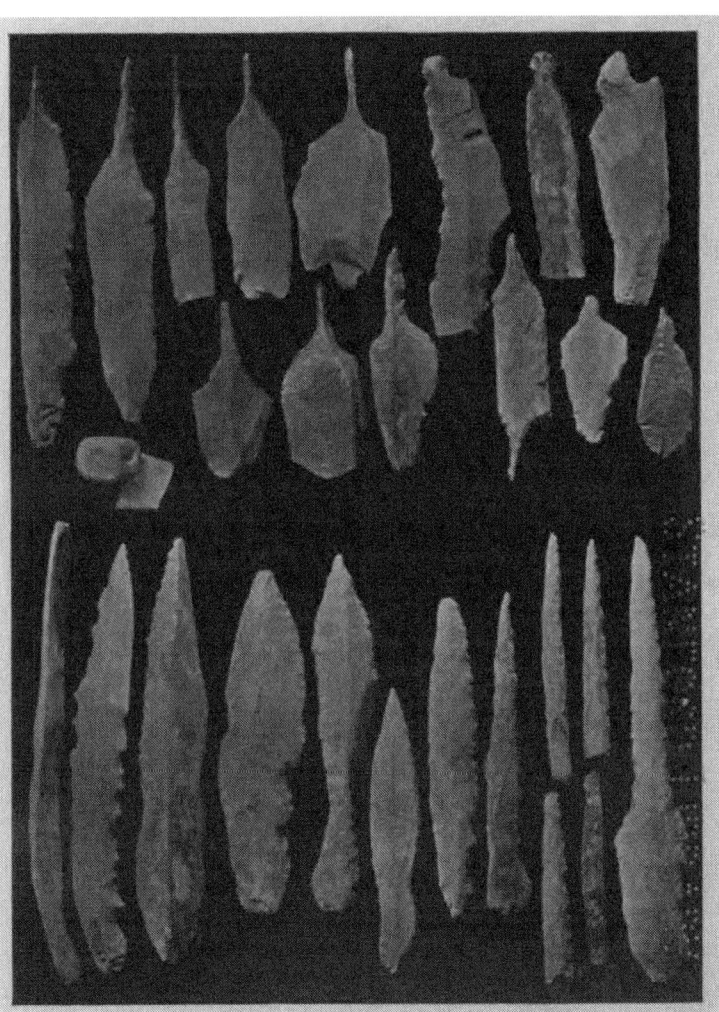

170   WORKED FLINTS FROM THE WADY AHMAR.

WORKED FLINTS FROM THE WADY AHMAR.

Ragaita, one of the Ababdeh told a fellah that he could take a short cut to the camp, and so save himself the longer walk by the very winding wadys. This was unknown to me. About seven in the evening, Yusuf, the young Abādi sheykh, came to say that this man had not reached the camp. We waited a short time, and then a search was organized. I tried to make our Bedawyn camel-men join in the hunt for the missing man, but without success. They said he was in God's hands, and refused to move, even when offered a considerable sum if they found him. All the Ababdeh were out through the night, and when we reassembled in the morning a second man was missing. It was the worst country I have ever seen for twisted valleys, and the Ababdeh said that it was a chance if the men could be found. A fast had been proclaimed, and it was with some difficulty that I could make them take a meal, in order to keep up their strength for the hunt. It was even harder to get the fellahin to eat, though they had done little more than walk up and down and shout. "What?" they said; "can we eat when two of our number are lost?" I found out subsequently that they had had a large meal in the night, when the Ababdeh had been away. During the night we tried to follow Moses' plan for pointing out the camp, and fired the bushes of the valley; but the wind was so high that it beat down our pillar of cloud and of fire, so that it could not be seen outside our own valley, and bushes carried to the hill-tops were almost blown away.

When it was daylight I went to where the man had left the Wady Ahmar, to track him if possible, and had just followed his trail over one hill when I heard a shout, and a man came running towards me with the news that the two lost men had arrived in the camp. I tell this incident because I cannot in the least understand it. The two men found that they were hopelessly lost. They had never been in the country before, and it was very dark; yet in the dark both went straight to the only water-hole within a day's march. They did not know where it was, and, before they were lost, had no idea of the direction in which it lay; yet from different points their senses led them straight to it, when quickened by the immediate prospect of death. They knew that some one must come for water, and our camel-men found the two sitting by the well. I talked it over with them, and found that they were very frightened, but had no idea how they had reached the water.

Our next camp was in the Wady el Gow, at its junction with the Wady Taliyeh. At the junction of the Wady el Gow and what the Bedawyn called the Wady es Sened—though hardly in agreement with the maps—stood a number of rather poor stone circles; and in the Wady el Gow a considerable number of what must be tomb circles. The inner circle of stones was in one case only 37 in. × 53 in., and with a little stone pavement around it and stones placed on end (see plan, no. 173). Another kind of monument had a straight row of stones placed on end, with another row more or less parallel to it; the two ends were rounded, and then the whole space had been filled in with large stones. This had the appearance of a burial-place, but we did not find any bone remains. In the strangest structure the space was only from 12 to 15 in. wide. Two rows of stones were still standing, and the structure was built with considerable care. The under-layers were placed lengthways, and the upper stones at right angles to the long axis.

Near the stone circles there was a smelting furnace (see no. 172). A hole was dug in the earth to a depth of 30 in., and around it a circular wall was built up to a height of 26 in., and above that a thinner wall was continued. The outer face of the wall was continuous. This made a little ledge where the thinner wall began. There was also a ledge of 11 in. where the first layer of

172   SECTION OF A FURNACE.

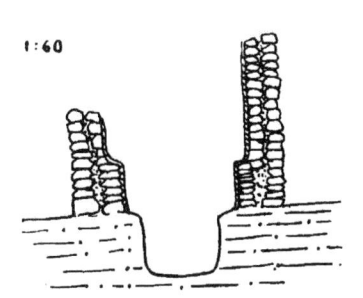

173   PLAN OF A TOMB CIRCLE.

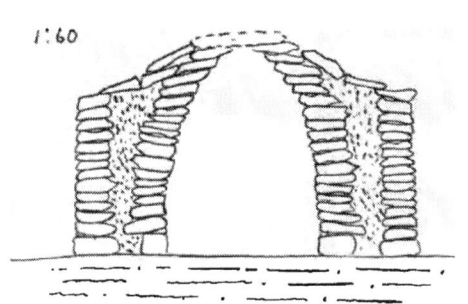

174   SECTION OF A NAWAMI.

175   METHOD OF BINDING THE CHISEL-SHAPED ARROW-POINTS.

176.

177. 178.
THREE VIEWS OF THE KAWABIS NEAR THE WADY SOLAF.

stones came above the pit in the ground. Two blast-holes were left—one a short distance above the ground, and a second one, 15 in. higher up, at right angles to it. The first hole, which pierced the thicker part of the wall, was 10 × 11 in.; the second one, which pierced the thinner part of the wall, was 15 × 21 in. The thickness of the wall measured 40 in. in the lower part, 18 in. only at the upper. The top of the wall was broken away in places, and showed it was built of double rows of stones filled in with gravel. The lower part of the furnace had a green glaze over it, in which particles of quartz were embedded.

We came back from the Wady el Gow and entered the Wady Umm Alawi. Near the Wady Nasb we found a large number of circles of stones bordering smooth bits of ground, and to a slight extent in little terraces. We dug over these, and found a considerable depth of ashes, and in some of the spaces was a quantity of fragments of hand-made pottery, and one worked bit of stone. At one end there was also a pile of stones, under which we found some bone fragments and some more of the hand-made pottery. These, I think, were hut circles.

We soon entered the Wady Nasb, and, passing through a thick, jungle-like swamp and many tamarisk-trees, we came on some beehive-shaped Nawamis—see section, fig. 174, and views, nos. 176-8. The section will explain the construction. The work is done with great care and evidently to measurement. These tombs are of very early date; the contents are shown of full size in no. 179. We found only one stone bead, disc-shaped, of carnelian, much like those known in the prehistoric period in Egypt. The copper instruments are also of very early form. Sir William Ramsay, who tested them, says that they are practically pure copper, with very slight traces of tin. The piece of twisted wire was for a time a puzzle, but I have since ascertained that such wire was known during the prehistoric period in Egypt.

A very characteristic ornament is the shell arml
which was cut from a large sea-shell. With the
ception of one Egyptian bead of carnelian, all
beads are of shell. The majority are cut from lai
shells, but there are many small shells with holes bor
through their ends. The arrow-heads are of the fl
chisel-shaped type, not particularly well made (no. 175

These tombs were grouped along the sides of
wady in the manner shown in no. 177. The doorwa
are a characteristic feature of the tombs. They are t
small to be of any use; but it was necessary to plac
flat stone inside to prevent small animals from enterii
The door is always on the west side, but varies a f
degrees in direction. I noticed that the doors point
to Mount St. Catharine, and that the doors of the tom
in the Hebran pointed to Mount Serbál.

At the head of the Wady Umm Gorfain there i:
large group, which we dug over next. In these
measurements were surprisingly accurate, when
rough nature of the uncut granite is considered.
twenty tombs the wall varied in thickness to the ext
of only an inch or two.

At the head of the Wady Umm Dhelleh there i:
large stone circle, of the regular hut-circle type. Ins
the ring of stones the ground is raised several inch
The doorway has two large stones, one at each sic
but the other stones vary considerably in size. I
not see as many of the hut circles as I did of the tor
circles, which were very numerous. No very lai
stones were used in the construction of either hut
tomb circles. The largest stones were in some grou
of stonework that I could not quite explain, unless th
were cemeteries with the tombs very thickly grouj
together. The finest examples of this last class are in
Wady Hebran. The stones have almost the appearai
of a fortress from outside, but inside they look like circ
touching each other, and piled over with loose stones

179 SHELL BRACELETS AND BEADS, FLINT ARROW-HEADS, AND COPPER TOOLS FROM THE NAWAMIS.

CHAPTER XVII

MOUNT SINAI AND GEBEL SERBÁL

BY C. T. CURRELLY

WHEN we reached the coast at Tor we found a letter from the Minister of Public Works asking me to go again to the Wady Magháreh to remove the sculptures and inscriptions from the cliffs. The Bedawyn were destroying these important records one by one, and Professor Petrie had represented to the authorities that if these sculptures were not removed to Cairo at once it was very probable that all would vanish. I wrote immediately in answer that, as soon as the work at Tell el Maskhuta was finished, I would return to Sinai and do my best to get the different inscriptions down from the faces of the cliffs on which they were carved.

For about a month we were at Tell el Maskhuta, clearing out and planning the fortress that Dr. Naville long ago identified as the Pithom of the Hebrew bondage. When the work for the Egyptian Research Account was finished, the majority of our men returned to Quft, but a few were kept, that they might assist in removing the inscriptions from the cliffs of the Wady Magháreh.

In the beginning of May Mr. Frost and I returned to Tor, which was now swarming with pilgrims. The quarantine enclosure is divided up into large compounds. Each alternate space is left empty, in order to isolate the different companies of pilgrims, who live during the period of quarantine in rows of tents or huts in their own enclosure, without having any access to the rest of the camp. A picket of soldiers is placed at the gate to prevent any disturbance or attempt to break bounds.

After a furious row over the camels we started from Tor for the Wady Magháreh. I told the Bedawyn that we wished to go by the Wady Hebran, and they agreed to take that route. I soon saw, however, that they had no intention of going that way if they could avoid it, and were trying to push on beyond the entrance to the Wady Hebran, so as to make it troublesome for us to force them to return and take the route on which we had agreed. Fortunately, I noticed which way they were heading, and insisted on their taking the proper direction. This route is longer than that going straight up the G'aa, and the Bedawyn are fond of bargaining for the longer route and taking people by the shorter one. The sides of the Wady Hebran are very steep, and the scenery is wild and grand. Once through the fine gorge at the mouth of the wady the eye is relieved by a number of palms and other vegetation, seen at intervals. We camped in a grove of tamarisks.

At the Wady Ithmed the Wady Hebran turns to the north almost at a right angle, and, rapidly rising, becomes a rough, broken stream-bed, down which the water must have flowed in rapids and cataracts when it was being denuded. The road is rather difficult for some distance as it approached the water-shed that divides the Hebran from the Feirán. Here are a great number of Nawamis, many of which are of excellent workmanship and proved to be in a good state of preservation. I noticed that here also these beehive-shaped tombs had their little doors pointing to the mountain. The saddle-like ridge was regularly dotted with them. The descent into the Wady Feirán is much less rough than the pass on the Hebran side. The Feirán valley runs in a north-westerly direction parallel with the G'aa for about thirty miles, and then turns to the south-west, almost at a right angle, and descends to the sea. It is the grandest wady

THE CENTRE FOR DEFENCE

I have seen. The cliffs are so high and so near the perpendicular, the turns are so sharp and unexpected, and in the part under Mount Serbál the vegetation is so luxuriant, that it suggests fairyland.

When we were encamped on the plain of Er Raha we felt how impossible it was for even a few hundred people to remain in so barren and cold a place; and we were anxious to examine the Wady Feirán, to see how far it would appear likely to have been the camping-ground of a people who remained in one place for nearly a year.

To me it seems that there is only one possible route from Egypt, and that the Feirán is the only place where the Hebrews could remain with their flocks during the time of their organization into a people. If they remained in the Feirán, the Gebel Serbál is the mount from which the Law was delivered. From my own experience in moving a body of men through the country, I am sure that the whole question is one of water-supply. This must determine the route and the camping-places. In Num. xxxiii there is a list which seems to give the names of the places when the Hebrews camped during their march. There appears to be little difficulty in identifying the places as far as the camp by the Red Sea, ver. 10.

The important question is, to which mountain they were journeying. As far as I know, every one who has been in Sinai agrees that the Amalekites must have assembled their tribes in the Wady Feirán, for there is hardly another place where the tribes could risk the serious undertaking of a muster in force. Such a muster not only means the calling of the inhabitants, who are scattered over thousands of square miles, into one valley, but their donkeys, goats, and sheep must come with them. This difficulty appears the greater when we consider that the majority of the wells are at least a day's journey apart; and that from sixteen to forty camels can drink one well dry. The first few families who reach a well on the road exhaust it; and after that, when the people from the greater distances come, they find the wells near the meeting-place empty, and must hurry on to reach the central point before they or their flocks die. If there is a large quantity of water at the rendezvous, the watering can be managed; but if thirty people and flocks arrive together, at even a comparatively well-watered place, they will drink up the available water-supply at once. There are springs around the Gebel Musa, and, for some part of the year, there is a considerable supply of water in the Wady Nasb; but the valley is about a day's journey from Er Raha, and it is one thing to procure water when families are scattered in familiar territory, with little to do other than to attend to the wants of themselves and their flocks, and quite a different matter when men may not scatter, and when bodies of fighting men must be moved. Few of those who have written on this question have considered how very slowly sheep travel, especially if they are forced on day after day and are compelled to feed as they go along.

The tribes of Sinai may have assembled at another place; but I am sure they could not scatter again, as they would have used up the water-supply behind them, and the wells take long to refill. To-day, as it must always have been, the Wady Feirán is the one centre of the peninsula. Though it is territorially in the possession of the Welad Saidi, men from all tribes have some hold on it, in the form of rights concerning a tree or some bit of land. Hither all come at certain times, for this is the great home of the peninsula. Here there is water in plenty—clear, sparkling water from the rock and to sit on the cool, damp ground in deep shade can be appreciated only by those who have journeyed along the stifling valleys, where the blistering rocks throw back the hot rays of the sun. This is the home of the tribes. In the Feirán they must have assembled, an before it taken their stand when their country was threatened. If they won, they remained sure of water for themselves and their flocks till sufficient had collected in the wells to allow them to scatter. If they lost, the survivors in small bands must have struggled to the north-east across the Tîh.

This fixes one place in the Biblical narrative—Rephidim. It must lie near the Feirán oasis on the way from Suez, somewhere in the Wady Feirán, the Wady Mukatteb, or the Seih Sídreh.

The account in Exodus gives four stations in the march—Elim, the wilderness of Sin, Rephidim, and Sinai. In Numbers it is Elim, the camp by the Red Sea, the wilderness of Sin, Dophkah, Alush, Rephidim, and Sinai. The people must have come in a moderately solid body. A tribal march cannot be in a straggling column, or the fighting men at any one point will be too few.

Just before leaving Sinai I found out an important fact. When we were taking the inscriptions away from the Wady Magháreh, it was necessary to have water for the mules at the sea-shore. The Bedawyn said that it must be carried there; but a Sudány soldier from the Tor Bashibazuks, who knew the country, told me that if a pit were dug anywhere near the shore it would fill with fresh water. We tried it at 'Aqabah, and found that on the other side of the peninsula there was also an under-drainage of fresh water running to the sea. It was evident that for some reason the Bedawyn did not wish me to know of this water-supply. Is it not probable that Moses, who knew Sinai well, brought the Hebrews from Elim along the coast, where they would be sure of this water-supply, and also where one side of the column would be safe from attack? This would enable him to march as he wished each day, and by keeping the women and children near the sea, he could have all of the fighting force together in one long column.

When sufficiently far south Moses turned inland
the Feirán, and they at once ran short of water, appa
ently at the end of their first day's march. In th
connection it is necessary to remember that the Hebrev
had no large animals; the donkey must have been tl
only beast of burden, as camels were not in general u:
in Egypt until the time of the Ptolemies, and catt
could not have lived in the desert at all. This prevente
the people from carrying quantities of water. If, hov
ever, we consider that they kept along the coast, the
might make short marches and be constantly on tl
defensive while they were approaching the district th:
Moses knew would be defended, and from whose valley
the enemy might at any moment rush forth.

This may explain the difference in the two account
Different halting-places along the coast would hav
little that was distinctive about them, and though tl
records of an exceedingly accurate scribe might mentio
the places, a more general record would not, as tl
wilderness of Sin would be considered a sufficientl
definite designation.

The battle was fought at Rephidim, somewhei
between the Feirán oasis and the sea, possibly in tl
lower Feirán valley.

In the narrative the next day's march is to Sina
It seems strange that any one should try to make th
mean anything but the one strategic point around whic
everything must move. A tribe could not have reache
even the borders of the mountains connected with tl
Gebel Musa in one day, and there is not enough wat
to support them there, even if they could have made tl
march. But there is no reason for such a move; tl
people have come a distance which is long, when coi
sidered as a tribal movement, and they are tired. Hei
is the garden of the country, where rest and shade ma
be enjoyed, and where the flocks may fatten after tl
long march. Moreover, Moses wishes to constitute

people with a set of laws and some definite government, and there is no place where this can be done better than in the rich oasis of the Feirán.

Palmer was carried away by the idea that the great plain of Raha was the only place in the peninsula where such a vast assembly could have witnessed the giving of the Law; but he based his arguments on a conception of numbers which we know to be absolutely impossible. How he made such a mistake is hard to see; and in his descriptions of the Feirán he mentions that there is a tradition still lingering, that a certain rock there is the one from which Moses brought the water. In addition to the story he mentions a custom as going with it. The Bedawyn still throw little stones to the rock, as the Hebrews are said to have done when they sat down, satisfied after their long drink, and played with little stones. In my opinion a story which is connected with a custom has considerable weight, and this is the original story told by the monks in the Feirán monastery. The present monastery is named after St. Catharine, whose body is said to have been found on the neighbouring mountain.

The view that Gebel Musa is Sinai is supported by tradition alone. But how old is that tradition? The great early convent is in the Feirán, and when that of St. Catharine was built, it was tributary to the older community. Also, the slopes around Mount Serbál are dotted with the cells of monks who lived there during the early period of Christianity.

When I was with the monks at Mount Sinai, I questioned them about what coins they had found. They showed me their collection, and I saw that only those from the Feirán were of an early date. I think that all the evidence goes to show that while the Roman Empire retained control of the peninsula, the Gebel Serbál was looked upon as the Mount of the Law; but that after the Saracens gained control over Sinai and

seized the rich Feirán, the monks were obliged to leav
and the traditions that remained concerning Sinai no
gathered around the convent of St. Catharine.

The Lady Silvia visited Sinai between the years 3
to 388. Her descriptions do not suit the Gebel Mus
but they seem to apply to the Gebel Serbál. On t
other hand, the distances imply that she went to t
Gebel Musa. Some of these distances, however, seem
be wrongly stated, and I think that all of them ha
been inserted by a later scribe at a time when the clair
of the convent of St. Catharine had become establishe

If, however, the question be examined apart from a
tradition, we would naturally ask why the man wl
seems to have been such a marvellous general shou
have led his people past a valley of plenty, and caus
them to sit down in a waste as barren as the Raha plai
The account states that the Hebrews were ready
grumble. I do not think it is possible to keep a peoj
through a winter on the plain of Er Raha. One nig
when we were there the water in our tanks froze to t
depth of an inch, and in spite of our heavy clothes
suffered considerably, and our men were badly exhaust
with the extreme cold. If we are bound to force into t
narrative a miraculous food and drink, I do not thi
anybody would wish to postulate an alteration in tei
perature, and women and children could not live in tl
plain without such a change.

Mount Serbál, on the other hand, appears to be
suitable and reasonable place for the requiremer
involved. I am not in a position to say how far t
change in the *ayin* in the word may count; but
Lepsius is right, the name Serb-baal, "the palm-grov
of Baal," would imply that from early times it was
holy mountain. The name "Mount of God," as giv
in the Hebrew account, has the appearance of bei
an original name of the mountain, and not a name us
after the giving of the Law. The fact that the Sinai

inscriptions focus at the Serbál would lead to the supposition that it was a place of worship also in later times.

As far as the early Christian tradition is concerned, Eusebius and other early writers state that the Hebrews remained in the Feirán, and the great mass of monastic cells on the slopes of Mount Serbál must mean that the hermits who came and dwelt there thought that they were living around the sacred mountain. It is altogether too much like a modern idea to suppose, because this was a holy mount to the inhabitants of the peninsula, and thus sacred to a "heathen" deity, that the Hebrews would look at it with repulsion. The feeling of the time was altogether the reverse. A sacred thing was sacred to all, and in the same land to-day the Muhammadan Bedawyn consider that the church of the monastery of St. Catharine has miraculous powers; with this in view they come and remain for hours in the church, in the hope of getting children and other blessings. One sheykh of my acquaintance believes that a miracle happened to him in consequence of a long stay in the holy place, Christian though it is.

Many have considered that the two points of the Gebel Musa, the top and the point called Sef-saf, correspond to the two names Horeb and Sinai. My friend Professor McLaughlin, however, tells me that Horeb is without doubt the older name, and that Sinai dates from a much later time.

When most of the arguments in support of the Gebel Musa theory are examined, it will be found that the plain of Er Raha is the one on which all lay most stress, because it is large enough to hold the two millions. Now, however, when Professor Petrie has at last settled the vexed question of the numbers, that argument has no force. Robinson, who places the giving of the Law on Gebel Sef-saf, sums up the description in the narrative in three divisions: (1) a mountain summit overlooking the place where the people stood; (2) space sufficiently adjacent to the mountain for so large a multitude to stand and behold the phenomenon on the summit; (3) the relation between the space where the people stood and the base of the mountain must be such that they could approach and stand at "the nether part of the mount," that they could also touch it, and that further bounds could appropriately be set around the mount, lest they should go up into it or touch the border of it. The first point speaks against the Gebel Musa, which cannot be seen from below; it may well apply to the Serbál. The second formerly was considered to be against the Serbál, but with the reduced numbers it may apply equally well to the Feirán or to Er Raha. The third head apparently would apply to almost any mountain in the peninsula; and if the Feirán theory holds, the people, in all probability, stood near where the ruined monastery now stands, at the entrance to the Wady Aleyat, and were forbidden to climb up into the mountain.

The photographs (nos. 180-183) give an idea of the wonderful beauty of the Feirán. A stream about nine inches square flows out of the rock, and then wanders down the valley, sometimes flowing beneath the surface, or again, springing up, continues as a tiny stream or broadens out into a little swamp. The palms, some large and some small, show vistas beyond, while behind all are the rugged mountains. In some parts of the valley these rise gradually above each other, while in other places the valley is bounded by a gigantic cliff. The *sidr* trees and the misty bushes of the *tarfa* add variety to the vegetation.

The ruins of the old convent are on a little hill, called El Maharrad, near the mouth of the Wady Aleyat. Its ruined walls of stone and mud brick point to its having been a building of considerable size. We obtained a few coins, and the Bedawyn say that a large

180 181
182 183

VIEWS IN THE WADY FEIRÂN.

number are found among the ruins. The coins show that, as far as the use of money is concerned, the flourishing period was immediately after the time of Constantine, the latter part of the fourth century. The monks of St. Catharine now have a man living in a little house, in order to maintain their hold on the property on which the old monastery is built. He cultivates a small garden, and stays for a year or more at a time, in order to keep the Bedawyn from encroaching.

Nearly every Bedawy family has some hold on the Feirán, and many of their little huts are scattered through the palm-groves. The huts usually have mud walls; the roofs are of palm-branches, supported by palm-trunks. In some places there are quite well-made walls of mud brick that surround the little patches of cultivated ground. There are several acres of corn and tobacco. The water that comes from the rock is led down the eastern side of the valley close to the edge of the cliff, and drawn off here and there for irrigating the fields. The dates of the Feirán are excellent. The ripe fruit is packed into goat-skins, often with a very aromatic herb which the people call *sheah*. These and the dates from Tor form the greater part of the fruit of the peninsula. There is also a small fruit, about the size of a cherry, that grows very plentifully on the *sidr* trees. It has an acrid, pleasant taste, and is much valued by the people.

Along the east side of the valley are great masses of clay, that were probably deposited when the waters were dammed back and formed a lake. In this clay-bed many tombs are still visible. They are about thirty inches square, and run far enough into the bank to receive a coffin; the front was then bricked up. These have the appearance of Roman tombs. There is another form of tomb in which, instead of digging out the space for the coffin, a structure is erected of stones to receive rows of coffins. Sometimes there are two rows of coffins provided for, one above the other, and at right angles; the under layer is put in from the front, and the upper layer from the side. Such tomb-structures are built on the steep side of a hill, and are flat-topped. I noticed that many of the tombs in the clay had an offering of the grass-like plant at the entrance, and the Bedawyn said that the tombs were still used. The one tomb of importance is in a cemetery of the ordinary Bedawy type. It is an ordinary sheykh's tomb, and when the Bedawyn pass it supplications are occasionally addressed to the dead chief.

From the Feirán we proceeded through the Wady Mukatteb to the Seih Sídreh, and into the Wady Magháreh. The men who were bringing the tools down to Ras Burdéys by boat had not arrived, but came in a few days. The first difficulty was to make the Bedawyn work at all; and when they thoroughly realised that I would not allow them to go on with their mining till the inscriptions were removed, they began to fight for exorbitant pay. I was pretty certain that they would not work long, and that what was not done during any little spurt of energy that might be worked up would probably not be done at all. With this in view I hired all the men I could obtain, in order to start on nearly all the inscriptions at once; and it was well that I did so, as I ended with only one Bedawy and three Sudány slaves. I found the work rather difficult. During the first day the points or edges were snapped off all the chisels. Some of the rock was so hard, a tool would make scarcely any impression, while other inscriptions were so crumbly that it was almost impossible to touch them without the rock breaking away. The surface had weathered hard, but just behind it the slightest touch seemed enough to make it crumble to sand. Another difficulty was to make the Bedawyn careful of the inscriptions. Had it not been for the few workers of

CUTTING OUT THE SCULPTURES

Professor Petrie's who came down with me, some of the inscriptions would certainly have been badly broken. These men, however, appreciated the importance of what was being done, and succeeded at last in making the Bedawyn work carefully. I had hoped that the rock would chip with blows of a chisel; but I found that this was very difficult, and much of the cutting was done by pounding the stone to powder along the trench that we made.

The inscriptions were on the face of the rock. In a few cases it was possible to work from the top to get behind them; but even then a great part of the cutting behind the inscription had to be done from the sides. It soon became difficult for the men to get into a position to work, and it was necessary to blast the rock away from the sides, so that they might have room to swing their hammers. I was afraid of damaging the inscriptions, and was consequently rather over-cautious with the blasting. As it was, we soon used up what little powder was in the district; and as sending to Suez and back was eleven days' journey, we were forced to make our own powder, as the Arab miners were doing. At a ruinous price a few pounds of sulphur were obtained, saltpetre was taken from the rocks, and charcoal was made from some twigs. These were mixed with a little water, well pounded, and set out to dry.

During all this time a terribly hot wind was blowing, and the Wady Magháreh, which is enclosed, became a perfect cauldron. For nearly a week the thermometer must have been at about 120° Fahr. in the shade. This may have been responsible for the marked disinclination to work shown by the Bedawyn. I postponed paying the men, but gave each man a few piastres to purchase food from others of the tribe. Even then many left after about two weeks, willing to lose their pay rather than remain.

As the work progressed it became necessary to drill

holes above the inscriptions, and, using chisels for spikes, to hang slings of heavy rope from them, into which the stone might slip in case a crack should develop, and the stone drop. The plan answered well, for not one inscription fell to the ground.

A number of sacks were in readiness with which to protect the faces of their inscriptions during their transport. These came in useful for building platforms of gravel bags, and for strengthening the bases of the scaffolding. In one case, however, it was necessary to blast away a great mass of rock from the top of an inscription, and then swing a platform over the cliff, anchored by chisels deeply cut into the rocks above. When the stones were cut out, they were either boxed or stoutly lashed to large trays, and then were lowered to the wady floor. In some cases there was considerable difficulty, but fortunately the lowering was accomplished without any mishap. The municipality of Suez had kindly lent for this work a heavy cart and two stout mules, with the help of which it was comparatively easy to transport the blocks to the sea.

I was not sorry when the last load went off, for running up and down the Magháreh cliffs under the terrible sun, scolding men all day, and then setting to work to make boxes or trays, either by moonlight or with a lantern, was tedious and tiring work.

Fortune was singularly kind during the whole time. Though many of the inscriptions came down in pieces, this was due to their being already cracked; and we had only one accident to a stone, and that was of very little importance. With the men also there was one accident only, in which a Bedawy nearly lost his life; but before we left he was well again. In the transport our good fortune was even more marked. It was not until the last stone was on the shore, and the mules were being unhitched, that one of them dropped dead. The awful heat had been too much for even a Suez mule.

As the last stone was being loaded into the boat which had come from Suez to take them up, a storm arose and blew the boat out to sea, where it was tossed about for days, till at last the storm, the severest there had been for thirty years, abated, and the boat reached Suez in safety.

While we were at work, Mr. Frost found a small piece of inscribed stone where some blasting had thrown down a pile of fragments of the rock. A man was put to search this pile, and we found numerous pieces of the Khufu inscription which had previously been destroyed. Fortunately we secured a piece that showed the face of the king.

CHAPTER XVIII

TOR TO 'AQABAH

BY C. T. CURRELLY

DURING our stay in Tor an expedition to the gulf of 'Aqabah, and from there to Petra and Jerusalem, had been planned. Two days after the last stone left the Wady Maghâreh, Doctor and Mrs. Rüffer and Mr. Carver arrived, and we started at once. We wished to visit the Gebel Musa again, and also to see the Wady Solaf. The second view of the Feirán made it seem even grander than it had appeared on my first visit.

Near the entrance to the Wady Solaf we found many beehive Nawamis. Two are of particular interest, as they are spoken of as sheykhs' tombs, and have the same grass-like offerings before the small openings as those already mentioned. Mudakhel, the best sheykh in Sinai, who was with us, said they were graves of very long ago, before the days of Islam. It seemed curious that any two of these beehive tombs belonging to a very early period should be singled out and venerated. Most of these Nawamis were on the sides of the wady, some little distance up from the stream-bed.

There was also a tomb made by modern Bedawyn in imitation of one of the beehive tombs. The form of the door was carefully copied; but the ability to make a beehive structure out of rough stones is not possessed by the modern inhabitants of Sinai. There was something almost pitiable about it. Probably over seven thousand years have elapsed since the Nawamis were

BEDAWY GENEROSITY

built; yet many are still standing, in spite of the goats climbing over them. I do not think that modern Bedawyn, out of the same material, could build one that would stand a week, if they could build it at all.

From the Wady Solaf we crossed the Naqb el Howa, "the pass of the wind." This is a narrow pass with a very steep ascent, and must have been difficult to traverse, if not impossible, before a rough path was made by the monks. The path leads to the Wady Seileh, and thence to the plain of Er Raha.

We had a good start from the monastery, and going up the Wady esh Sheykh a short distance, we turned into the little Wady Soweiriyeh, and then crossed some more open rolling country to the Wady Sa'al. In the open country we saw a line of Bedawyn tents. Tents are very few in number, and during nearly six months in the peninsula I saw five groups in all. It is said that they are removed from the more frequented wadys as the old-time hospitality demands the sacrifice of a sheep should a stranger come. To avoid this the Bedawyn rarely pitch in a wady that is likely to be visited; for whatever generosity and hospitality may once have existed, they are no more, though at times the old phrases indicating them are used. When I first arrived at Tor a man came strolling down to where we were camped, with his camel-stick in his hand. I had not seen one in use before, and as this one in form exactly corresponded to the *Uas* sceptre of the monuments, I asked the man if I might look at it, and then if he were willing to part with it. He at once said, "It is yours," and refused to take any money for it. In vain I tried to make him sell it or take it back, and finally I told my man Yusuf to pay him for it privately. Things at once changed. From an open-handed lord he turned into a beggar; and though Yusuf gave him what both knew to be four times the regular price of the stick, he fairly whined for more.

The Wady Sa'al is an imposing and remarkably fine gorge. We were riding along, when a turn in the wady brought us to a great wall of cliff straight in front of us. As we approached we ascended a little ridge, and saw that a small opening went through what seemed to be an entire barrier, but at such an angle that the break was not noticeable from below. We came to the gap, and suddenly found ourselves looking into a gigantic bowl hollowed out in the rocks (see nos. 184 and 185). Away below was a flat sandy plain, and at a considerable distance from where we were standing was an oasis, the Ain Hudherah. Much of the charm of the place was doubtless due to its gorgeous colouring. The rocks were heavily stained with iron, and the effect was that of marble on a gigantic scale.

We managed to climb down the rocks, and walked across the sandy plain at the bottom of the bowl towards the oasis. There is a good supply of water that comes out of a square cutting in the rock. We examined this, and found that it was only a few feet long. As far as I could see, the work was of Roman time. A very old Bedawy, who was almost naked, was attending to the trees of the oasis, and regulating the water by means of small mud canals. The camels came around by another route, and as soon as our water-skins were filled we continued our journey, often looking back towards the beautiful mass of green, dotted with the red blossoms of the pomegranate.

From the Ain Hudherah we travelled through some beautiful scenery (no. 186). Next morning we found that we had left the sandstone and were in gneiss and dyke rocks again. Early in the day we came upon a she-camel with its young; the little one, Mudakhel said, was about two hours old. The legs were very long and hairy at the knees; their ungainliness was accentuated by the creature's attempts to stand. Without a moment's delay it had begun to get its awkward legs into a

184   AIN HUDHERAH (HAZEROTH).

185 THE GREAT BOWL OF ROCKS AROUND
        AIN HUDHERAH.

186 LEAVING AIN HUDHERAH FOR THE WADY
        GHAZALEH.

position to support the body, but without success. The sheykh said that on the morrow it would stand, and that in two or three days it would walk; but that it was only after seven days that it would travel, and then it would go very well. The early morning sun was hot, and it was interesting to notice how the mother managed to keep the little thing within her own shadow. She had to stand a considerable distance away, and it required constant care on her part, while watching the futile struggles of her offspring, so to move that her shadow would be over it.

About ten in the morning we came to where the road to Syria branches off. Here there was a little water. We turned to the right and entered one of the finest passes in the peninsula, the charm of which was its narrowness and crookedness. A touch of green gave a pleasant relief to the reddish colour of the rocks. The heat was intense, and seemed to be appreciated by the immense numbers of locusts that swarmed around the bushes. I asked one of our Bedawyn what the noise was. He answered, "Birds."

About three o'clock we reached the sea, where we remained for a day, as our camels were very tired. The camp was pitched in a palm-grove that reached to the water's edge. There was a sudden change in the scenery. We had been in the grand but hard and monotonous valleys, where the last thing that could be imagined was motion, and almost in a moment we were in a gently moving palm-grove by the sea, where the camels feeding among the trees and bushes on the low shore made pictures on every side.

As the cruel sun gave place to the gentle moon, and the soft breezes made a low sound in the palms, it seemed as if we had suddenly awakened on some dreamy atoll of the Southern Seas. The sudden change explained to me what had been a puzzle for a long time. The desert valleys had had a strange effect, which I knew was not produced by their lines, nor did it come from their monotonous colour. Now it was clear to me that our eye, being naturally accustomed to a perpetual motion in landscape, ceases to notice it as such, and actually receives a shock when perfect stillness lies upon every object. At this place there is an Egyptian fort, and the Bashibazuks there seized the opportunity to pour out a long list of complaints to Dr. Rüffer, hoping that he would intercede for them at headquarters, so that they might have more pay. So, from the atoll in the Southern Seas we were brought back to the familiar begging Orient.

The road on to 'Aqabah follows the coast with but little deviation; once it turns inland, but soon comes back to the seashore. The whole beach is a mass of shells, great and small; sometimes for miles there are strips where the sand can scarcely be seen for them. At very short intervals, also, there are heaps of shells, that mark where the Bedawyn had made a meal on shell-fish. With the shells and the dry seaweed lie fragments of coral, with which the beach is strewn.

Near the bend of the gulf of 'Aqabah there is a tiny island called Geziret Farun, on which there is a Turkish castle of early date. Between the castle and the island a pearl-fishing boat was moored, and the men came over to us in their little dug-out canoe, which they paddled with a disc of wood fastened to a round stick. We visited their boat, and found it full of odds and ends from the sea—shells, a big turtle-shell, half-dried fish, a dudong's skin stretched out to dry, and scores of other things that they had found on the coral reefs. They do a little diving for pearls, and informed me that they could dive to a depth of ten fathoms. They have the sea-telescope, and while searching the bottom use the canoe, which they punt with great skill. These men are all pirates on occasion; and if a boat runs on the coral reefs the crew have a hard time of it, if they are not well-enough armed to beat off the pirates. The examples of these pearl-divers that I saw were certainly villainous enough. They make a home along the coasts by Yambo or Jedda, and go away for long cruises. They are physically well made, and from constant exposure to the sun, and a plentiful use of oil, their skins are of the richest and softest chocolate-brown, and are often seamed all over the shoulders and the back in an extraordinary way.

The walls of the castle show very poor workmanship, many of them being mere rubble; and all are thin, and must have been of little protection against any weapons heavier than arrows. The cisterns, however, are well made, with very flat vaults that appear to be still perfectly solid. From this castle it is a very short distance around the head of the gulf to the modern town of 'Aqabah.

Just at the head of the gulf there are large mudbeds that are soft underneath, though they look solid enough on the surface. While crossing one of these my camel began to sink with extraordinary rapidity. I jumped down and began to pull off his saddle, and shouted for my camel-man, who was some distance behind. I do not think that the beast had ever been in such a place before, but he behaved admirably, staying perfectly quiet till we had the saddle off, and then rolling over on his side, and so freeing his legs, which had sunk deep into the mire. This raised my opinion of the camel, which usually appears to be so stupid. The Sudánys have a good explanation for the supercilious look that is so marked on the camel's face; they say that to man has been given the knowledge of the ninety-nine beautiful names of Allah, but the camel knows the hundredth and will not tell it.

The village of 'Aqabah is built around the stone fort. The houses are of mud brick, and about as miserable as can be imagined. The people seemed all to be idling about, dressed in rather elaborate and showy clothes. During the days of the great pilgrim caravans there was considerable activity in the town, which is now altogether lifeless.

About three companies of Turkish soldiers were encamped just behind the town in rough shelters, and on its southern side there was a magnificent palm-grove. We had been promised an escort of cavalry from 'Aqabah to Petra, and thought, from the courteous way in which we were received, that everything was kept in readiness for us to proceed on our journey. We were asked to encamp in the palm-grove; a sentry was stationed over our baggage, and a ring of soldiers placed around us to keep away the villagers, who soon swarmed around.

We soon found, however, that we were not to proceed, and that we were virtually prisoners. The commander of the troops was very courteous; but there was a ring of sentries around us, and although we might go about with some freedom during the day, at night we must remain within the small ring of soldiers. It was rather trying, as we had expected to be in the cooler valleys of Palestine a few days later; and now we had to face the prospect, whether near or remote we could not tell, of the unwelcome journey across the barren Tīh.

In spite of the annoyance, one exquisite pleasure was ours. From where we sat there was a view through the palm-trunks out over the soft, moon-lit sea, where shoals of tiny fish were leaping in silver curves ahead of the sharp white streak that told of a pursuing shark.

We were soon convinced that, though we had an official order to proceed, an unofficial one had been sent to stop us from going on to Petra. As soon as we were allowed to leave we turned back to the Egyptian frontier, reluctantly facing the prospect of a journey across the barren Tīh. The frontier is a few hours only from 'Aḍabah, where the ascent to the great plateau begins.

Before the Suez Canal was cut, great caravans of pilgrims from Egypt came across the Tīh from 'Aḍabah, on their way to Mecca. A rough road was made for them, and near 'Aḍabah a bridge was built. The plateau of the Tīh is dreary in the extreme. During our journey across we did not see a single tent or a beast grazing; but everywhere the long, level line of the upper chalk cliffs, broken here and there, but again returning to the same level. The ground is like the Libyan plateau, covered with chocolate-coloured flints that have settled into a hard pavement. The upper chalk as it wore away left behind it great masses of flint nodules, and these have split up in the sun to the small flakes that form the pavement, which is so level that it has almost the appearance of being rolled. Strewn over this are thousands of flakes and implements from palaeolithic times (see fig. 163). The flint seems to be good, and there are quantities of large pieces; yet the implements are all small and of decidedly poor workmanship. The majority have the orange patina well known on Libyan flints. One or two flints were of the regular celt pattern, but the majority were small scrapers. Flakes that would join together were by no means rare, and it looked as if the surface had remained undisturbed during the whole time since they had been struck.

Some years ago Professor Sayce stated that the probable route of the Hebrews lay across this desert, and that the Mount of the Law was not in the peninsula at all. This seems to me to be absolutely impossible, for the people could not get across this desert with flocks and herds.

At Nakhl there is a fort and a tree, but not a palm-tree, as the name would lead one to suppose. A few Egyptian soldiers are kept here, and there was some excitement over a murder. The murderers had been captured, and the tribe had been given the privilege of compounding for the offence by the payment of a hundred camels. This they had declined to do, so justice was to take its course. The commander of the few soldiers told me that some grain is cultivated on the plateau in certain spots, and that it is buried in holes until the owner requires it. He placed the number of the population of Sinai very high, and brought in one of the men who was charged with the murder to substantiate his statements. This man was one of a war-party against the Turkish Bedawyn fifteen years ago; he gave the numbers of his party as one hundred and eighty, and said that they were from two sub-tribes only. The soldiers claimed that there were ten thousand men in the peninsula, while our sheykh, Mudakhel, put the numbers at about six thousand men. The numbers are almost impossible to ascertain, as the people near the borders are always moving. I think that sometimes there are as many as the ten thousand men in the peninsula, while at others they are much fewer. A Sudány soldier, who had been in the country a long time, and who knew the tribes very well, gave me a rough list as follows:

Aleyqat and Hameda	2,000 men.
Owarma and Sowàlah	200 ,,
Welad Said	300 ,,
Mezàynah	1,000 ,,
Karashi (he called it " Gurrarcia ")	(?)

He said that the Tīh tribes were so much mixed that he did not know their numbers; but he thought that about half were on the Turkish side and half on the Egyptian border. An old man, the brother of the sheykh of the Aleyqat, agreed to these numbers. From my experience in the country I should have put the numbers lower, as I so seldom seemed to meet new men; the same appeared to turn up everywhere.

The Aleyqat and the Hameda are under one sheykh.

Their territory extends from the north down below the Wady Magháreh. The Owarma and the Sowàlah live in the Gebel Ramleh and around Serabít el Khádem. The Welad Said hold the Feirán. The Mezàynah live around Ras Muhammad, towards the gulf of 'Aqabah, and the Karashi live around the Gebel Musa and towards the Feirán. I think that the population of Sinai is always just what the country will support; and if the numbers of soldiers sent from Egypt on the different expeditions be a guide, the population must have remained about the same through several millenniums.

From the Tih we dropped into the Gebel Ramleh, the desert of sand. Just after the rainy season (and there may be as many as twenty rainy days during the winter) there is a considerable quantity of vegetation, and the flocks receive enough nourishment to enable them to give a little milk for a few weeks. I was told that this was one of the reasons why it had been so difficult to keep the men at work removing the inscriptions; for tales of plenty were coming in from the Gebel Ramleh, and the men were longing for the luxury of milk and clarified butter. Proceeding northwest we at last reached the quarantine station, and the next morning the quarantine launch came over and took us to Suez.

MAP 4.

PLAN OF THE TEMPLE OF SERABIT EL KHADEM.

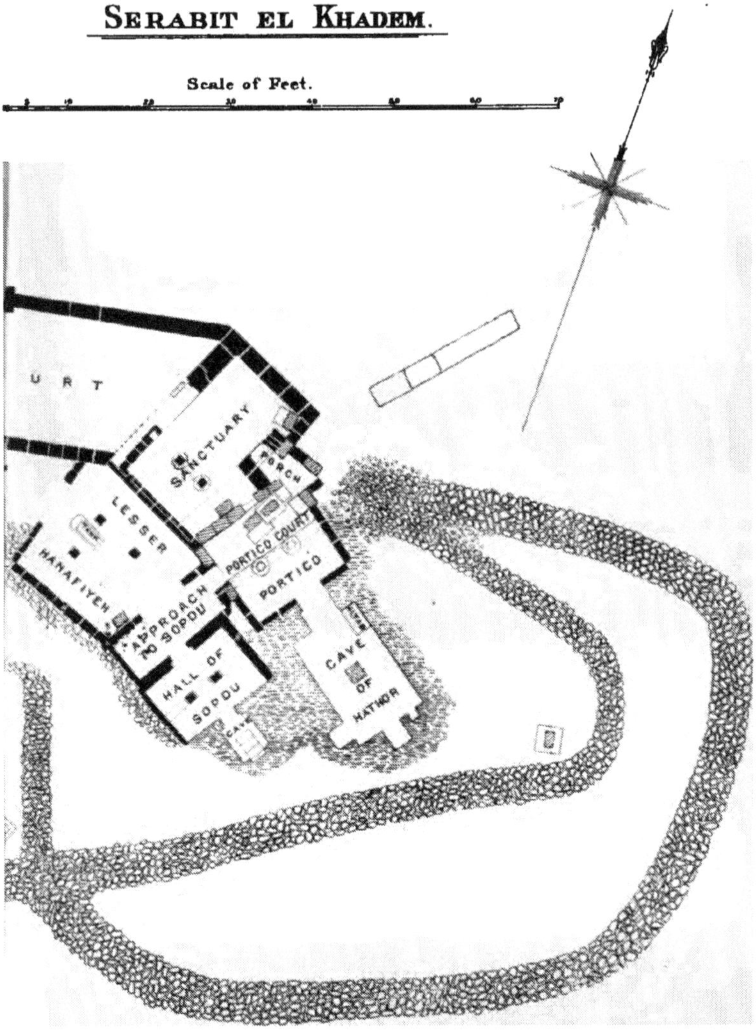

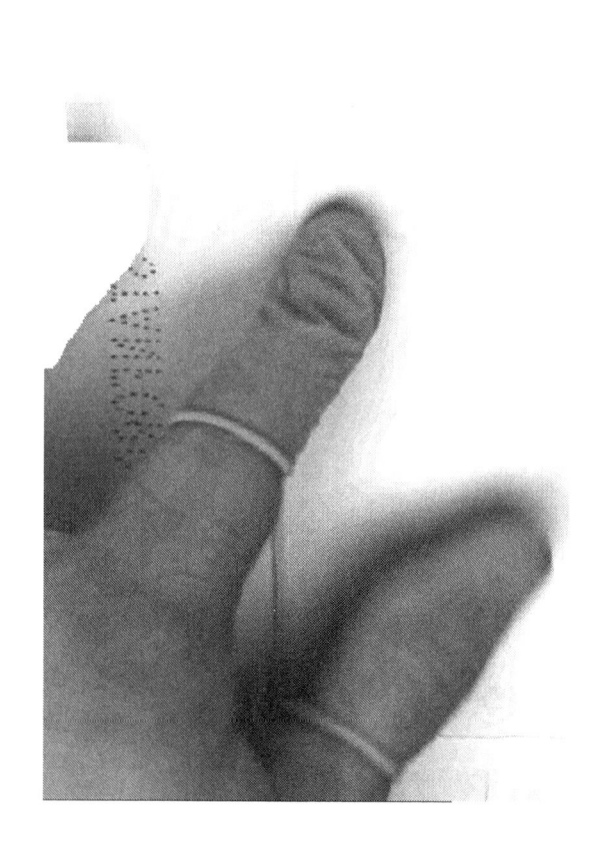

INDEX

Aa en perui hez, 112
Aahmes, 102
Aahmes, queen, 102, 137, 140, 142, 147
Aamu, 115, 118, 124, 131, 138
Aaron, story of, 232
Ablutions in temple, 105-7, 190
Aboriginal race in Sinai, 6
Abu Ghaneym, Sheykh, xi, 4, 7, 22, 30, 42
Abu Qudeyl, xi, 4, 5
Abu Zenymeh, 17
Acacia, 29
Ahau boats, 112, 118
Ahmar, Wady, 239
Ain Hudherah, 262
Alabaster vases, 137
Alaf, two meanings of, 211
Aleyat, Wady, 254
Alphabet, new, 61, 129-32
Altars in cave, 95, 98, 134
 ,, of incense, 95, 133, 189
Am merti, 114
Amalekites, 247
Amen, figure of, 90
Amenemhat I, in group, 96-7, 123
 ,, ,, statuette of, 97
Amenemhat II, figure of Hat'hor, 124
 ,, ,, on altar, 95
 ,, ,, stele of, 98
 ,, ,, tablets of, 60, 98
Amenemhat III, altars of, 95, 98
 ,, ,, expedition of, 117
 ,, ,, figure of, 84
 ,, ,, figure of Hat'hor of, 124
 ,, ,, lintel of, 77
 ,, ,, pillar of, 94
 ,, ,, rock inscriptions of, 27, 38, 45-6, 60, 156

Amenemhat III, steles of, 66, 82-3, 85, 92-3, 96, 98
Amenemhat IV, columns of, 93
 ,, ,, rock inscriptions of, 63
 ,, ,, steles of, 92, 98
Amenhotep I, building of, 80, 93-4, 102
 ,, ,, door of, 93
 ,, ,, offerings of, 142, 147
Amenhotep II, building of, 107
 ,, ,, offerings of, 142
 ,, ,, pillars of, 79, 86
Amenhotep III, building by, 108
 ,, ,, cattle hunt scarab, 150
 ,, ,, cup of, 138
 ,, ,, *menats* of, 142
 ,, ,, steles of, 73, 76
 ,, ,, vases of, 140
 ,, ,, walls of, 74, 82
 ,, ,, wands of, 144
Amen·meryt, 102, 142
Ameny, 95, 98, 105
Ameny·senb, 94
Animals, hunt of, on bowls, 151
 ,, wild, protection from, 40
Ankh'ab, 97, 124
Apotheosis of king, 181
'Aqabah, 265
Arabs, *see* Bedawyn
Archbishop of Sinai, 237
Arrow-heads, flint, 244
Ashes of sacrifices, 99, 186
Ashtaroth, 192
Ass drivers, 117
Assa, expedition of, 114
 ,, inscriptions of, 46
Aten under Ramessu I, 127
Axis of temple changed, 87, 103-4

271

INDEX

Ayun Musa, 8
   ,,   ,, Roman remains at, 9

Baba, Wady, 18
Baboon, rude figure of, 123
"Baker," 117
Bantantha, figure of, 128
Basalt flow, 35-7, 58-9
   ,, pounders, 50
Batah, Wady, 57, 65
Bauerman, Mr. H., 27
Bead, spiral, 150
Beads in Nawamis, 243
   ,, of shell, 240
   ,, various, 152
Bedawyn, burial of, 230, 232
   ,, character of, 2, 236, 261
   ,, conversation of, 32
   ,, dress of, 234
   ,, family life of, 32
   ,, health of, 30
   ,, law of murder, 236
   ,, liberty of, 31
   ,, marriage of, 236
   ,, meals of, 233
   ,, occupations of, 234
   ,, population, 268-9
   ,, religion of, 232
   ,, settling in Egypt, 199
   ,, smoking, 226
   ,, weapons, 235
   ,, weaving of, 235
   ,, women, 32
Benjamin, defeat of, 220
Berrah, Wady, 230
Bes, head of, 150
   ,, vases, 137-8
Bethel stones, 63-8, 73-4
Beyts, Messrs., 4
Boatmen, 118
Boats, *ahau*, 112
   ,, terms for, 5
Bowls, offerings of, 140-1
Bracelets, 143-4
Brazen sea, 107
British School of Archaeology, vi
Broom-rape, 12
Burdeys, 21
Bureaucracy of Egyptians, 109
Burnings at funerals, 101
   ,, on high places, 100-1
Burnt sacrifices, 100, 186

Bush, Mr. H. B., x, 4, 5, 22
Button, Mr., ix

Calcite, 18
Calendar, Egyptian, 165
   ,, Muhammadan, 164
   ,, Russian, 164
Camel's skull on hill, 37
Camels, charges for, xi, 5, 21
   ,, endurance of, 225
   ,, engaged through sheykh, 4, 21, 23
   ,, essential factor, 3
   ,, feeding of, 225
   ,, grazing, 62
   ,, loading of, 6, 11
   ,, saddles of, 226
   ,, weakness of, 5, 6, 226
Camel-child, 28
Camel-men, stealing by, 4
Camp in desert, arrangements of, vii, xi, 3, 9, 11-2, 22, 26
Carboniferous sandstone, 20, 35
Carver, Mr., 260
Cats on ring-stands, 145-6
   ,, ,, tablets, 148
Cave, 94, *see* Sacred Cave
Caverns collapsed, 15-6
Cemetery, Arab, 28, 53, 229, 256
Census lists in Palestine, 217-8
   ,, ,, misunderstood, 210-3
   ,, ,, of Israelites, 209
Cheetah, figures of, 148
"Chief in department of the interior," 110
"Chief of boats," 113, 118
"Chief of elders," 114
"Chief of the gang," 115
"Chief of the land," 114
"Chief of the north land," 111
"Chief of the store-house," 114
"Chief of transport," 112
"Chief physician," 113
"Chief scribe," 113
"Chief seal-bearer," 111
Chiselling of rock, 40, 161-2
Chisels of bronze, 161-2
Chronology, fixed points in, 166
   ,, interest of, 163
   ,, of dynasties, 175
   ,, of Manetho, 171-3
   ,, of Old Kingdom, 174

INDEX

Circles of stones, 53, 242, 244
Clay bed in Feiran, 255
Climate, uniformity of, viii, 206-7, 228
"Collectors," 116
Column, octagonal, of Hat·hor, 135
   ,, papyrus, glazed, 150
Columns, fluted, of Amenemhat IV, 93, 135
   ,, of Hatshepsut, 84
"Commander of recruits," 114
"Commander of the palace gate," 111
Commissariat, ancient, 111
Composite documents, 196-8
Co-natural action, 202
Cones in shrine, 135, 189
Conical stones, worship of, 135, 189
Conquest of Sinai by Egyptians, 42
Contracts, 5, 7, 21-2
"Controller," 113
"Cook," 117
Copper borer, 52
   ,, chisels, 52
   ,, in Nawamis, 243
   ,, ore, 240
   ,, slag, 18, 51-2
   ,, smelting, 51, 161, 240
"Copper smelters," 117
Corn grinders, 52
Cornice, 78 9
   ,, of porch, 91
Court, 86
Cow of Hat·hor, figures of, 137, 151
Creation, story of, 233
Crete, chronology in, 173
Criticism, literary, dangers of, 195
Crucibles, 51-2, 162
Crushers of stone, 159
Cubicles for dreaming in, 70, 74-8, 191
   ,, subterranean, 76
Cubit measures, 8, 76
Cultivation at Serabit, 155
Currelly, Mr. C. T., ix, 2, 64
   ,, ,, chapters by, 224-69

Dance, sacred, 183
Daphne, dreaming at, 68
Dates of Feiran, 255
Dates, *see* Chronology
Debbet el Qeray, 28
Denudation of raised plain, 10
   ,, of sandstone, 35

Denudation of valleys at Serabit, 57
"Deputy of chief seal-bearer," 111
"Deputy scribe," 114
Destruction of sculptures, 46-8
   ,, of offerings, 138
"Deviser of minerals," 116
Dhaba, Wady, 24, 56, 58, 73, 157
Dill, Professor, on ancient dreaming, 68
Divers in Red Sea, 264
Diversity due to ancestry, 197-8
   ,, implies use of documents, 201
Division of labour in Egypt, 110
Dog star, *see* Sirius
Donkey drivers, 117
Drainage in successive directions, 57
Dreaming in sacred places, 67-9, 190
Dynasties, list of, 175

Ear, votive, 150
Echini, spines of, 52
Eckenstein, Miss, x
Egypt, contrast with Sinai, 1
Egyptian roads, 8
   ,, view of Israel, 221
Egyptians brought to work in Sinai, 2, 4, 224
"Elder of the treasury," 112
"Elders," 115
Elders, seventy, 214
Elim, 13, 205
Enclosure wall of temple, 74
Enclosures of stones, 66
Entrance to temple, 75
Epidauros, dreaming at, 68
Erasure of figures, 90
Erthameh, Wady, 231
Et-hal, Wady, 16
Etham, 204
Ethiopian type of IIIrd dynasty, 43
Evans, Dr. Arthur, 173
Exodus, conditions of, 194-222
   ,, route of, 203-6, 247-51, 267
Expeditions, system of, 118
"Eyes and ears of the king," 114

Families, size of Israelite, 211
Faults in marls, 15
Feet outlined on rock, 14
Feiran, Wady, 246-8, 254
Ferruginous bed, 35, 58-9

INDEX

Flint arrow-heads, 244
," knife, 136
," palaeolithic, 227, 267
," used in mining, 50, 160
," worked, 15-6
Food supplies, xi
Foreign influence in design, 141
"Foremen," 115
"Foremen of miners," 116
Fort, so-called, 38
Frazer, Dr., *Golden Bough*, 181
Frost, Mr., x, 229, 237, 245, 259
Furnace, smelting, 18, 240, 242

G'aa desert, 225
Game boards on rock, 14
Gardiner, Mr. Alan, vi
Gebel Hammam, 10
General, 113-4
Geziret Farun, 264
Gharandel, Wady, 12, 29, 205
Gideon, 220
Glazing in two colours, 142
Gneiss, grey, 24
Gods, mixture of, 71
," of a district, 71
," worshipped by local rites, 71
Goshen, 203, 208
Gow, Wady, 242-3
Granite dykes in Tartir, 34
," headlands of Wady Sidreh, 23
," seaworn, 20, 23, 35
," weathering of, 23
Gravel of pluvial age, 15-6
Greek influence in design, 141
Griffith, Mr. F. Ll., 127
"Guards," 115
"Guards of the store-house," 113
Guétin et Charvaut, Messrs., x
Gypsum rock, 11

Haematite, 35, 59, 72-4
Hammamat, expedition to, 116
Hammer stones, 51-2, 240
Hanafiyeh, Lesser, 87, 105
," of Hathor, 85-6, 105
," of mosques, 107, 190
Hat'hor, cow of, 137
," figures of, 84, 125
," tablets of, 147
," worship of, 191
," *see* Pillars

Hatshepsut, building by, 102-5
," figures of, 84, 89
," tablets of, 147-8
," vases of, 139
Hawk of Senusert I, 97
," ," Sneferu, 96, 122
Heaps of stone by road, 13-4
Hebran, Wady, 244, 246
Heirship of kings, 177
Henti festival, 177, 180
Her en perui hez, 115
Heroöpolis, 204
Her per Aamu, 115
Her per kaiu, 115
Heru, 115
High places for worship, 100, 188
Hisan Abu Zenneh, Mangaz, 13
History, care for, in Egypt, 171
Homr, Wady, 28
Horeb, 253
Hor·ur·ra, stele of, 73, 82
Hoyle, Dr., on *felidae*, 148
Hull, Dr., v
"Husband of the treasury," 112
Hymn-book, a composite document, 196-8

Incense, altars for, 95, 133, 189
"Inspectors," various, 114-5
Intercalary day not used, 164
"Interpreter," 114-5
Iqneh, Wady, 20, 37-8
Iron-stone, *see* Ferruginous bed
Ishmael, story of, 233
Ishtar, 192
Israelites, census lists of, 209-13
," course of Exodus, 203-6, 247
," documents of, diversity in, 197-9
," educated, 199
," error in numbers of, 208
," families, size of, 211
," in Egypt, 199
," numbers of, 207
," population of, 207-18
," used writing, 132
Issa, story of, 232
Ithmed, Wady, 246
Iuka, General, 60

Jacob, blessing of, 216.
," dream of, 68

INDEX

Jew murdered, 13
Jewish worship, popular, 100-1, 193
Jews, mixed origin of, 197
Justinian, 237

Ka·hotep, 66
Kai, 116-7
Kemnaa, 66
Kenuna, 80
Khallyl Itkheyl, camel-man, 6, 21-2
Khamileh, Wady, 24
Khebdet, or Khebtata, 118
Khemti, 117
Khenensu, 94
Khent, queen of Senusert I, 97
Kherp, 111-2
Kherp aha, 111
Khery a mer sahu, 111
Kheti, 117
Khufu, sculpture of, 46, 259
Khurdiyeh, Wady, 29
King, apotheosis of, 181-5
  „ identified with Osiris, 181-5
  „ mock, substituted, 182, 184
  „ slain periodically, 182-5
  „ slain when ill, 181
Kings, frequency of offerings by, 149
  „ group of four, 96, 123
  „ list of, dated, xiii
  „ *see* Shrine of Kings
Koptos, columns at, 135
Korah, rebellion of, 214, 216

Labour, division of, 110
Labwa, Wady, 230
Lahyan, Wady, 27
Laver, washing at, 106, 190
Leap year, not Egyptian, 164
Leben, Gebel el, 23
Levels of strata, 58
Levi, 124
Levites, census of, 215
  „ originate in Palestine, 216
Limestone, nummulitic, 14
  „ regular strata of, 17
Literary criticism, dangers of, 195
Local sculpture, 125, 129-30
Lost men, 241
Lotus cup, 138
Lotus-leaf pendant, 150
Lua, or Luy, 124
Lyons, Captain, x, 56

Macdonald, Major, 7, 20, 53
Mafkat in turquoise, 41
Maghareh, Wady, flints in, 16
  „ „ geology of, 34-6
  „ „ name of, 20
  „ „ removal of sculptures from, 256-9
Maharrad, El, monastery, 254
Maket, 124
Mallos, dreaming at, 68
Malta, temple in, 136
Man in Sinai of pluvial age, 15
Manetho, history of, 171
Manna, 230
Maps of Sinai, v, 56
Markha, Gebel el, 18
Marl beneath limestone, 15
Maskhuta, Tell el, 245
Matrona, shrine of, 68
Mealing stones, 52
Medum, hawks at, 123
Men lost in desert, 241
Menat, necklace of, 152-3
  „ offerings, 141
Men·kau·hor, tablet of, 37, 40, 45-6
Mentuhotep in group, 96-7, 123
Mentu·nekht, 127
Mer adetu, 113
Mer akhenuti, 110
Mer āt, 114
Mer depet, 118
Merenptah, bracelets of, 143
  „ repairs by, 78, 108
  „ ring-stands of, 145
  „ vases of, 138
  „ wands of, 145
Mer gemaau, 112
Mer mashau, 113
Merru, 124
Mer sa, 115
Mer sahu, 111
Mersekha, *see* Semerkhet
Mer sesh, 113
Mer ta, 114
Mer ta mehu, 111
Mer uru, 114
Merytamen, 102, 142
Mes en aati, 116
Mesenti, 116
Midianites, position of, 205
"Miner, superior," 116-7
"Miners," 117

INDEX

Miners, huts of, at Maghareh, 38-9, 51, 67
Mines at Maghareh, 59-61
　,, at Serabit, 154-9
　,, foreign inscriptions at, 130
Mining, methods of, 48-9, 61, 154-61
　,, season for, 169
Miracle, misuse of word, 201
Model of temple, 74
Monastery of Serbal, 254
　,, of Sinai, 237
　,, of Tor, 225
Month shift of Sirius rising, 177, 180
Months, Egyptian, 165
Monuments, destruction of, 46-8
Mopsus, shrine of, 68
Mosaism, a reformation, 193
Moses, 200
　,, prayer to, 237
Mosques, ablutions in, 107
Mould for casting, 51
Mount of the Law, position of, 251
M'teyr, camel-man, 6, 11
Mudakhel, sheykh, xi, 2, 260
Mukatteb, Wady, 228, 256
Murkheiyeh, El, cliffs, 17
Murray, *Osireion*, 181
Musa, Gebel, 237-8, 250-4
Muslim washings, 106-7
Musri really Sinai, vii, 195

Nabathaean coinage, 33
Nakhl, 267
Naqb el Buderah, 19
Naqb el Howa, 261
Nasb, Wady (eastern), 243
　,, ,, (western), 25
Nawamis, 243, 246, 260
Nefertari, Aahmes, queen, 102
　,, Merymut, queen, 125
Nekht, scribe, 89
Neter kherti, 117
Neter kherti em hat, 116-7
Neter sahu, 110
Nile, fall of, 174
Nimr, Dr., x
Non-natural action, 202
Nummulitic limestone, 14

Odgers, Dr., lecture on dreaming, 68
Offerings, destruction of, 138
　,, list of numbers of, 149

Oracular dreams, 67-9, 190
Organization of Egyptians, 109
Osiris, king identified with, 181
Outer steles, 82
"Overseer of the house of the superior miners," 115
"Overseer of the house of the Syrians," 115
"Overseer of the treasury," 115

Palaeolithic flints, 227, 267
Palestine Exploration Fund, 56
　,, popular worship in, 100
Panehesi, cup of, 137
　,, stele of, 77
Papyrus column, glazed, 150
Patterns, foreign, 141
　,, on bowls, 151
Pavements around steles, 82
Pearl divers, 264
"Peasants," 117
"People of monuments," 117
"People of the temple of Amen," 117
Pepy, inscriptions of, 46, 174
Pesy, 117
Petrie, Mrs., x
Pihahiroth, 204
Pillars, 76, 79, 89
　,, of Hathor, 75, 77-80, 86, 105, 135
Pithom, 204
Plagues in wilderness, 215
Plants figured on bowls, 151
Pluvial age, 15
Polychrome glazed vases, 151-2
Polytheism, breadth of, 70-1
Population, growth of, 218-9
　,, of Israel, 207-18
　,, of Palestine, 217-8
　,, of Sinai, 207, 268
Porch, Mr., x, 16
Porch of Sanctuary, 91
Porphyry dyke, 20
Portico Court, 73-4, 93
　,, of Hathor, 93, 98
　,, of Shrine of Kings, 84
Pottery buried by miners, 52
"Princes," 114
"Prospector," 116
Ptah, 76
　,, on stele, 130

INDEX

Ptah-ur, 156
Pylon, 73-4, 79-80, 108

Qarqah, El, 14
Quarantine station, 5
Quarrelling among Bedawyn, 2
Quartz found, 240
Queen's head dated, 129
  ,,   ,, of local work, 125
Quft men brought to Sinai, 2
Qurneh, 15

Ra'abiyeh, 7
Raamses, city of, 204
Ragaita, Wady, 239
Raha, Er, plain of, 239, 247, 251-2
Rainbow, story of, 233
Rains, viii, 12, 30, 39, 206
Ramessu I, steles of, 127-8
Ramessu II, bracelets of 143
  ,,   ,, building by, 108
  ,,   ,, figures of, 150
  ,,   ,, reworked *hanafiyeh*, 87, 105
  ,,   ,, ring-stands of, 145
  ,,   ,, sistrum of, 147
  ,,   ,, statues of, 128
  ,,   ,, steles of, 127-8
  ,,   ,, vases of, 140
  ,,   ,, wands of, 145
Ramessu III, bracelets of, 143-4
  ,,   ,, polychrome vases of, 151
  ,,   ,, sistrum of, 147
  ,,   ,, steles of, 76, 108
  ,,   ,, vases of, 140-1
  ,,   ,, wands of, 145
Ramessu IV, bracelets of, 143-4
  ,,   ,, inscriptions of, 81, 89-91, 108
  ,,   ,, offerings of, 143
  ,,   ,, sculpture of, 90
  ,,   ,, wands of, 145
Ramessu V, bracelets of, 143-4
  ,,   ,, offerings of, 108
Ramessu VI, bracelets of, 143
  ,,   ,, building by, 90
  ,,   ,, inscription of, 108
Ramleh, Wady, 229, 269
Ra-n-user, tablet of, 45, 47
Ravines in sandstone, 58
Recess in rock, roofed, 83
Red Sea, road by, 17

Religion of Semites, quoted, 101
Rephidim, 249
Reservoir, so-called, 60
Retem bushes, 29
Retennu, 118, 131
  ,, brother of chief, 118
Ring-stands, 145
Roads, Egyptian, 8, 11, 62-3, 102
Rock shrine, 63
Roman pottery in cave, 108
Roofing in sanctuary, 91-2
  ,, of chambers, 75-89, 91
  ,, system of, 78
Rüffer, Dr. and Mrs., 260

Sa, gang, 116
Sa'al, Wady, 261-2
Sa en bet, 118
Sa en mennu, 117
Sa en per Amen, 117
Sab, 112, 114
Sacred Cave, 72-4, 94, 98
Sacrifices, ashes of, 99, 186
  ,, Semitic, 187
"Sage scribe," 112, 114
Sahu, 111
Sahura, tablet of, 37, 40, 44, 46-7
Salamin, Wady, 13
Saleh abu Risq, camel-man, 6
Salt at Maghareh, 52
Sanctuary, 73, 89, 92, 108
Sandstone, Carboniferous, 20, 35
  ,, Cenomanian, 36
  ,, cliffs of, 58
  ,, tilted bed of, 19
Sa-nekht, mine of, 48
  ,, tablet of, 37-8, 43
Sar, 114
Sau, 115
"Scribe," 112
"Scribe of the treasury," 113
"Sculptor," 116-7
Sculpture, destruction of, 46-8
  ,, earliest, 41-3
  ,, local style of, 125, 129-30
  ,, removal of, 48, 245, 256-9
  ,, style of, 41-5
  ,, subjects of, 93
Sea bed raised, 7, 8, 10, 18
"Seal-bearer," 111
"Seal-bearer of the God," 110, 114
Season for mining, 169

INDEX

Sebat, daughter of Senusert I, 97
Sebek·her·heb, 66, 156
Sebek·hotep, official, 63
Sed festivals, 176
  ,, ,, irregularity of, 178
  ,, ,, list of, 178
  ,, ,, periods of, 176
Sehez saru, 114
Sehes us neferu, 115
Sekhti, 117
Selameh, guard, 25
Seleucia, dreaming at, 68
Semerkhet, tablet of, 37, 41
Semitic incense offerings, 134, 189
  ,, sacrifices, 101, 187
  ,, unknown to Egyptians, 114
  ,, writing, 200
Sened, Wady Es, 242
Sen·nefer, prince, 80
Senusert I, group of kings of, 96, 123
  ,, ,, hawk of, 97, 124
  ,, ,, lintel of, 77, 97
  ,, ,, stele of, 65
Senusert II, statuette of, 98
Senusert III, statuette of, 98, 124
  ,, ,, stele of, 72
Serabit el Khadem, bethels at, 63
  ,, ,, mines at, 60
  ,, ,, plans, 55
  ,, ,, structure of, 57
  ,, ,, temple of, 72-108
  ,, ,, Wady, 57
  ,, ,, worship at, 186
Serapeum, 67
Serbal, Gebel, 37, 251-4
Serval, figures of, 148
Sesh, 112
Sesh en perui hez, 113
Set·nekht, stele of, 75, 108
Set, stele of, 98
Sety I, bracelets of, 143
  ,, ,, building of, 108
  ,, ,, glazed cartouches of, 150
  ,, ,, sculptures of, 141
  ,, ,, steles of, 72, 74, 76
  ,, ,, vases of, 140
  ,, ,, wands of, 145
Sety II, bracelets of, 143-4
  ,, ,, *menats* of, 142
  ,, ,, on pylon, 80, 108
  ,, ,, ring-stands of, 146
  ,, ,, sistrum of, 147

Sety II, vases of, 140
Seyyal acacia, 29
Shasu settling in Egypt, 199
Shatt, Esh, 5
Shebeikeh, Wady, 16
Shell armlets, 244
  ,, beads, 240
Shellal, Wady, 19
Shenty, 113
Sheykh Abu Ghaneym, 4, 7, 22, 30, 42
  ,, Abu Qudeyl, 4, 5
  ,, Mudakhel, xi, 2, 260
  ,, Wady esh, 231-2, 239, 261
Shishak, 195
Shrine at roadside, 63
  ,, of Kings, 84, 104
Shur, 205
Side door of temple, 85
Sidreh, Wady, 16, 20, 23, 53
Sigeh, game of, 14
Signary, 131
Silvia, pilgrimage of, 252
Simmons, Mr. Lintorn, 27
Sinai, Monastery of, 237
  ,, Mount, position of, 251
Sinefert, 156
Siq, Wady, 24
Sirius, regulating calendar by, 165
  ,, rising of, 165, 179
Sistrum offerings, 146-7
Slag heaps in Seih Baba, 18
  ,, ,, in Wady Nasb, 27
  ,, of copper, 51-2
Sleeping at sacred sites, 67-9, 102
Smelting furnaces, 18, 240, 242
Smith, Robertson, 101
Smoking of Bedawyn, 226
Sneferu, figure of, 84, 96
  ,, hawk of, 96, 122
  ,, opens Serabit mines, 97
  ,, sphinx of, 130
  ,, statuettes of, 96, 123
  ,, tablets of, 37, 40, 44, 46-7, 97, 137
Sneferu, shipmaster, 98, 124
Snellus, Mr., 224
Snow in Sinai, 230-1, 237
Soleif, Wady, 231, 261
Sopdu, Approach of, 88
  ,, Cave of, 89
  ,, figure of, 84
  ,, Hall of, 89, 105

INDEX

?du, Shrine of, 104, 192
?his, see Sirius
weiriyeh, Wady, 261
elling of names, ix
?hinx of local work, 129
  ,, of Tahutmes III, 88, 105
?rings at Ayun Musa, 8
  ,, at Gebel Musa, 248
tatue formerly removed from Serabit, 128
teles, carving of, 121
  ,, character of Egyptian, 65
  ,, copied from Bethel stones, 65
  ,, decay of, 83
  ,, not rearranged, 85, 92, 104
  ,, pavements of, 82, 104
  ,, sockets of, 82
Stone circles, 53, 65, 242, 244
  ,, rows, 242
  ,, tools, 159-60
Stones, group of, 64
  ,, piles of, 64
  ,, upright, 63-8
Stores from England, 3
Strata, collapse of, 15
  ,, faulted, 15
  ,, fissured with dykes, 20, 34
  ,, levels of, 36
  ,, tilted, 15-7, 19
Sudany type of IIIrd dynasty, 43
Sudr, Wady, 10
Suez, 4, 5
Sunnu, see *Ur sunnu*
Supernatural, term misused, 202
Survey at Serabit, 55
Sutekh, figure of, 127
Suwiq, Ras, 56, 59, 67
  ,, Wady, 25, 58
Syrian worship of conical stones, 135
Syrians, 115, 118

Tablets of cats, 148
  ,, of Hathor, 147
Tahutmes I, offerings by, 102
  ,, ,, vases of, 137, 139
  ,, ,, wands of, 144
Tahutmes III, building by, 102-7
  ,, ,, fragments of, 90
  ,, ,, lintel of, 81
  ,, ,, mine of, 49
  ,, ,, name with Hatshepsut, 103, 139

Tahutmes III, pillars of, 79
  ,, ,, pottery of, 61
  ,, ,, sphinx of, 88, 105
  ,, ,, tablets and steles of, 37, 47, 73, 79, 81, 85, 87, 92, 147-8
  ,, ,, vases of, 139-40
Tahutmes IV, building of, 107
  ,, ,, pillar of, 78
  ,, ,, tablet of, 60, 156
Taliya, Wady, 242
Tanks, 85, 88, 105-7, 136
Tartir ed Dhami, 34
Ta'usert, bracelets of, 143-4
  ,, *menats* of, 142
  ,, offerings by, 108
  ,, ring-stands of, 146
  ,, vases of, 140
Tawaddud, 106
Tayibeh, Wady, 16
Tefnut named, 140
Tell el Amarna, 126
Temple, axis of, 87, 102-3
  ,, described, 74
  ,, history of, 96
  ,, model of, 74
  ,, successive fronts of, 75-81
Tenos, dreaming at, 68
Tents, pitching, 9
Tep, chief festival, 180
Tha en perui hez, 112
Thorns, 29
Three days' journey in the wilderness, 203
Thyi, queen, head of, 126
Tih plateau, 10, 12, 58, 66, 73, 267
Tomb circles, 242
Tombs, direction of, 244 (*see* Nawamis)
  ,, in Wady Feiran, 225
  ,, modern forms of, 53, 229-30
Tools of copper, 52
  ,, ,, stone, 159-60
Tor, description of, 224, 245
Trefoil, blue-glazed, 150
Tribal system of work, 22-3
Tribes of Sinai, 268-9
Turin papyrus of kings, 167
Turkish guard at Aqabah, 266
Turquoise, 36, 41, 49, 51, 61, 69
  ,, Mistress of, 70
Twelve year festival, 179, 182

INDEX

Uba, 114-5
Uha, 116
Umm Agraf, Wady, 24, 57, 59, 229
Umm Alawi, Wady, 243
Umm Dhelleh, Wady, 244
Umm Gorfain, Wady, 244
Umm Luz, Gebel, 239
Umm Riglayn, Gebel, 36, 56-7, 59, 65-6, 74
Umm Themam, Wady, 20, 37
Una, inscription of, 174
Upright stones, 64
Upuat, jackal god, 45, 183
Ur sunnu, 113
Ury, 115
Usertesen, *see* Senusert
Useyt, Wady, 14
Uz neferu, 114

Valleys at Serabit, formation of, 57
Vases, forms of, 140
   ,,   offerings, 137-40
Votive ear, 150

Wall around the temple, 74, 82, 108
 ,, of stones in valley, 38
Wands, 144-5
Washings in ritual, 106-7
Water-supply, along coast, 249
  ,,   ,, amount of, 12
  ,,   ,, ancient, 206
Water-supply, ruled movements of Israelites, 247, 250
  ,,   ,, scanty wells, 247
  ,,   ,, tanks for, 10
Water-supply, Ain Hudherah, 262
  ,,   ,, Ayun Musa, 8
  ,,   ,, Esh Shatt, 5
  ,,   ,, Feiran, 255
  ,,   ,, G'aa, 227
  ,,   ,, Gebel Musa, 248
  ,,   ,, Gharandel, 12
  ,,   ,, Maghareh, 206
  ,,   ,, Wady Nasb, 25
  ,,   ,, Wady Tayibeh, 17
  ,,   ,, Wady Useyt, 14
Weill, Capt. Raymond, v, vi, x
Werdan, Wady, 10, 29
Wilson, Sir Charles, v, x
Wind storm, 29, 259
Wire twisted, 243
Woman's head glazed, 150
Women, position of, 32
Workmen brought from Quft, 2, 4, 224
Writing, common in Syria, 200
  ,, new system of, 61, 129-32, 200
Wudu ablutions, 106
Wutah, Wady, 12

Zebeyr, Wady, 25
Zeser, tablet of, 37-8, 44

BRITISH SCHOOL OF ARCHAEOLOGY IN EGYPT, AND EGYPTIAN RESEARCH ACCOUNT

PATRON: THE EARL OF CROMER, G.C.B., G.C.M.G., K.C.S.I., ETC., ETC.

GENERAL COMMITTEE (*Executive Members*)

Lord AVEBURY	*Prof. ERNEST GARDNER	*J. G. MILNE
WALTER BAILY	Prof. PERCY GARDNER	Sir C. SCOTT MONCRIEFF
HENRY BALFOUR	Rt. Hon. Sir G. T. GOLDIE	ROBERT MOND
Prof. T. G. BONNEY	Prof. GOWLAND	Prof. MONTAGUE
Rt. Hon. JAMES BRYCE	Mrs. J. R GREEN	WALTER MORRISON
Prof. J. B. BURY	Dr. A. C. HADDON	Dr. PAGE MAY
*SOMERS CLARKE	JESSE HAWORTH	Prof. H. F. PELHAM
EDWARD CLODD	Dr. A. C. HEADLAM	F. W. PERCIVAL
W. E. CRUM	*Sir ROBERT HENSLEY	Dr. PINCHES
Prof. BOYD DAWKINS	D. G. HOGARTH	Dr. G. W. PROTHERO
Prof. S. DILL	Sir H. H. HOWORTH	Sir W. RICHMOND
*Miss ECKENSTEIN	Baron A. VON HÜGEL	Prof. F. W. RIDGEWAY
Dr. GREGORY FOSTER	Prof. MACALISTER	Mrs. STRONG
Dr. J. G. FRAZER	Dr. R. W. MACAN	Mrs. TIRARD
ALAN GARDINER	Prof. MAHAFFY	E. TOWRY WHYTE

Treasurer—*F. G. HILTON PRICE *Honorary* ⎱ Mrs. F. PETRIE
Director—Prof. FLINDERS PETRIE   *Secretaries* ⎰ *Dr. J. H. WALKER

The need of providing for the training of students is even greater in Egypt than it is in Greece and Italy; and the relation of England to Egypt at present makes it the more suitable that support should be given to a British school in that land. This body is the only such agency, and is also the basis of the excavations of Prof. Flinders Petrie, who has had many students associated with his work in past years. The large results of this centre of work in the subjects of the prehistoric ages, the early dynasties, the relations of prehistoric Greece with Egypt, the papyri, and the classical paintings, have shown how much need there is of maintaining these excavations in full action. The present year's work on the Temple of Onias, a Hyksos cemetery and fort, the cemetery of Goshen, and a town of Rameses in Succoth, has carried on the course of historical discovery, and active support is required to ensure the continuance of such work.

Office: **EDWARDS LIBRARY, UNIVERSITY COLLEGE, LONDON**

WORKS BY W. M. FLINDERS PETRIE

THE PYRAMIDS AND TEMPLES OF GIZEH. (Out of print.)
TANIS I. 19 pl., 25s. *Quaritch.*
TANIS II. Nebesheh and Defenneh. 64 pl., 25s. *Kegan Paul & Co.*
NAUKRATIS I. 45 pl., 25s. *Quaritch.*
HIEROGLYPHIC PAPYRUS FROM TANIS. (Out of print.)
A SEASON IN EGYPT, 1887. 32 pl. (Out of print.)
RACIAL PORTRAITS. 190 photographs from Egyptian Monuments, 45s. *Murray, 37, Dartmouth Park Hill, N.W.*
HISTORICAL SCARABS. (Out of print.)
HAWARA, BIAHMU, AND ARSINOE. (Out of print.)
KAHUN, GUROB, AND HAWARA. (Out of print.)*
ILLAHUN, KAHUN, AND GUROB. 33 pl., 16s. (Out of print.)*
TELL EL HESY (LACHISH). 10 pl., 10s. 6d. *Alexander Watt.*
MEDUM. 36 pl. (Out of print.)
TEN YEARS' DIGGING IN EGYPT, 1881-1891. 6s. *R.T.S.*
TELL EL AMARNA. (Out of print.)
KOPTOS. 28 pl., 10s. *Quaritch.*
A STUDENT'S HISTORY OF EGYPT. Part I., down to the XVIth Dynasty. 5th ed. 1903. Part II, XVIIth and XVIIIth Dynasties. Part III., XIXth to XXXth Dynasties. 6s. each. *Methuen.*
TRANSLATIONS OF EGYPTIAN TALES. With illustrations by Tristram Ellis. 2 vols., 3s. 6d. *Methuen.*
DECORATIVE ART IN EGYPT. 3s. 6d. *Methuen.*
NAQADA AND BALLAS. 86 pl., 25s. *Quaritch.*
SIX TEMPLES AT THEBES. 26 pl., 10s. *Quaritch.*
DESHASHEH. 37 pl., 25s. *Quaritch.*
RELIGION AND CONSCIENCE IN EGYPT. 2s. 6d. *Methuen.*
SYRIA AND EGYPT. 2s. 6d. *Methuen.*
DENDEREH. 38 pl., 25s.; 40 additional plates, 10s. *Quaritch.*
ROYAL TOMBS OF FIRST DYNASTY. 68 pl., 25s. *Quaritch.*
DIOSPOLIS PARVA. 48 pl. (Out of print.)
ROYAL TOMBS OF EARLIEST DYNASTIES. 63 pl., 25s.; 35 additional plates, 10s. *Quaritch.*
ABYDOS. Part I. 81 pl., 25s. *Quaritch.*
ABYDOS. Part II. 64 pl., 25s. *Quaritch.*
METHODS AND AIMS IN ARCHAEOLOGY. 66 blocks, 6s. *Macmillan.*
EHNASYA. 25s. *Quaritch.*
ROMAN EHNASYA. 10s. *Quaritch.*

Of works marked * a few copies can be had on application to the Author, University College, London.

CPSIA information can be obtained
at www.ICGtesting.com
Printed in the USA
BVHW051924130120
569355BV00002B/28/P

9 781375 672412